Analyzing Streams
of Language

Analyzing Streams of Language

Twelve Steps to the Systematic Coding of Text, Talk, and Other Verbal Data

Cheryl Geisler

Rensselaer Polytechnic Institute

PEARSON
Longman

New York   San Francisco   Boston
London   Toronto   Sydney   Tokyo   Singapore   Madrid
Mexico City   Munich   Paris   Cape Town   Hong Kong   Montreal

Senior Vice President and Publisher: Joseph Opiela
Vice President and Publisher: Eben W. Ludlow
Executive Marketing Manager: Ann Stypuloski
Production Manager: Donna DeBenedictis
Project Coordination, Text Design, and Electronic Page Makeup: WestWords, Inc.
Cover Design Manager: Wendy Ann Fredericks
Cover Designer: Keithley and Associates, Inc.
Cover Art: © Don Bishop/Getty Images, Inc.
Manufacturing Buyer: Lucy Hebard
Printer and Binder: Hamilton Printing Company
Cover Printer: Phoenix Color Corporation

Library of Congress Cataloging-in-Publication Data

Geisler, Cheryl.
    Analyzing streams of language : twelve steps to the systematic coding of text, talk, and
other verbal / Cheryl Geisler.
        p. cm.
    Includes index.
    ISBN 0-321-16510-1
    1. Linguistic analysis (Linguistics)   I. Title.

P126.G464 2003
410--dc21

                                                                                        2003047733

Please visit our website at http://www.ablongman.com/geisler

ISBN 0-321-16510-1

1 2 3 4 5 6 7 8 9 10—HT—06 05 04 03

CONTENTS

Preface

Chapter 1
Anchoring in the Literature

Chapter 2
Designing the Analysis

Chapter 3   Segmenting the Data

Chapter

4   Coding the Data

Chapter

5   Achieving Reliability

Chapter 6   Calculating Frequency

Chapter 7   Seeing Patterns of Distribution

Chapter
8   Exploring Patterns Across Dimensions

Chapter
9   Following Patterns over Time

10 Evaluating Significance

11 Detailing Results

12 Presenting Results

PREFACE

What Is Verbal Data?

Verbal data are the phenomena of language, data made up of words, often in a continuous stream. Verbal data may come from the stream of *oral interactions* that a researcher records and transcribes—conversations, interviews, speeches. Or verbal data may come from the stream of *written interactions*, words already written down—published texts, letters and other informal writing, document archives. Increasingly, verbal data may also come from the stream of *electronic interactions* that surround us—e-mails, chats, web pages, to name a few.

What Verbal Data Can Tell You

Many fields use verbal data in one form or another:

- The management researcher uses verbal data when she conducts research using open-ended interviews, whether she asks her questions in person, over the phone, through a written questionnaire, or through an on-line poll.
- The composition researcher uses verbal data when he studies the interactions among students and teachers, no matter whether they are the oral interactions of the traditional face-to-face classroom or the written interactions of more recent distance-learning classrooms.
- The rhetorician uses verbal data when he delves into the archives of a national park, data that may include newspaper reports of the time, the first director's notes and letters, and even the roadside markers that called visitors' attention to early sites.

When faced with a stream of language, many researchers despair of seeing any regularity to verbal data. Words, it is often assumed, are too mushy and soft to support reasonable claims. These researchers would be surprised to find out from those who have studied language closely that language is highly regular—that, for instance, a culture can be characterized by the number of seconds speakers typically wait before taking the next turn in a conversation; that the stories told on the street have a well-formed and recurring structure; that speakers use a whole host of referential discourse to point to what they are talking about.

Researchers who study language have, in fact, told us a great deal about how verbal data works: how it is structured at the level of the phrase and clause; how it works itself out through the give and take of conversation; how it provides for coherence and novelty in extended discourse; how it acts rhetorically in the world, to *do* as well as *say*. Human beings as well as the communities and organizations they form produce an almost endless stream of oral and written language, and this language can be used as evidence for a wide range of inquiries. *Analyzing Streams of Language* uses this basic knowledge about language to help researchers in the humanities, social sciences, and management to use language phenomenon as the basis for reasonable research claims.

About This Book

Analyzing Streams of Language is a practical guide for analyzing verbal data of all kinds, providing a step-by-step methodology for exploring and describing streams of language. It shows you how to approach language systematically. The focus is on building a descriptive analysis that can be articulated, makes sense, and is reliable.

With *Analyzing Streams of Language,* you will learn how to construct an in-depth analysis of verbal data, how to get beyond the surface to see what is really going on. This book will take you through the entire analytic process from exploring the literature, through designing the analysis, coding the data, examining patterns, evaluating their significance, and finally presenting the results. This methodology is foundational to a wide variety of disciplines. It has applications not only in my home discipline of composition and rhetoric, but also in education, management, anthropology, and sociology.

Analyzing Streams of Language is designed to meet the needs of readers at a variety of stages of research. It can be used as the main text in a graduate course on research methods, as a reference manual by individual researchers, or as a handbook by faculty looking for help in guiding students through dissertations using verbal data. You do not have to have an extensive background in language analysis to use *Analyzing Streams of Language*. Without jargon, we walk step by step through the analytic process, using simple terminology and commonly available computer applications.

Analyzing Streams of Language takes advantage of commonly available electronic resources. It integrates computers into the analytic process from the get-go, incorporating commonly available and inexpensive software (Microsoft's *Word* and *Excel*) into each stage of the analysis. One of the most exciting features, formulas in *Excel* developed explicitly for the tasks of analyzing verbal data, will save you hundreds of hours of time in doing your analysis. Other electronic resources also supplement the printed text: sample data for you to analyze, sample analyses to serve as models, and pointers to useful web resources.

Philosophical Perspectives

Data analysis is a practical activity—it is made up of practices, ways of doing things, ways of getting by and making do. Data analysis is also, however, a philosophically contentious activity. The last 25 years in the human and social sciences have seen a lessening of reliance on the controlled studies of experimental methods and greater attention to the naturalistic inquiries often categorized as qualitative research. Verbal data is often associated with one side of this methodological divide, with qualitative data analysis. A leading sourcebook even goes so far as to associate qualitative data with the "form of words rather than numbers" (Miles and Huberman, 1994, p. 1).

Placing words in opposition to numbers, seeing them as alternative means for the symbolic mediation of claims, is not a logical necessity, however. When we say, for example, that teachers talk more than their students in the average classroom, we are making quantitative claims about verbal data. Whether a researcher chooses to add numbers to be more specific about this quantitative relationship may vary. In my experience, most people see a difference between a teacher's talking a little more than students (say 15–20% more) and talking three times as much (300%). The analytic techniques introduced in this book will give you the simple quantitative know-how to see the difference between the two in your own data; but they will also help you to develop more intuitive descriptions.

The dichotomy between qualitative and quantitative research often divides over other and more substantive issues than the use of numbers. Perhaps the most fundamental issue concerns whether verbal data are collected as they naturally occur or whether the researcher has intervened to create the conditions under which the data was solicited. This is the distinction between naturalistic inquiry and experimental inquiry. In naturalistic inquiry, researchers enter a site to record oral data or to copy written data as it naturally occurs or occurred. Historians, for example, collect verbal data from document archives and, for the purposes at hand, are not seen as affecting the data they collect. Researchers recording political debates for later analysis are not usually seen as having an effect on the debates themselves (although, if the analyses are delivered in televised post-debate interviews, a case can be made for their impact).

In experimental inquiry, by contrast, the researcher deliberately intervenes in a research site to create conditions under which a hypothesis can be tested: Students in one classroom, for example, might be subject to a new kind of pedagogy while another class uses a more traditional method. In such experiments, verbal data may indeed be collected: Transcripts from the two classes, for example, may be used to tell a great deal about the differences between the methods, evidence that might be lost by relying solely on outcome measures like student grades.

The analytic methods presented in this book are rooted in naturalistic inquiry, but also find a useful place in the arsenal of the experimental investigator. For those readers using an experimental design, Chapter 2 on "Designing the Analysis" may be irrelevant, since design has been built into the data collection effort rather than developed afterward as is often the case with naturalistic inquiry. For those readers using a purely naturalistic method and uninterested in seeing the significance of their patterns against a larger backdrop, Chapter 10 on "Evaluating Results" may be irrelevant. By and large, however, researchers from across the naturalistic-experimental divide will find much of use in this book.

A distinction related to that between naturalistic and experimental inquiry is that between descriptive and inferential methods. Descriptive methods for analysis are often coupled with naturalistic methods for data collection. Descriptive analysis focuses on providing a detailed description of the data itself. Inferential analysis, often coupled with experimental designs for data collection, tries to go beyond the data analyzed to make inferences about the phenomenon in general.

Descriptive techniques can range from narratives that attempt to maintain the chronological sequence and perspective of the participants themselves through more topological systems, which take the data sequence apart to describe it using a set of descriptive categories. Some descriptions combine both, providing a narrative for how the data change over time and in categories.

Inferential analysis is less concerned about the specifics of the data gathered for the study itself and more interested in what can be said about the phenomenon in general. The Census Bureau, for example, is less interested in the details of the lives of a sample of 600 citizens than with what can be inferred to the general population based on these 600. Nevertheless, inferential work need not be opposed to solid descriptive work. The techniques presented in this book focus on developing solid descriptions of verbal data that make sense both in terms of carefully defined categories and as a narrative told over time.

In some philosophical systems, especially those associated with the radical contextual perspectives described later in this section, researchers take issue with inferential methods. Seeing each situation as unique or historically situated, they see no possibility of developing universal generalizations. I remain agnostic about this issue. It seems important, for most purposes, to be able to draw some relationship between the data being described and the general state of the world—even stories told on the street draw some moral or conclusion for their listeners. Trying to see this relationship need not involve the making of universal claims, but neither does it exclude it. This issue is more fully explored in Chapter 10 on "Evaluating Results" and Chapter 12 on "Presenting Results."

Another significant philosophical distinction that arises in the analysis of verbal data concerns the decision on whether to take an internal or external perspective on the inquiry. The positivist tradition of research assumed, without question, an external perspective on a research site, assuming that only an outside observer could develop a legitimate understanding of the underlying patterns. Insiders were assumed to be too immersed in the situation to see the big picture.

More contextually based systems of inquiry, based on a better developed understanding of the contextually bound nature of language, suggest that this reliance on external perspectives often misses much of importance in the human world. The practice of using informants, developed by anthropologists doing field work in other cultures, is a key technique for trying to get at the meanings that participants themselves ascribe to the words they use rather than to impose an external meaning-making framework upon them.

While some researchers do claim that meaning is so contextually bound that no one outside a given context can claim to have a legitimate understanding of what is going on, it is more common to take a less radical position. The problem with radical contextuality is, in fact, that it precludes scholarly activity itself since scholars are, by definition, outsiders to the situations they study. A more common position is to recognize some validity for both external and internal perspectives, to posit the human ability to move among them, and to recognize that while, at times, only the participants in a situation know what's really going on, at other times, they are the last to know—or to want to know!

In this book, the relationship between external and internal perspectives is presented as a continuum along which verbal phenomena may range. In most face-to-face conversations, for example, external observers can very well distinguish between the turns taken by one speaker and another. When such conversations are transcribed, however, it may take a little more familiarity with the context to decide when Bill is talking and when it's not Bill, but Roger. It may take even more familiarity to be able to decide when Bill's remark is intended to be negative rather than positive. And it may only be an insider who can reasonably decide whether what Bill is saying is novel or whether it is just the same old thing.

Deciding whether to take an internal or external perspective on a particular analysis is not a trivial matter when it comes to the analysis of verbal data. The meanings and significance of a set of words may be more or less transparent to outsiders. This issue is taken up in more detail in Chapter 5, "Achieving Reliability."

The distinction between empirical work and scholarly work is another distinction relevant to the analysis of verbal data. Empirical work is research based on observations of the world around us. In its aspirations to describe that social/human world, it shares a common history with the physical sciences who also base their claims on empirical observations. Scholarly work, by contrast, need not be based in empirical observation. A long tradition of work rooted in philosophy uses the insights of reason as a source of scholarly claims. The data that comes from written texts is generally more closely allied with the scholarly tradition rather than the empirical one. At one time, in fact, texts vied with empirical observations as sources of evidence about what was real. The post-modern equivalent is the debate about whether there is anything beyond the text.

Very often the distinction between scholarly and empirical work is made based on the distinction between systematic method and intuitive analysis. These two distinctions are not, however, isomorphic. An argument based on observations of the world is as likely to be intuitive as it is to be systematic. And we do not have to go far to find scholarly studies that are very systematic.

In this book, our focus is on combining the insights of intuition with enough of the systematics of methodology to provide reasonable grounds for argument. This approach can be used with all types of verbal data, whether it be taken from the stream of oral interactions that have traditionally been considered the stuff of empirical work or taken from the stream of written texts that have typically been considered the domain of scholarly inquiry. The two traditions have quite distinct methods for writing up their work as we'll discuss in Chapter 12, "Presenting Results." But, as this book will argue, the standards for evidence and careful definition can be shared across this divide.

The final distinction to be addressed here is the distinction between the "soft" and "hard" sciences. Without fail, this distinction is invoked polemically—the speaker inevitably sees him- or herself as doing "hard" science rather than something "softer" and therefore less legitimate. Where the boundaries are drawn shifts considerably: Sometimes the hard sciences are the physical sciences as opposed to the social sciences and humanities. In this case, all verbal data is located on the soft side. At other times, the term "hard" is used to describe a social scientific approach to distinguish it from the more intuitive approach taken by colleagues in the humanities. In this case, work using verbal data can be found on both sides of the divide.

Polemics aside, the key issue in the debate between hard and soft concerns the respective role of method and intuition in the analytic process. Hard science approaches will stress the discipline of method, with analysis shaped by a methodology that is well-specified, replicable, and "objective" in the sense that the same analyst will produce the same conclusions given the same data. Soft science approaches will stress the insight of intuition, with analysis shaped by the meaning-making capacities of the human, in a way that very much depends on insight and experience, often inarticulate and very far from replicable.

As described more fully in Chapter 5, "Achieving Reliability," all analysis of verbal data starts with an intuitive understanding of what words mean. Such meaning-making cannot be specified in a way that fully meets the standards of objective knowledge: Meaning shifts from context to context and every verbal analyst must come to terms with this variability. Intuition is a key tool in this process, not the enemy to be overcome.

Nevertheless, there are many ways in which a verbal analyst can "see" what she wants to see and ignore the unexpected. And there are many ways in which the analyst can fail to mount a convincing argument for what she has seen. This book tries to protect you from such outcomes. Seeing patterns in verbal data, and describing the results in such a way as to be meaningful and convincing to other researchers in your field is what we are about.

Comparison to Other Approaches

Many research traditions rely upon the analysis of verbal data and have developed specific analytic approaches. In this section, we clarify the relationship between the process outlined in this book and these other traditions.

My experience with the analysis of verbal data began in earnest with training in *protocol analysis*. Used in cognitive science, researchers using protocol analysis ask participants to "think aloud" as they complete a task and then transcribe and analyze the resulting protocol. In general, this verbal data is assumed to provide evidence of internal psychological processes with each segment of the data stream being assigned to a cognitive category.

The techniques outlined in this book are consistent with protocol analysis. That is, the stream of verbal data can be segmented into idea units and each unit assigned to a category of cognitive processes, the basic procedure for protocol analysis. The approach taken in this book is by no means restricted to protocol analysis, however. Using the procedures outlined in Chapter 4, "Coding the Data," categories are not limited to cognitive categories, nor is it necessary to code the entire data stream as outlined in Chapter 3, "Segmenting the Data."

The analysis of verbal data is often taken to be synonymous with a second research approach known as *content analysis*. Common in studies of advertising and the media, researchers use content analysis to determine the relative frequency of certain concepts—how much violence is portrayed on television, for example. Typically, content analysis involves stripping out function words ("the" and "when," for example), taking out the inflections ("ed" and "ing," for example), and then doing pattern matching on certain lexical items taken to be associated with the phenomenon of interest (the word "argument," for example, might be associated with the phenomenon of violence).

Many of the techniques outlined in this book are consistent with content analysis. The pattern matching techniques described in Chapter 4, "Coding the Data," can be used to do a content analysis. Much research using content analysis does not, however, take context into effect, or make provisions for determining the reliability of their analysis using procedures like those outlined in Chapter 5, "Achieving Reliability." The usual assumption is that the meanings of words can be treated as fixed—that "argument" is always associated with the phenomenon of violence, for example. Such an assumption can be severely stressed when undertaking research across cultures or even in specific subcultures—like the academic subculture where "argument" can be synonymous with good reasoning and far from the connotations of violence common in the context of mass media. Researchers looking to do sound content analysis will thus consider the effect of contextual variation on their analysis and consider making provisions to achieve reliability as outlined in Chapter 5.

Conversation analysis, a third approach to dealing with verbal data, has been developed to deal with the patterning of oral interactions in conversation. Concern focuses on speaker allocation (who has the floor) elicitation-response patterns (questions usually followed by answers), and other rules of engagement. Often, these patterns are looked at for their relationship to specific contexts: In school, for example, teachers are expected to ask questions for which they already know the answer, a practice that would be looked at as highly suspect in other contexts.

The techniques outlined in this book use many of the insights from conversation analysis as a starting point for investigating verbal phenomenon. Here we are generally less concerned with developing a systematic understanding of conversational phenomena per se and more concerned with using an understanding of how those phenomena work as a basis for answering other questions. Understanding the elicitation-response patterns in typical classrooms, for example, we might undertake to analyze the power relationships in peer tutoring situations. Not all verbal data comes from conversations, but when it does, we can use the insights of this research tradition as a starting point for our work as outlined in Chapter 3, "Segmenting the Data."

Discourse analysis is another research tradition that aims to develop fundamental understanding of specific verbal phenomenon, in this case, continuous discourse. Such discourse is often written, but can also be oral. Using discourse analysis, researchers attempt to describe what makes a discourse coherent, how listeners determine reference, how writers use metadiscourse to talk with their readers. As was the case with conversation analysis, the techniques in this book take advantage of the insights of discourse analysis as a foundation for other analyses. Coherence, cohesion, reference, and metadiscourse are all key concepts used in segmenting and sampling verbal data that forms continuous discourse as outlined in Chapter 3.

Finally, as we noted earlier, *qualitative analysis* is often taken as identical with analysis based on verbal data. Although many strains of qualitative analysis exist, most involve coding segments of verbal data as a way of locating phenomenon of interest. The verbal data need not have come from the research site itself—it is possible, for instance, to code one's research notes—but transcriptions of oral conversations, especially interviews, are also not uncommon. The techniques outlined in this book are, for the most part, highly compatible with qualitative research traditions. Some researchers would balk at using the kinds of descriptive statistics introduced in Chapters 6, "Calculating Frequency;" others would not. More would question the concept of significance testing introduced in Chapter 10, "Evaluating Significance." For the most part, however, qualitative researchers looking for systematic guidance on the analysis of verbal data will find much of use here.

How To Use This Book

The analytic process described in this book is made up of twelve steps in six phases:

1. Getting a design for the analysis (Chapters 1 and 2);
2. Preparing the verbal data for analysis (Chapter 3);
3. Coding the verbal data to reveal the phenomenon of interest (Chapters 4 and 5);
4. Detecting patterns in the coded data (Chapters 6, 7, 8, and 9);
5. Measuring the significance of these patterns (Chapter 10); and
6. Making claims about these patterns (Chapters 11 and 12).

If you wish, you may work through this process using a data analysis project on which you are currently working. Or you may simply want to delve into chapters dealing with specific issues—coding, for example (Chapter 4) or temporal patterns (Chapter 9). You may also want to consult specific techniques, which are found throughout the text and can be located through the table of contents.

For those researchers just starting out, projects at the end of each chapter suggest well-defined activities that can be engaged in, more or less one week at a time, to lead to an initial analysis of a data set. This is a remarkably good way to get your feet wet in an area, to begin to explore a phenomenon, and to refine directions for something like a dissertation. If you already have data in hand, you might reasonably expect to get to the start of a solid analysis by the end of this process. Even if you have only a nascent interest in a topic, however, you can make significant progress by getting some experience with data in a way that will help you refine your interest and choose a dissertation topic. And if you already have a defined interest, you can take a big step forward by producing a pilot analysis that might be an important component to a dissertation prospectus.

This book makes innovative use of common computer applications, Microsoft Word and Microsoft Excel, as analytic tools. Such applications are powerful though relatively inexpensive and easy to learn. Techniques throughout the book provide you with step-by-step explanations for using these tools for your analysis. This book also directs you, where possible, to Internet resources that will make your analysis easier.

Other features of the book will help you to make best use of the material:

OBJECTIVES, at the opening of each chapter, are brief paragraphs that will tell you exactly what you will learn to do in the chapter.

TEST YOUR UNDERSTANDING provides quizzes following the presentation of the material in each chapter to challenge you to test your understanding. They might be assigned as homework and reviewed in class.

TRY IT OUT is a series of exercises that give you a chance to try out techniques on a small sample of data and compare results in class.

PROJECTS at the end of each chapter ask you to apply the techniques in the chapter to your own data. Unlike the exercises, projects build from one chapter to the next, leading to the completion of a full project by the end of the book.

FURTHER READING, bibliographies at the end of many chapters, direct your attention to other resources on the topic.

KEY FORMULAS IN EXCEL, found in Appendix B, provides a quick reference guide to Excel formulas useful for the analysis of verbal data.

COURSE WEBSITE, *http://www.ablongman.com/geisler,* provides a host of regularly updated materials relevant to teaching and learning with this book. A list of these resources can be found in Appendix C.

 VIDEO CLIPS found on the course website, provide live demonstration of the techniques introduced in this book. The movie camera symbol throughout the chapters call attention to these video clips, and a list can be found in Appendix C.

ANSWER KEY, found on the course website and listed in Appendix C, provides answers for Test Your Understanding exercises.

SAMPLE WORKBOOKS, downloadable from the course website, provide templates for major analytic procedures. You can download them and edit them to suit your purposes. They are listed in Appendix C.

Why This Book?

The process outlined in this book has developed through a combination of my own struggles to develop an analytic methodology that makes sense in my own research and my efforts to guide doctoral students. The attempt to write it down arose from my specific desire to direct greater attention to research methodology, especially in the field of rhetoric and composition, and to demystify the process by which reasonable claims about verbal data can be made. My search through the literature turned up a persistent lack of practical advice for those starting out as researchers, as well as a lack of guidance to those of us who train the next generation of researchers. I strongly believe we need to uncover the often hidden practices that make up the tacit knowledge of our research traditions. In my experience, this kind of practical knowledge makes research rewarding and exciting. I hope you agree, and I wish you luck in your analytic endeavors!

Acknowledgments

The process of first learning to analyze streams of language and later to show others has been—and will continue to be—a lifelong endeavor for me. Luckily, it has never been a lonely process. I begin my acknowledgments with the English faculty at Carleton College, particularly Owen Jenkins who first made me pay attention to words, and to Harriet Sheridan who showed me how they make meaning. Later, at Carnegie Mellon, David S. Kaufer introduced me to the synthesis of linguistic and rhetorical traditions whose impact is evident throughout these pages. Sharing the struggles of analysis, Christina Haas and Nancy Penrose have given me the encouragement of lifelong friendships.

My biggest debts lie, however, with my graduate students. In interaction with them, they taught me both what needed to be said and why. I owe debts to those whose dissertations I have directed at Rensselaer Polytechnic Institute (RPI): Christine Noel Henwood and Cynthia Louise Haller (1995), Roger Munger (1997), Lee Honeycutt (1998), Barbara Lewis (1999), and Terese Monberg (2002); to those who took the first version of Verbal Data Analysis at Rensselaer: Kellie Barnes, Jennifer Estava, Maureen Murphy, and Michelle Wallace; to those who have braved the first draft of this manuscript at the University of Louisville: Christopher Carter, Tony Edgington, Chris Erwin, Kelli P. Grady, Darci Thoune, and Karen Ware; and to those who braved the most recent incarnation of the book back at RPI: Kellie Cater, Virginia Martin, Pat Nugent, Deb Sarlin, Shaun Slattery, Huatong Sun, and Ashley Williams. Their struggles and encouragement are reflected in this text, and I am grateful to them.

My thanks to the English department at the University of Louisville where, during Fall 2001, I served as Thomas R. Watson Visiting Distinguished Professor of Rhetoric and Composition and finally got started on this book; to my colleagues in communication and rhetoric whose intellect and collegiality have been a precious resource; to reviewers Graham Smart, Anne Beaufort, and Johndan Johnson-Eilola for their confidence in the project; to the folks at Longman, Eben W. Ludlow who saw the promise of the project and Donna DeBenedictis who brought it through production; to Jared Sterzer and others at WestWords who attended to every detail of language and image; to Mark Stein for his confidence and support; and to Naomi Elizabeth Geisler Stein and Bella Rosalena Geisler Stein, my darling companions in reading.

Cheryl Geisler

Analyzing Streams
of Language

Anchoring in the Literature

In this chapter, you will anchor your research interests in the literature already published in your field. You will develop techniques for locating foundational and recent work in order to develop familiarity with the practices of using verbal data in your field. You will also learn how to read back from a study into the techniques by which it was done, a process we call reverse engineering.

The Literature

When engineers start to design, they seldom begin from scratch. If you were an engineer trying to develop a new coffeemaker, for instance, you might start out sketching out a few interesting ideas, but before long, you would want to take a close look at the coffeemaker in your kitchen. Grab that screen driver! Take it apart, see what it's made of, imagine the order in which it was assembled, puzzle out the mechanism, examine it for signs of wear and tear.

This is the process called *reverse engineering* and in this chapter you'll apply its lesson to anchor your research in the literature in your field. Your purpose is twofold. First, pick out a work (article, chapter, book) that appeals to you for the way it addresses issues that are of interest. This will serve as a starting point for your own research, tentative but anchored. Second, you will begin to take the work apart to see how it was put together, imagine the order in which it was assembled, puzzle out the mechanism, and examine it for signs of wear and tear.

The rationale behind anchoring your research in the literature lies in understanding that good research does not arise in a vacuum, but builds upon the research that went before. You can think of your field as a conversation you are trying to join: People say things, others respond. Topics come up, get discussed, and then are set aside. Questions are asked, thought about, answered or abandoned. A line of thought is proposed, explored, resolved.

In taking up your own research project, you are attempting to extend this kind of ongoing conversation in your field. Often, a strand of research is initiated by a foundational piece of research that got people to pay attention to an issue they hadn't thought much about before. Other researchers will then come in with other research projects that build upon, extend, or question the conclusions of the foundational work. This line of research will continue until the issues in the research are resolved or until the line of inquiry is abandoned. By finding a piece of research to serve as an anchor point and then reverse engineering the research to see how it was put together, you will take important steps toward developing a contribution to your field.

Finding an Anchor Point

If you have been working on a line of research for awhile, you will already be familiar with some of its foundational work and some recent work. If so, you may wish to anchor your work in something you already know. But no matter how long you have been working in a field, there are always times when you will want to go back to these basics for anchoring yourself in a literature. You may want to find a foundational piece of work on which a strand of research in your field has already been built, or a more recent piece of work that is solid and intriguing.

In any case, the best way to find a anchor point for your research is through word-of-mouth referrals by people working in the area. This might be a faculty member or even a more advanced graduate student. Talk to them about your interests and ask if they can recommend something for you to read. In this way, you take advantage of their deep understanding of the area to bootstrap your own research process. To supplement word-of-mouth referrals, try some of the following techniques.

Locating Foundational Work

Foundational work is work that serves as the foundation for an ongoing line of research. You can use a couple of ways to locate foundational work.

In your prior reading, have you come across an analysis that stuck in your mind, that was intriguing, that you thought was "neat"? Use a Cited Reference Search (see page 3) to see if it has been cited by other researchers. If it has, it is probably a foundational piece that would make a good starting point for your work.

Or, find an edited collection in an area of interest to you and check the references for each chapter. Is there a work that is repeatedly cited with a title that makes it seem relevant to your work? This may well be a foundational work.

Locating Recent Work

If a strand of research has been ongoing for some time, you may wish to anchor your research in a more recent piece of solid research rather than go back to the beginning of the research strand. To find more recent work, try one of the following tips:

- Use a bibliographic database to look for recent articles on a topic of interest to you (see page 5).
- Browse the journals in your field. Look at the table of contents for the last 4–5 years. Pick an article of interest.
- Search for recent books on your topic at Amazon.com. Also look at the other books they suggest might be of interest. Make sure the work is scholarly.
- Use a general search engine like Google (*http://www.google.com/*) and search for your topic. Look for links to citations or for on-line documents that look like they come from credible sources.
- Check the conference program of a recent conference in your field.
- Find scholars and researchers who are working on topics of interest to you. Use one of the strategies provided to find published articles by this author.

Using a Cited Reference Search

A Cited Reference Search will provide you with the citations of all the works citing the one in which you are interested. Thus, a Cited Reference Search will allow you to see how many times a particular work has been cited, by whom, in what venue, and over what period of time. If you find that a particular work has been cited in the journals in your field over a relatively long period of time, and, perhaps, by some of the leading researchers, you can be sure that it is a foundational work.

Many university libraries provide access to the citation indexes for the sciences, social sciences, and the arts and humanities through the ISI Web of Science (*http://www.isiknowledge.com*). Research using verbal data is usually indexed in either the Social Science Citation Index or the Citation Index for the Arts & Humanities.

Doing a Cited Reference Search is a two-step process. In step 1, as shown in Figure 1.1, you provide the bibliographic information for the work in which you are interested: author's name, the approved abbreviation for the cited journal, and the year in which the work was published. For instance, if we wanted to see how many times Charles Bazerman's article, "Physicists Reading Physics: Schema-Laden Purposes and Purpose-Laden Schema," published in 1985 in *Written Communication* has been cited, we would complete the search request as shown in Figure 1.1. Notice that for the journal, *Written Communication,* we have used the approved abbreviation WRIT COMMUN. A complete list of approved abbreviations can be found by clicking on the <u>list</u> link underlined in this search screen.

Once you have filled in the information for the Cited Reference Search, click on LOOKUP to go to the next step.

In Step 2, select the reference you wish to view. As you can see in Figure 1.2, there are a total of 41 references to a Bazerman article published in 1985 in *Written Communication,* 38 with the correct citation (volume 2, page 3), one with an incorrect citation (volume 2, page 2) and one with an incomplete citation (no volume number).

To view individual references, select all three of these and then click on SEARCH.

The Web of Science then provides us with the citations for the 41 articles that have referenced Bazerman's article: 9 in *Written Communication,* 3 in *Tesol Quarterly,* 3 in the *Journal of Documentation,* 3 in *College English,* 2 each in *College Composition and Communication, Discourse Processes, Journal of Pragmatics, Research in the Teaching of English,* and the *Review of Educational Research,* and 1 each in a host of

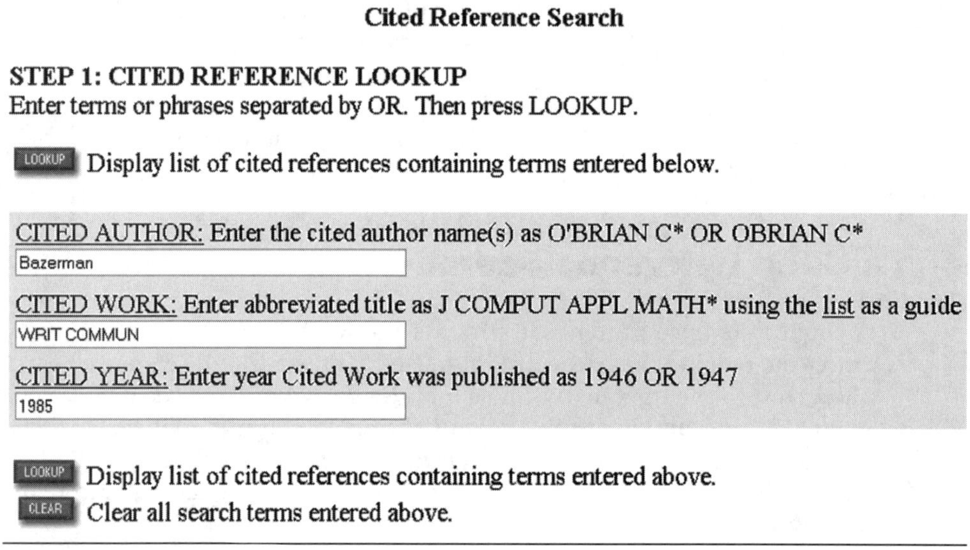

Cited Reference Search

STEP 1: CITED REFERENCE LOOKUP
Enter terms or phrases separated by OR. Then press LOOKUP.

LOOKUP Display list of cited references containing terms entered below.

CITED AUTHOR: Enter the cited author name(s) as O'BRIAN C* OR OBRIAN C*

Bazerman

CITED WORK: Enter abbreviated title as J COMPUT APPL MATH* using the list as a guide

WRIT COMMUN

CITED YEAR: Enter year Cited Work was published as 1946 OR 1947

1985

LOOKUP Display list of cited references containing terms entered above.
CLEAR Clear all search terms entered above.

Figure 1.1   Step 1 of a cited reference search—providing bibliographic info.

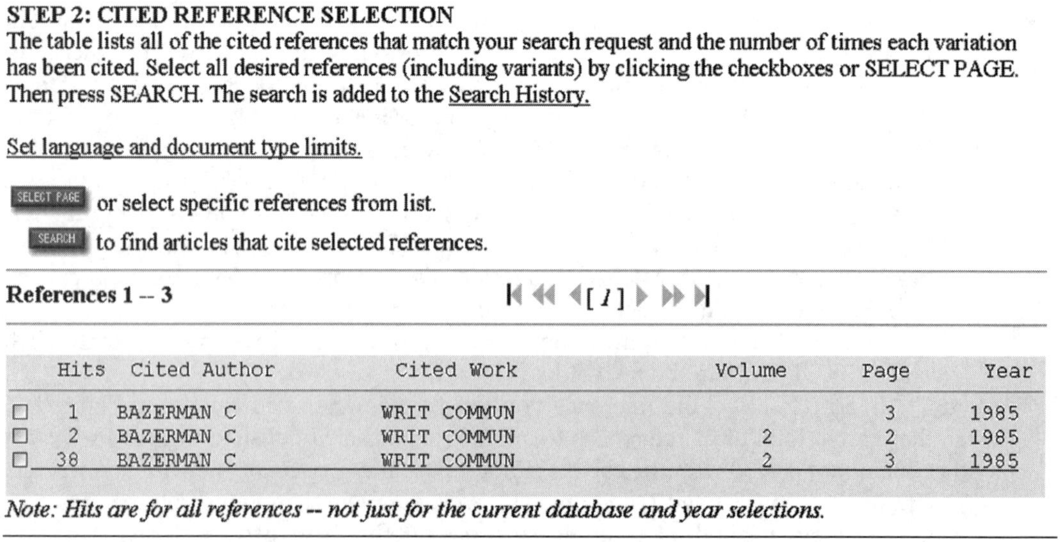

STEP 2: CITED REFERENCE SELECTION
The table lists all of the cited references that match your search request and the number of times each variation has been cited. Select all desired references (including variants) by clicking the checkboxes or SELECT PAGE. Then press SEARCH. The search is added to the Search History.

Set language and document type limits.

SELECT PAGE or select specific references from list.

SEARCH to find articles that cite selected references.

References 1 -- 3 |◀ ◀◀ ◀[*1*]▶ ▶▶ ▶|

	Hits	Cited Author	Cited Work	Volume	Page	Year
☐	1	BAZERMAN C	WRIT COMMUN		3	1985
☐	2	BAZERMAN C	WRIT COMMUN	2	2	1985
☐	38	BAZERMAN C	WRIT COMMUN	2	3	1985

Note: Hits are for all references -- not just for the current database and year selections.

Figure 1.2   Step 2 of a cited reference search—selecting a reference.

other journals. This pattern of citation suggests that Bazerman's article would be a good choice for a foundational work.

Using a Bibliographic Database

Many university libraries provide access to on-line bibliographic databases that make it relatively easy to locate recent work on a topic. Many of these databases provide summaries of the works indexed; some of them provide links to the full text.

The first step to using a bibliographic database is to specify the search, probably by a keyword related to your topic. If you wanted to find a more recent work on advanced reading strategies than the Bazerman article, for instance, you could use the bibliographic database, Electronic Collections Online (ECO) available through Online Computer Library Center (OCLC) FirstSearch, to search for articles with the keyword READING STRATEGIES. As you can see in Figure 1.3, we have specified the last four years, 2000–2003.

The next step is to use the resulting links to refine your search. The results for the READING STRATEGIES search turn up 276 records, with a very wide range. You might decide that the link to an article by Paul, Charney, and Kendall on reception studies in the rhetoric of science looks like it's in the ballpark. The detailed record, shown in Figure 1.4, provides a link to the full text, the citation information, an abstract, and, off-screen, a list of keywords.

At this point, you might decide to read the Paul et al. article to see if it's of interest, peruse their reference list to find other works of interest, or do another search in ECO for one of the keywords used by Paul et al. to index their article.

▣ ❓	Current database: **ECO**	
News Help		

	Search Clear	
Search in:	ECO ▾ ⓘ	
	An OCLC collection of scholarly journals (**Browse Journal Titles**)	
Search for:	Reading Strategies	Keyword ▾ 🔲
and ▾		Keyword ▾ 🔲
and ▾		Keyword ▾ 🔲
Limit to:	All Publisher Collections ▾	
	All Subject Collections ▾	
	Year 2000-2003 (format: YYYY-YYYY)	
Limit to:	☐ ▤ **Full text** ❷	
Limit availability to:	☐ ↷ **Subscriptions held by my library (YRM, RENSSELAER POLYTECHNIC INSTITUTE)** ❷	
match any of the following	**Library Code** **Find codes ...**	
Rank by:	No ranking ▾ ❷	
	Search Clear	

Figure 1.3   Step 1 of a bibliographic search—specifying a keyword.

Ownership: **FirstSearch indicates your institution subscribes to this publication.**
- Libraries that Own Item: 204   🐾 RENSSELAER POLYTECHNIC INSTITUTE
- 🔳 Search the catalog at Rensselaer Research Libraries
- Local Holdings Information: vol: 2- 1988-

External Links: ▪ ▐ILLiad▌ Send Request to ILLiad

Full Text: 🔘 View PDF Full Text (ECO)

Copyright: This material is protected by the United States Copyright Act of 1976 and the Berne Convention Implementation Act of 1988. Material in this publication may only be printed and/or saved to another word processor or the internet, reproduced, stored or transmitted, in any form or by any means, with the prior permission in writing of Sage Publications, Inc.

Author(s): Paul, Danette ; Charney, Davida ; Kendall, Aimee
Affiliation: Brigham Young University; University of Texas at Austin; University of Texas at Austin

Title: **Moving beyond the Moment: Reception Studies in the Rhetoric of Science**

Source: *Journal of Business and Technical Communication* 15, no. 3 (2001): 372-399
Additional Info: Sage Publications; 20010701

Standard No: ISSN: 1050-6519

Language: English

Abstract: Studies in the rhetoric of science have tended to focus on classic scientific texts and on the history of drafts and the interaction surrounding them up until the moment when the drafts are accepted for publication by a journal. Similarly, research on disasters resulting from failed communication has tended to focus on the history of drafts and the interaction surrounding them up until the moment of the disaster. The authors argue that overattention to the moment skews understanding of what makes scientific discourse successful and neglects other valuable sources of evidence. After reviewing the promises and limitations of studies from historical,

Figure 1.4   Step 2 of a bibliographic search—using a detailed record.

The most productive of these strategies may be the first: looking at the reference list put together by Paul et al. Published authors in the field, especially ones published in a respected journal in a recent year, have probably put together a better list of leads to recent work than any search you could construct in a bibliographic database. Here you might look for a recent edited volume on the topic and for other recent articles. Any of these might prove to be just the anchoring point you're looking for.

Choosing a Good Anchor

To anchor your analysis of verbal data in the literature of your field, the work you choose for your anchor must itself be based on an analysis of verbal data. While this may not be as hard as it sounds, there are some things to keep in mind as you're searching for a foundational or recent work for this purpose.

As we noted in the preface, verbal data is data in the form of words, often a continuous stream, either transcribed from a recording of oral interactions— conversations, interviews, speeches—or verbal data already written down, both the designed discourse of published texts and the more serendipitous texts of electronic interactions (e-mails, chats, etc.). Many different types of research from many different research fields are based upon such data.

When you are looking for an anchor point for your research, make sure the claims made in the work are based on some form of verbal data. These claims may be claims about verbal phenomena themselves—such as the claim that classroom conversations are dominated by teacher talk. Or they may be claims about other kinds of phenomenon, but which can be verified by looking at verbal data— such as the claim that teams are more collaborative when they have six members or less.

1.1 Test Your Understanding

A review article can often help you to locate foundational work and recent work in an area of interest. My review article, "Writing and Learning at Cross Purposes in the Academy," downloadable at the course website, contains references to the following works. Use it to:

1. separate the works into areas
2. identify foundational work for each area
3. select the most promising recent work in the area

Be prepared to explain your choices.

a. Ackerman, 1991
b. Brown and Day, 1983
c. Brown, Day and Jones, 1983
d. Copeland, 1985
e. Durst, 1987
f. Emig, 1977
g. Garner, Belcher, Winfield, and Smith, 1985
h. Langer and Applebee, 1987
i. Langer, 1986
j. Nelson, 1990
k. Newell, 1984
l. Penrose, 1992
m. Schumacher and Nash, 1991
n. Schwegler and Shamoon, 1982
o. Sherrard, 1986
p. Spivey, 1984
q. Spivey, 1991

For discussion: What are the benefits of using a review article to anchor in the literature? What are the potential dangers?

Reverse Engineering

Once you have located an anchoring point for your research, one based on verbal data of some sort that investigates a phenomena you find intriguing, you need to develop an insider's perspective. Like the engineer, you must develop a deep appreciation for your coffeemaker, not seeing it simply as something you get coffee from each morning, but seeing it as a system that accomplishes work with certain techniques and materials for certain purposes. To reverse engineer a work, consider its various aspects: the **contribution** it makes, your **interest** in it, the **data** on which it is based, the **claims** it makes based on this data, the **categories** used for the analysis, and the **patterns** detected by the analysis. Each of these aspects is discussed in more detail next.

Contribution

The general purpose of scholarly work is to contribute to the state of knowledge (and sometimes practice) of a research community. Contribution can come in many forms: Sometimes a work opens up a new area that other scholars have not yet looked at; sometimes a work confirms the claims made in prior work; sometimes a work serves to correct or question claims made earlier. Each of these cases will be considered a contribution to the state of knowledge because the research community is in a better state of knowledge after reading and accepting the work than it was before (at least so the author claims).

In some fields, a further link is made between a more advanced or adequate state of knowledge and the condition of society. In particular, the claim is made that better knowledge and understanding will bring benefits to society as a whole. A better understanding of how physicists read physics, for example, might help us to better devise an educational system that includes advanced reading strategies; it might even reshape the way scientific articles are written.

In other fields, the claim for social benefits is less clear, although it can often be inferred: A better reading of the rhetorical strategies used in *Hamlet* may make no more claim to benefit than the usual benefits to be had from a more satisfying reading. But such benefits may be enough to justify the time and resources dedicated to the research.

Interest

In advancing the state of knowledge in your field, you should not imagine yourself as leaving behind your personal interest. This personal interest will serve as the driving motive behind your research, often providing you with the insight and edge that spurs on good work. There is no conflict between making a contribution to a field and pursuing issues of personal interest, though you must often work to see their connection.

Thus, an important starting point for reverse engineering is to identify your own personal motives for being interested in what the article is talking about. Often, if you look at a piece of research, you will find that the author provides you with insight into his or her own personal motives for taking up the issue. Recognizing the author's personal motives and thinking through your own motives will often point the way for finding the focus of your own research agenda.

Data

In reverse engineering a work, look at the kind of verbal data that has been used. As we noted earlier, verbal data may be transcripts of oral interactions or written and archived texts; it may be taken from a relatively current stream of language, or it may come from streams of language that flowed long ago.

Some authors are explicit in identifying the verbal data they have used for their analysis; with others, you have to make some inferences to figure out what they looked at. In either case, however, you can be sure that some verbal data has been considered—what was it?

Claims

Work based on verbal data may either make general claims or claims about specific texts or interactions. A work may claim, for example, that in general, women's contributions to electronic discourse are more tentative than men's. Or a work may describe the very specific rhetorical strategies used by Fanny Hill in her novels. The first kind of work is often more foundational, whereas more recent work may tend to look at specific instances to verify the general claims made earlier.

Categories

You will find that works vary widely in terms of the systematicity of the categories they use for analysis. The emphasis in this book is on developing explicit categories so that your readers will understand the basis for the claims you make. You will find, however, that many authors are more intuitive in their analysis. Some give you some description of the kind of way they categorized verbal phenomena, but others simply give you description and leave you to infer the categories through which these descriptions were produced. For the purposes of anchoring your research in the literature, either kind of analysis—systematic or intuitive—will do, although if you can find analytic categories, you will want to keep them in mind as you develop your own analytic techniques.

Patterns

The final aspect of the work to consider is the patterns the author describes. Do things change over time, increasing, decreasing, or following some more complex trajectory? Do things change over space, with stronger patterns associated with certain persons, places, organizations, or other social units? Do things change one with the other, so that as one thing increases or decreases, so too does a second thing? Does one thing cause another, so that when one has occurred, the second is definitely or at least likely to occur?

1.2   Try It Out

One of the main purposes of reverse engineering an article is to begin to understand the process by which it was created. Read one of my recent articles, "Upon the Public Stage: How Professionalization Shapes Accounts of Composing in the Academy," downloadable from the course website, to identify:

a. Kinds of verbal data used
b. Categories for description
c. Patterns found

Try It Out (continued)

Next estimate, in terms of weeks of full-time work, how much time it took me to (a) get this verbal data, (b) develop the categories for description, and (c) see the patterns.

For discussion: Compare your estimates with others in your class. Reflect upon what you have learned from this reverse engineering, what you'd like to know more about the analytic process, and how you might apply your knowledge in your own research.

PROJECT: REVERSE ENGINEERING YOUR ANCHOR

Reverse engineer a work that you find interesting and appealing as an anchor for your analysis. A sample reverse engineering workbook is available at the course website. For oral presentation, consider:

INTEREST: Introduce the article and tell us why you are interested in it. Also tell us, if you can, why the author was personally interested in this line of research.

CONTRIBUTION: Describe the contribution this work makes to the strand of research in which you are interested—as far as you understand it. What appear to be the issues in this strand of research? What contribution to its field does the work claim to make? Of what benefit to society, if any, does the work claim to be?

DATA: Describe the kind of verbal data used in this article and why, as far as you can tell, the author selected this data for analysis.

CATEGORIES: Describe the analytic categories or descriptions by which the data was characterized.

CLAIMS: What are the overall claims the author makes about this data?

PATTERNS: Describe the kinds of patterns the author found.

RESOURCES: Now think about the work from the point of view of your own analysis. What kind of work did the author have to do to produce this work? How long do you think it took? What resources did he or she need? How does this compare with the time and resources available to you?

REFLECTIONS: Finally, reflect upon what you have learned from this work, what you'd like to know more about, and how you might apply your knowledge in your own research.

For Further Reading

In the field of composition and rhetoric, you can find the tables of contents for the leading journals on-line as follows:

College Composition and Communication, issues since 1998, are indexed at the journal's website *http://www.ncte.org/ccc.*

College English, issues since 1997, are indexed at the journal's website *http://www.ncte.org/ce.*

Computers and Composition is indexed at the journal's website *http://corax.cwrl.utexas.edu/cac.*

JAC (Journal of Advanced Composition) is indexed at the journal's website *http://jac.gsu.edu.*

Journal of Business and Technical Communication is indexed in ContentsFirst of OCLC FirstSearch (*http://firstsearch.oclc.org*). Full texts of the articles are available through ECO (Electronic Collections Online), also from OCLC FirstSearch (*http://firstsearch.oclc.org*).

LLAD (Language and Learning Across the Disciplines) is indexed and full back issues are available at *http://wac.colostate.edu/llad.*

Philosophy and Rhetoric, recent issues are indexed at the journal's website *http://muse.jhu.edu/journals/par.*

PRE/TEXT is indexed at the journal's website *http://www.pretext.com/pt/pt_bkissues.html.*

Quarterly Journal of Speech, recent issues are indexed and summarized in *http://www.natcom.org/pubs/QJS/Summaries.htm.*

Research in the Teaching of English is indexed and annotated at *http://www.ncte.org/rte/annotatedbib.shtml.*

Rhetoric Review, recent issues are indexed at the journal's website *http://www.rhetoricreview.com.*

Rhetoric Society Quarterly is indexed at the journal's website *http://rhetoricsociety.org.*

Written Communication is indexed in ContentsFirst of OCLC FirstSearch (*http://firstsearch.oclc.org*). Full texts of the articles are available through ECO, also from OCLC FirstSearch (*http://firstsearch. oclc.org*).

CHAPTER

Designing the Analysis

 In this chapter, you will develop a design to guide your analysis. Based on the way you anchored your interest in the literature in the last chapter as well as the mucking about you have done at your site, you will articulate your questions, build a descriptive framework, decide how to focus your analysis, and then make decisions about how to sample cases, making sure to build in comparisons.

Design of Analysis

Many researchers taking a naturalistic approach to data collection simply jump right in. Guided by interest and gut instinct, they gather volumes of data, only limited by the time they have available and what's available. Other naturalistic researchers and those guided by an experimental paradigm *design* their data collection. Deciding ahead of time, they articulate research questions, define an object of study, and plan a strategy for judicious sampling. In either case, however, if verbal data is involved, both kinds of researchers inevitably end up with more data than can be analyzed in a time frame that seems reasonable—whether it be a few weeks, a semester, or a year. At this stage developing a design for the analysis becomes important.

More is at stake in designing the analysis than just feasibility. How you choose the cases to analyze and how you construct the comparative frameworks in which the analysis takes place form the foundation of your study's credibility. You must be able to explain how the cases you have selected are related to the questions that drive your study. You must be able to articulate your process of sampling. And, in most cases, you need to show how the comparisons you make are meaningful and relevant to the issues at hand. To meet these challenges to credibility, you need to design your analysis.

Design is often thought of as the polar opposite of mucking about. When you muck about in a research site, you go in without many expectations; you may have a sense that something is interesting; or you may find yourself in a site for other reasons and then realize that there are interesting research issues at hand. Such mucking about is critical to design, not its antithesis. Without a first-hand acquaintance with a research site:

- you do not know what's going on at the site,
- you cannot know what kind of objects are available for study,
- you will not be able to build in the comparisons that are most relevant, and
- you will not understand the kinds of cases on which you might focus.

These are the issues involved in designing an analysis, the issues addressed in this chapter.

Much of the advice in this chapter can be employed at one of two stages in a project. A first point for design comes when you have gathered your data and need to develop a strategy to direct your analysis. The data you have gathered may be comprehensive. Perhaps you have tried, to the best of your ability, to collect all texts and tape record all interactions. Or the data may come from a preexisting archive, whether it be the paper archives of a historical collection or the electronic archives of a chat room. In all these cases, you have more data than you can possibly analyze in a reasonable period of time. The strategies in this chapter are directed at helping you select among your data for further analysis.

Another possible point for using the advice in this chapter follows what we have called the mucking about period—the time when you have entered into a situation, become familiar with it, and seen something interesting. At this point, you may construct a design using the techniques in this chapter in order to guide your data collection. This kind of early design will not relieve you of the need to refocus your design when you come to the stage of data analysis, but it may considerably reduce the amount of data you face when analysis time rolls around.

Constructing a Descriptive Framework

Having mucked about in a situation—having gathered your data or found it in an archive—you should have a sense of what's going on: who's involved, what they do, what resources they have available, how things shift over time. To design an analysis, you begin by articulating that knowledge through what Miles and Huberman have called a descriptive framework: a graphic representation of the components of the situation in which you're interested.

A few years ago, for example, I became interested in a senior capstone design course in mechanical engineering. I had mucked about in the course in my role as the director of the writing-intensive program of which this course was a part. The descriptive framework in Figure 2.1 is a graphical representation of these weekly

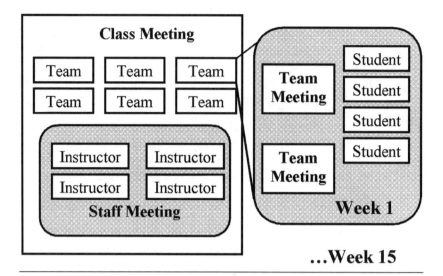

Figure 2.1   A descriptive framework for a capstone design course.

events and their participants. Eventually I had gathered a great deal of data about each of the components of the course:

> For each of 15 weeks, teams of students meet with the instructors in the course for a 90-minute class meeting: I had recorded these class meetings.
> In addition, each team met twice, once with one of the instructors and a second time on their own. We had recorded the team meetings and gathered all the texts from four of these teams.
> Each student also prepared work on their own. To track this work, we collected process logs from all team members. We also met for weekly interviews with a team contact as well as one other team member on a rotating basis.
> Finally, I knew the instructors attended a one-hour staff meeting each week in addition to whatever course preparation they did on their own. We attended and recorded each of these staff meetings and held a longer interview with instructors at the beginning and end of the course.

A good descriptive framework will describe the universe of phenomenon in the research site. To do this, begin with the major verbal events. In the descriptive framework in Figure 2.1, for example, three events have been identified: class meetings, team meetings, and staff meetings.

Second, a good descriptive framework will identify the relevant participants in the events making up the universe of phenomena. In Figure 2.1, for example, we see that students attend the team meetings as well as the class meetings; that instructors join the students in class meetings but also meet on their own in staff meetings.

Third, a good descriptive framework will specify the significant relationships among its entities. It will, for example, show the categories of which participants are members—such as the teams of which students are members in Figure 2.1. It can also indicate other kinds of relationships such as hierarchy, opposition, and association—that an instructor "mentors" a team, that teams "compete" for the best design, that team members may "belong to" the same fraternity.

All these relationships might be characterized as spatial because they describe the interconnections among various entities in the spatial dimension. In addition, a good descriptive framework will have a temporal dimension. It should, for instance, indicate temporal routines—as Figure 2.1 shows how the class meeting, staff meeting, and team meetings combine to make up a weekly routine that repeats itself 15 times during the course of a semester. Or, it might describe temporal change—for instance, that a design team moves through three phases in the course of their work.

2.1 Test Your Understanding

The descriptive framework in Figure 2.1 does a good job of indicating the category memberships that shape the phenomenon in space and the temporal routines that punctuate the phenomenon over time. It does not, however, represent other kinds of spatial relations (hierarchy, opposition, and association). Modify this diagram, downloadable at the course website, to include one or more of these additional relationships.

For discussion: Is it possible for a descriptive framework to represent all the relationships in the universe to be studied? If not, how can a researcher choose what to include and what to leave out in her descriptive framework?

Articulating Research Questions

In your previous work on anchoring in the literature, you developed the beginning of an understanding of what your field knows or thinks they know about the phenomenon that interests you, the phenomenon depicted in the descriptive framework. Tacitly, you used this knowledge to make decisions about where to draw the boundaries of your universe and the kinds of entities and relationships to include within it. Before you go further in your design, you need to articulate that knowledge in the form of a research question or questions that will drive your analysis.

One source of research questions is your own curiosity and need to know. Look at your descriptive framework. What is it you want to know about this phenomenon? Is there something you suspect that is going on here? Is there something you feel a need to know more about? A second important source of questions is the literature in which your work is anchored. What does this literature suggest is going on here? Can you confirm or disconfirm this understanding?

Does your field know something, but need to know more? What is it they really need to know?

In general, there are three kinds of questions that can be answered by the kind of descriptive analysis you will take forward in this book:

QUESTIONS OF KIND: What kind of thing is this? What is it made up of?

QUESTIONS OF ASSOCIATION: What is this thing associated with? When this occurs, what occurs with it? What is absent?

QUESTIONS OF TIME: How does this thing vary over time? What are its routines? How does it evolve?

As you articulate these questions, you might be tempted to include a fourth kind of question, a question of cause, to drive your research. Be careful about this. Strictly speaking, descriptive analysis cannot give a definitive answer to questions of causality: Did this cause that? But we can make some headway on causality with questions of association—is this associated with that?—because there can be no causality without association. And we can also go some distance toward causality by using questions of time—does this precede that?—because there can be no causality without precedence. Thus, if you find yourself wanting to ask questions of causality, try to rephrase them as questions of association or questions of time.

Defining the Focus for Analysis

From the universe of data mapped out by a descriptive framework, you need to select one or more foci for further analysis. The focus defines the object at the center of whatever you would consider to be an appropriate answer to your research questions. For instance, if you want to answer the question, how does a design evolve over time?, appropriate answers would involve the object "the design." Thus, the design would be your focus.

The kinds of objects you may take as the focus of your analysis can vary considerably. Much analysis takes the *individual* as its focus. Such analysis asks, "What has this individual been doing?" Using a focus on the individuals in the capstone design course, for example, we might select the following data to analyze:

- all the texts written by an individual,
- all the interviews we had with the individual, and
- all the contributions that the individual made in class and in team meetings.

Other analysis focuses on certain kinds of *events*. Such analysis asks, "What happened here?" In the data set for the capstone course, for example, we might decide to focus on the team meeting as an *event* and pull the following data for further analysis:

- transcripts of all team meetings,
- selections from all interviews in which the team meetings are discussed, and
- all texts used during the team meetings.

Some analysis focuses on specific *activities* that occur in the situation. This analysis asks, "What gets done here?" Such analysis cuts across the individuals and events in a situation, and may even involve other quite different situations. In the capstone data, for example, we might focus on the activity of engineering design and select the following data for further analysis:

all the texts and sketches a team constructs for a design,
all the segments of team meetings in which the design was discussed,
all discussions in the staff meetings about student design work in general, or a particular team's design, and
interviews with the staff member responsible for mentoring the team through their design work.

By choosing a focus for analysis, you make a commitment to analyze certain phenomenon and to discuss that phenomenon in reporting your results—individuals, teams, activities, and so on. Such commitments need not be final or exclusive. That is, taking one focus for analysis for your current project does not preclude you looking at the data with a different focus later. One of the strengths of a naturalistic approach to research is, in fact, the way that the data it produces is rich enough to sustain a variety of analyses. And some complex projects can have more than one focus for analysis: You could look at both a team and at the individuals on that team, for example.

Sampling Cases

Once you have decided on a focus for your analysis, you will need to decide how to sample among the cases your site presents. In almost all situations, you will have more than one choice. In the situation diagrammed in Figure 2.1, for example, if you decide to focus on students, which students? If you decide to focus on team meetings, which team? If you decide to focus on a team's design activity, which design? If you decide to focus on a whole course, why this course?

Convenience Sampling

One of the most commonly used strategies for sampling cases is also the least defensible: convenience. Using convenience sampling, I might choose a student because he sits next to me. I might choose a set of meetings because they occurred at a time I can easily attend. I might choose a certain team because I already know some of the members. I might choose this course because it is one I already know about. Sampling by convenience, as these examples suggest, puts personal considerations ahead of other considerations that might be relevant to your study.

If convenience is your only answer to a question about sampling, you will lose a great deal of credibility. By the same token, however, convenience is almost never totally irrelevant in the design of a study. If your desired focus is difficult to access for whatever reason, you may need to consider what is possible for you. If access depends upon a history of interaction in a site that is difficult and costly to build, you may want to rely upon rather than abandon what you already have access to. For example, if you wish to study a medical school, as one of my doctoral students did, you might, as she did, study a medical school she had once been a part of rather than try to establish ties with a new school.

Convenience should never be the whole story for your sampling, however. A variety of other more defensible strategies exist that can serve to guide your choice of cases within a site as discussed in the following.

Typical Case Sampling

Can you select a case or cases that are typical in your site: a typical student, a typical team, a typical meeting, a typical course? To use the strategy of typicality you will need to have some kind of data available about the range of relevant variation in cases in your site. If most of the teams in the capstone design course, for example, are made up of both men and women, I may want to make sure to pick mixed-sex teams for my cases. Not all variation are relevant, of course: If I find out that most of the students in the course own cats, I still may not have to worry about whether or not the students on the team I choose are cat owners.

Best Case Sampling

If the phenomenon in which you are interested only occurs in some cases, you may want to employ a sampling strategy that maximizes you chances of finding it. If, for example, you are interested in describing successful design activities, and you know that about a third of the teams in any capstone design course will not be judged successful by their instructors, you may want to try to find a way to sample teams with a high probability of being successful.

Criterion-based Sampling

Best case sampling is a special variety of the more general strategy of criterion-based sampling. With criterion-based sampling, you specify a certain relevant criteria and choose all cases that meet that criteria. If, for example, I want to study mixed-gender communication patterns in student design teams, I might decide to study all the mixed-gender teams formed in a particular semester at a particular university.

Stratified Sampling

With a stratified sampling strategy, you take advantage of knowing something about the existing variations in a site. If you know, for example, that in a certain site most design teams are either all male or all female, but that a few teams are mixed gender, you may want to make sure that you study a certain number of each of these three kinds of teams: male-only, female-only, and mixed. If you know that some design teams succeed and others fail, you may want to make sure to interview students from both types of teams.

Random Sampling

With random sampling, you choose cases based on the patterns established by a randomly generated sequence of numbers. Using a random sampling strategy involves three basic steps:

1. Associate each case in your universe of potential cases with a number starting with 1 and continuing until all the cases are numbered. If you have 50 teams as shown in Figure 2.2, for example, you would number the teams from 1 to 50.
2. Use Excel to generate a random sequence of the size sample you want to select. If you want to select 12 cases, for example, you would need a random sequence of at least 12 numbers.
3. Select the cases associated with the random number sequence. If our sequence was 16, 50, 36, 9, 25, 1, 5, 27, 19, 29, we would pick Team 16, Team 50, Team 36, and so on.

#	Gender Composition	Score in Class	Coop	#	Gender Composition	Score in Class	Coop
1	Women-only	2	yes	26	Men-only	17	yes
2	Women-only	6	no	27	Women-only	19	no
3	Mixed	18	no	28	Men-only	35	no
4	Mixed	10	no	29	Men-only	1	yes
5	Women-only	46	yes	30	Mixed	18	yes
6	Men-only	1	yes	31	Women-only	14	no
7	Men-only	23	yes	32	Men-only	15	yes
8	Women-only	1	no	33	Men-only	11	yes
9	Men-only	44	yes	34	Men-only	39	no
10	Men-only	12	no	35	Mixed	49	yes
11	Women-only	11	yes	36	Men-only	49	no
12	Men-only	32	no	37	Men-only	14	yes
13	Men-only	20	yes	38	Women-only	4	no
14	Men-only	23	no	39	Men-only	34	yes
15	Mixed	36	no	40	Men-only	43	no
16	Women-only	11	no	41	Men-only	37	no
17	Men-only	18	no	42	Women-only	14	yes
18	Mixed	25	yes	43	Men-only	36	no
19	Women-only	11	yes	44	Men-only	18	no
20	Men-only	17	no	45	Men-only	8	yes
21	Men-only	47	yes	46	Women-only	19	yes
22	Men-only	38	no	47	Women-only	11	no
23	Men-only	3	yes	48	Mixed	46	no
24	Men-only	30	no	49	Women-only	37	no
25	Women-only	12	yes	50	Men-only	44	yes

Figure 2.2   The universe of 50 design teams.

To use Excel in step 2 to generate a random number list, begin by copying this formula

=ROUNDUP((RAND()*SIZE),0)

into a cell in Excel, replacing the variable SIZE with the size of the universe you are sampling. For example, if we want to sample from the universe of 50 teams as shown, we would edit the formula to be:

=ROUNDUP((RAND()*50),0)

Next, drag this formula down for approximately twice as many cells as you need the random number sequence to be. So, as you'll see in Figure 2.3, in order to get a sample size of 12, we have placed the formula in A2 and dragged it down to fill 18 cells.

To fix this sequence, copy the sequence and use the Paste Special command under Edit in the menu bar to paste just the values into the next column as shown in Figure 2.4.

The final step involves filtering out repeating values from your sequence. As you can see in Figure 2.5, some of the now-fixed values in Column B repeat earlier

A
Random Numbers
6
17
22
8
14
18
26
21
39
39
36
36
4
21
15
28
41
6

Figure 2.3   Random number generation in Excel.

	A	B	C	D	E
1	Random Numbers	Fixed			
2	6				
3	17				
4	22				
5	8				
6	14				
7	18				
8	26				
9	21				

Paste Special

Paste
- ○ All
- ○ Formulas
- ● Values
- ○ Formats
- ○ Comments
- ○ Validation
- ○ All except borders
- ○ Column widths
- ○ Formulas and number formats
- ○ Values and number formats

Operation
- ● None
- ○ Add
- ○ Subtract
- ○ Multiply
- ○ Divide

☐ Skip blanks   ☐ Transpose

[Paste Link]   [OK]   [Cancel]

Figure 2.4   Fixing the value of the random number sequence.

	A	B	C	D	E	F	G
1	Random Numbers	Fixed					
2	6						
3	17						
4	22						
5	8						
6	14						
7	18						
8	26						
9	21						
10	39	39					
11	39	39					

Advanced Filter

Action
- ○ Filter the list, in-place
- ● Copy to another location

List range: $B$1:$B$25

Criteria range:

Copy to: Sheet1!$C$2:$C$25

☑ Unique records only

[OK]   [Cancel]

Figure 2.5   Creating a nonrepeating random sequence.

values in the sequence; 39, for instance, occurs twice in a row. To get a sequence of unique values for the random sequence, select Advanced Filter under the filter command on the Data menu and copy to another location unique records only. You may now use the resulting list to select your 12 cases.

Comprehensive Sampling

The final strategy may not seem like a strategy at all, yet in some cases it is appropriate. In comprehensive case sampling, you choose all the cases available to you in a site. If there are 50 teams, you analyze 50.

Choosing a Sampling Strategy

Deciding what sampling strategy or combination of strategies to use is more an art than a science. The guiding principle is to choose the strategy that will best support the credibility of your eventual analysis. Obviously, if you are concerned with a phenomenon that is not widely encountered, you may want to use some variation of criterion-based sampling. If you wish to describe a best case phenomenon, it makes sense to use a best case sampling technique. But if you want to show how a phenomenon is distributed over the range of your data, you would not want to restrict yourself to best cases: a stratified, random, or even comprehensive sample may be best.

To make this discussion of sampling choice less abstract, consider the engineering capstone design data again. Suppose I want to describe the ways sketches are used in the engineering design process. And suppose I choose an example of the use of sketches from the opening lecture by the primary instructor, a lecture that stuck in my mind for the skillful and interesting way that the instructor used sketches.

When I complete my analysis and write up the results for my readers, what could I conclude? Minimally, I could suggest that the patterns in this case are examples of the kind of patterns that *may* occur when engineers use sketches to design. If I were to go further, however, and claim that these patterns were somehow typical, somehow best, or somehow characteristic of professional practice, the credibility of my claims would be undermined by my casual approach to the sampling strategy that lead to the case to begin with. For I had only picked an example that stood out in my mind without considering what made it exemplary—or typical, and so on.

A little more consideration of sampling would have gone a long way to putting my analysis on more solid ground. I could have, for example, used a comprehensive strategy to search my transcriptions for all interactions that involved the use of sketches and then tried to describe my case in terms of that comprehensive sample. I could have done a stratified sample, choosing to look at a couple of uses of cases by students in team meetings compared to a couple of cases used by instructors in class meetings. I could have used a random sample to pick 10 cases of sketch use. Any of these strategies might have put me on more solid ground with respect to the credibility of my results.

Many researchers object to using systematic sampling strategies to deal with naturally occurring data. In particular, random sampling will only be effective if you believe that the phenomenon of interest randomly occurs throughout your data. Much about verbal data is far from random. For this reason, you may be better off choosing a stratified sample, a best case sample, or a criterion-based sample. In any case, the most important lesson is to have an articulated sampling strategy and to be able to explain your strategy to readers in a way that enhances rather than undermines your credibility.

2.2 Try It Out

Suppose I have gathered data from 50 teams in the order shown in Figure 2.2. Complete the following table (downloadable from the course website) showing the gender characteristics of the following samples:

a. a convenience sample of 12.
b. a typical case sample of 12, with typicality defined by gender.
c. a best case sample of 12 with "best" defined as top-scoring.
d. a criterion-based sample of 10 using the criterion of experience.
e. a stratified sample of 12 stratified by gender composition.
f. a random sampling of 12 (use the following random number sequence: 16, 50, 36, 9, 25, 1, 5, 27, 19, 29 or one you generate on your own using the directions on pages 19–21).

Kind of Sample	Teams Sampled	# of Men-Only Teams	# of Women-Only Teams	# of Mixed-Gender Teams
Convenience				
Typical				
Best Case				
Criterion-Based				
Stratified				
Random				
Comprehensive				

For discussion: Given what you find, discuss the benefits and costs of each strategy.

Building in Comparisons

The core strategy in designing an effective analysis to answer your research question is to build in comparisons within the focus of your analysis. With comparisons, you are able to look at this focus in relationship to other phenomena that you take be *a priori* different. Such comparisons become essential in shaping the coding and pattern detection we describe in later chapters.

If you have a single focus for your analysis, or if you have used something other than a stratified sampling strategy, now is the time to build in the essential comparisons. If you have chosen to analyze a case because you think it is a best case, search for a case that has a high probability of not being very good. If you have chosen what you think is a typical case, look at the periphery of your data to search for cases that are less than typical. A fail-safe strategy always includes what appear to be negative cases or atypical cases for analysis.

Ideally, your comparisons come from the same data set as your core cases. Cases that come from the same data set but exhibit contrast help to define the boundaries of a phenomenon in a way that cases outside that set cannot. If, for example, we find the instructors in the capstone course consistently using sketches in ways different from the students, we may be on to something—both groups have a lot of context in common: the same course, the same design project, the same university, even the same field. If, despite all these commonalties, they consistently exhibit differences, then we may be on to something.

Cases for comparison may come, as the comparison of instructors versus students, from variations in the spatial dimension of a data set. Do not neglect, however, to consider the possibility of looking for temporal contrasts. Do you expect the phenomenon of interest to vary significantly over the time frame covered by your data set? If so, you may want to choose your contrasts accordingly. We might expect, for example, that the way sketches are used in the design process would vary significantly from the ill-defined early stages of design to the final stages of specification. In this case, we might want to compare samples from these two stages of design work.

The source of appropriate comparisons often comes from the literature in which you are anchoring your study. Does your literature take a certain situation as paradigmatic, typical, desirable? Can you build in a comparison with such a case in your data set? Or, if such a comparison is not available in your own data, can you find data elsewhere that might make an appropriate comparison? Could we compare, for example, the ways students use sketches to design with the way they are used in the published literature in engineering?

Setting up a Data Workbook

During the analytic process described in this book, you will store and manipulate your verbal data in a data workbook created in Microsoft Excel. Begin setting up your own data workbook by creating a new workbook and inserting worksheets to contain the preliminary components of your design.

Inserting Worksheets

When you open Excel, it will provide you with a workbook (as shown in Figure 2.6) with a set of empty worksheets reachable by the tabs at the bottom. To add additional worksheets, use the Worksheet command on the Insert menu as shown in Figure 2.7.

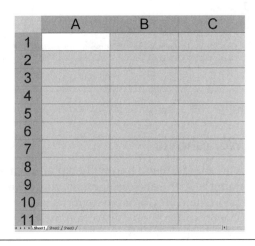

Figure 2.6   An empty Excel workbook with worksheets.

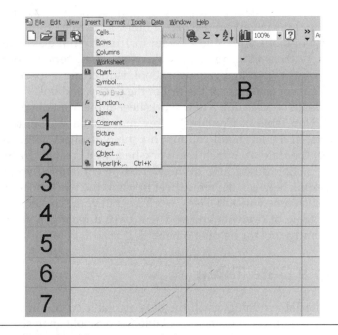

Figure 2.7   Inserting a new worksheet.

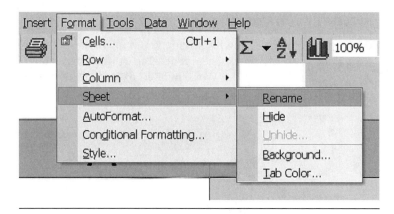

Figure 2.8   Naming a worksheet.

Naming Worksheets

Give each worksheet a name that will help you remember its contents. Get in the habit of naming a worksheet as soon as you create it in order to save yourself much confusion later on. To name a worksheet, select Rename from the options under the Sheet command on the Format menu as shown in Figure 2.8, and then type in the name you have chosen.

Setting up a Table of Contents

Although your data workbook begins life looking very empty, you will find that it fills up quickly and can become a morass in which to find your way. If you share your workbook with others—your instructor, your classmates, or a colleague on a project—these navigational problems can have serious consequences. One of the best ways to manage your workbook is to create a special worksheet that serves as a table of contents for the rest of the data workbook.

Begin by inserting a new worksheet at the front of your workbook and label it TOC (for Table of Contents). Now make a three-column list of all your worksheets. In the left-hand column, list the worksheet name. In the middle column, insert the date on which the worksheet was created. In the right-hand column, write a short description of the worksheet contents. If you want, you can insert a hyperlink between the worksheet title and the worksheet itself.

Each time you add a new worksheet to your workbook, make sure to add it to your table of contents and you will have a record of your work, a navigational tool, and a tool for helping others.

Setting up a Data Table

A Data Table catalogues all the data available to you in your data set. This establishes the universe of data available for possible analysis. As the sample table in Figure 2.9 suggests, it includes the following kinds of information:

Week	Date	Technical Meeting	General Meeting	Don	Joe	Sue
0	8/28/98					#1
1	9/3/98			#1		
	9/3/98		#1			
	9/3/98					#2
2	9/10/98				#1	
	9/10/98		#2			
	9/10/98					#3

Figure 2.9   Sample data table.

- The type of data, listed in columns across the top.
- The dates of collection/recording/publishing, listed in rows down the side.
- The weeks/months of the projects, numbered.
- The data label: For example, Technical Meeting #1.
- The accession number.
- This might be the number of the tape on which it was recorded, the document number under which it was filed, the name of the computer file in which it is stored.

PROJECT: DESIGNING YOUR ANALYSIS

Design the analysis of your project in your data workbook. A sample data workbook is available at the course website. Include and label the following worksheets:

DF: the descriptive framework or graphic representation of the situation from which your data is taken. You can use the Drawing toolbar in Excel to create this or import it from another graphic application.

DATA TABLE: a table listing of all the data available to you for analysis.

DESIGN: a. research question or question you seek to answer with your analysis;

b. description of the object at the focus of your analysis and the kind of data you have relevant to that focus;

c. description of the cases you've chosen, the method you've used for sampling, and a rationale for that sampling;

d. comparisons you have built into your sample and what you expect these comparisons to show;

        e. assessment of the strengths and weaknesses of your design in terms of feasibility and defensibility.

TOC: a table of contents that lists each of the new worksheets you have inserted.

For Further Reading

Bauer, M., and B. Aarts (2000). "Corpus Construction: A Principle for Qualitative Data Collection" in M. Bauer and G. Gaskell, *Qualitative Researching with Text, Image and Sound* (pp. 19–37). London: Sage.

Goetz, J. P., and M. D. LeCompte (1984). "Selection and Sampling" in *Ethnography and Qualitative Design in Educational Design* (pp. 63–92). Orlando: Academic Press.

Hamel, J., with S. Dufour and D. Fortin (1993). "Defining the Object of Study" and "Selecting the Ideal Case to Grasp the Object of Study" in *Case Study Methods* (pp. 40–44). Newbury Park, CA: Sage.

Miles, M., and A. M. Huberman (1994). "Focusing and Bounding the Collection of Data: The Substantive Start" and "Focusing and Bounding the Collection of Data: Further Design Issues" in *Qualitative Data Analysis: An Expanded Sourcebook* (pp. 16–49). London: Sage.

Silverman, D. (2001). "Ethical Issues in Ethnography," "Interviews," "Texts," and "Naturally Occurring Talk" in *Interpreting Qualitative Data: Methods for Analyzing Talk, Text, and Interaction* (pp. 54–56, 83–218). London: Sage.

CHAPTER **3**

Segmenting the Data

In this chapter, you will segment the data you have selected for analysis into units appropriate for analysis. After learning about how the units characterize various kinds of verbal data, you will use one or more of these units to select and segment your data.

Unit of Analysis

The analysis of verbal data begins when we segment the data into some unit for analysis. Unfortunately, too little attention has been paid to the unit of analysis. If we fail to segment our data into units of analysis before trying to place it into categories, we end up moving through our stream of data without awareness of its structure, to say "That's narrative" or "That's argumentative" whenever the fancy strikes us.

The trouble with this approach is that we don't know where the phenomenon lives. If someone asks us, "What is *it* that's narrative? What is *it* that's argumentative?" we have no answer: we have no unit of analysis. If we choose to segment the textual data by paragraph, however, we will have a ready answer: It's this paragraph that's narrative; it's that paragraph that's argumentative. The unit of analysis, then, identifies the level at which the phenomena of interest occurs.

Problems arise, however, when we choose an inappropriate unit of analysis. For example, it turns out that the paragraph is a very poor choice for looking at the phenomenon of discourse type. Because paragraph breaks are more a matter of typographical convention than meaning, they have a weak relationship to discourse boundaries. Boundaries for discourse types are, in fact, quite variable: A narrative may go on for pages or may be just a couple of sentences within a single paragraph that is otherwise argumentative.

As you might imagine, choosing an inappropriate unit for analysis can lead to enormous problems in coding data. Faced with a paragraph that contains both narrative and argumentative discourse, for example, a coder may not know whether to put it in one category or the other. Or if a narrative extends across paragraph boundaries, a coder may have trouble identifying it when looking at just one paragraph.

All such problems in coding can be alleviated by taking a more informed approach to choosing a unit of analysis appropriate to your phenomenon and segmenting your data accordingly. This chapter will help you develop an informed approach by reviewing some of the basic units of language and the kinds of phenomena with which they are often associated.

Basic Units of Language

In this section, we describe some of the basic units of language by which any stream of verbal data can be segmented. Then, in subsequent sections we discuss units characteristic of specific types of verbal data. Finally, we close the chapter by pointing to some of the problems you may encounter in segmentation and ways to handle them.

Words

A stream of verbal data is conventionally seen as made up of words and we write it down as a sequence of words. Oral interactions, do not, however, come to us as a stream of words; they come as a series of phonemes, the smallest units of distinguishable and interpretable sound. We as listeners do the mental work of hearing the words we transcribe.

Nevertheless, for the purposes described in this book, *words* can be taken to be the smallest unit of analysis into which any stream of verbal data can be segmented. Such segmentation is easy because of the typographical convention of placing spaces or some kind of punctuation before and after each word.

Using words as the unit of analysis in a comprehensive analysis can be challenging: It requires us to place every word in the verbal stream into a category. More commonly, words are used as the base unit of analysis for a selective analysis. Suppose, for example, we wanted to know how often human agents appear in the following text.

> Increasingly, the data of science education research are verbal data: transcripts of classroom discourse and small group dialogues, talk-aloud protocols from reasoning and problem-solving tasks, students' written work, textbook passages and test items, curriculum documents. Researchers wish to use data of these kinds to describe patterns of classroom and small-group interaction, development and change in students' use of technical language and concepts, and similarities and differences between school and community cultures, school science and professional science, the mandated curriculum and the delivered curriculum. *(Lem Ke, 1998)*

Using a selective approach, we could identify all human agents in the data and then calculate how often they occurred every 1,000 words. In our example paragraph, human agents are referenced 3 times as underlined in the passage and the passage is 83 words long. Calculating the rate per 1,000 words involves solving:

$$x/1000 = 3/83$$

or

$$x = (1000 * 3)/83$$

which can be solved to yield a rate of

$$x = 36 \text{ human agents per 1000 words}$$

In Microsoft Word, word counts can be easily determined by selecting the passage to be counted and using the Word Count command on the Tools menu bar that will yield the results shown in Figure 3.1.

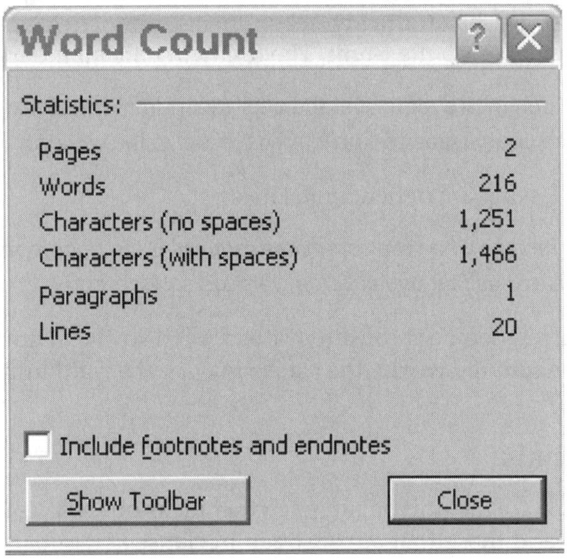

Word Count

Statistics:

Pages	2
Words	216
Characters (no spaces)	1,251
Characters (with spaces)	1,466
Paragraphs	1
Lines	20

☐ Include footnotes and endnotes

Show Toolbar   Close

Figure 3.1 *Determining word count in Microsoft Word.*

T-Units

Syntactically, the stream of language is structured as a set of *t-units,* the smallest group of words that can make a move in language. A t-unit consists of a principle clause and any subordinate clauses or nonclausal structures attached to or embedded in it. The following are all t-units:

> I ran to the store because we needed flour for the cake for Martha's birthday.
> Jen is the mail carrier who replaced the one we liked.
> Walking is my favorite form of exercise, the one with the least impact.

T-units are one of the most basic units of language. If the phenomenon in which you are interest is associated with the moves a speaker or writer makes, the t-unit may be the most appropriate unit for your segmentation. You might, for example, look at each t-unit in the transcript of a meeting of an engineering design meeting for the kind of move it makes: descriptions, proposals, questions, evaluations, and so forth. You could also look only at t-units that make proposals. The length of t-units has also been used as a measure of syntactic maturity.

Clauses

Clauses are the smallest unit of language that makes a claim—predicates something—about an entity in the world. A clause is a group of words containing a subject—the entity—and a predicate—the claim being made about the subject. When clauses stand alone, they are said to be independent. When they make sense only in conjunction with an independent clause, they are said to be dependent. As we have already seen, an independent clause with all its dependent clauses makes up the t-unit. The following are all independent clauses:

> the committee requested the prior report from the president
> once upon a time two children were lost in the woods

The following are dependent clauses:

> He refused *when the committee requested the prior report from the president*
> She told us *that two children were lost in the woods.*

If your phenomenon of interest is related to the claims that a speaker or writer makes about the world, the clause may be the right unit of analysis for you.

Nominals

Nominals are the unit of language that picks out objects in the world, both concrete objects and those that are abstract. In clauses, nominals can serve as subjects, but they may take other roles as well as the following examples suggest:

> *That cat* is obnoxious.
> *The day I was born* was cold.
> *June* is *a hot month* in *Kentucky.*

If your analysis is concerned with what is being spoken or written about, you may want to use the nominal as your unit of analysis. Nominals can help you identify the domains of knowledge from which speakers or writers draw; the worlds of discourse through which they move.

Choosing to analyze nominals is inherently selective—you make the decision not to look at the predicates that make up the clauses that, in their turn, make up the stream of verbal data. If you are going to look at nominals, you will probably want to choose some slightly larger unit (such as the t-unit) by which to segment the data, and then look at each nominal within that segment.

Verbals

You might also decide just to look at the *verbals*. Verbals are the unit of language that conveys action, emotion, existence. Inflected verbals—those with tense—fill the predicate slot in clauses, both independent and dependent, as in the following:

> When you *back up your hard drive regularly*, you *prevent data loss*.

Other verbals come as reduced verb phrases:

> The purpose *for backing up your hard drive* should be obvious.

In this example, "backing up" is actually serving as part of a noun phrase, but it is clearly a reduced form of the verbal "back up" used in the previous example. Some verbals like "back up" are idiomatic combinations of verb forms with prepositions, back + up, where the meaning is quite different from the sum of the parts. In these cases, the verbal is the entire idiom.

If you are interested in the schema being invoked, you will want to select the *verbal* as your unit of analysis. The verbal, "back up your hard drive regularly," for example, invokes a schema related to computer use in the same way that "went on a date" invokes a courtship schema. Using verbals, you can track the way schemas shift through your data set.

Because of their relationship to schemata, verbals are often indicative of genre choices, or shifting within genres from one part to another. In news reports, for example, hot news is often presented using present perfect tense:

> The government *has announced* support for the compromise bill.

Details are then presented in simple past tense:

> The compromise was worked out in committee yesterday.

In a similar fashion, in narratives, main events tend to be in simple past tense:

> She *went to see him* one day and she *said* "Has anybody been to see you?"

while really significant events may be presented in the historic present:

> And he *says* "No, but a right nice young lady came to see me"

Background events tend to be in progressive form:

> This friend of mine brought these photographs out, taken of the family through the years, and, *passing them around*, and *looking at them*, he said, "Oh! That's the young lady that came to see me when I was in bed."

If you are interested in genre, you may want to look at the predicate, particularly its tense, as a unit of analysis. A complete list of verb tenses with examples can be found at *http://www.gsu.edu/~wwwesl/egw/tenses.htm* if you need to refresh your memory.

Indexicals

Indexicals provide language with ways to anchor interactions to the specific context in which they occur. The essential indexicals are *I, here,* and *now*. With *I,* the speaker or writer points to him- or herself. With *here,* he or she anchors the discourse in place, and with *now,* he or she anchors it in time. Many other expressions depend upon our ability to identify the essential indexicals. For example, we cannot comply with the following command:

> Bring the book tomorrow.

without identifying the implicit *I* (to surmise what book might be relevant), the *now* (to figure out what is tomorrow), and the *here* (to know where to bring it). The essential indexicals scope out the beginnings of a common ground that interlocutors share, a common ground that can be increasingly enriched by further interactions.

Speakers and writers use the demonstrative pronouns, *this* and *that, these* and *those,* to point to objects, locating them physically or metaphorically with respect to the *here* of the discourse:

> Not *this* one; *that* one.

In a similar fashion, a writer or speaker moves from indefinite to definite articles, from *a* to *the.* The indefinite article serves to introduce an object into the shared common ground:

> I saw *a man* chasing after an ambulance.

Once introduced, the object can be pointed to with the definite article:

> Did *the man* catch it?

Pronouns serve a similar pointing function:

> No, *he* couldn't keep up.

If your analysis is concerned with understanding the development and nature of the common ground that speakers or writers create with their interlocutors, you may want to use one or more of the indexicals as your unit of analysis. Indexicals can also give you a handle on the extent to which interlocutors are coordinating with each other.

Personal Pronouns

Personal pronouns—*I, me, you, he, she, him, her, they,* and *them*—point to the world of interlocutors, which a speaker or writer takes as common ground. As we have already seen, pronouns are indexical. Focusing on the personal pronouns as a specific kind of indexical can give you clues about the scope of the human world in which writers or speakers see themselves as acting. Looking specifically at first person pronouns (*I, me*) can help you to examine the agency of the speaker or writer. Personal pronouns can be looked at for themselves (how many times did the speaker use *I*?), for what they refer to (where did the speaker talk about her family?), or they can be used to select other phenomenon for analysis (what kind of verbals does the speaker attribute to herself?).

Topical Chains

Topical chains in both spoken and written interactions are what allow participants to understand their discourse as about something. To some extent the topic of a discourse can be established by how it indexes objects in the worlds—listeners and readers will understand language that indexes the same object to be somewhat cohesive. But topical chains are the true workhorses of cohesion that writers and speakers establish.

Topical chains are constructed from t-units; each t-unit may either start a new topic or continue the same topic as the one before it. When a writer constructs a long topical chain, or when two interlocutors work together to extend one another's thoughts through a long topic chain, they develop the complexity of the topic.

Topical chains are identified by referentials:

pronouns	*it, they, he, she*
demonstratives	*this* and *that*
definite articles	*the*
other expressions	*such*

In oral discourse, the boundaries of topical chains are often marked (*OK, well*).

If you are interested in the conceptual complexity of discourse, the extent to which a topic is developed, or the depth of interaction on a topic, you may want to use the topical chain as your unit of analysis. You may also want to use the topical chain as a unit of analysis if you wish to do a selective analysis of discussions that concern a specific topic. Next to the t-unit, the topical chain is one of the most useful units for segmenting language.

Modals

Modals provide language users with a way to indicate the attitude or stance of the writer or speaker toward the message he or she is conveying. The stance can range from bald assertion:

Sally *will leave* tomorrow.

to assertions with less definite status

Sally *might leave* tomorrow.
Sally *could leave* tomorrow.
Sally will *probably* leave tomorrow.
Sally will *certainly* leave tomorrow.

In general, modality can communicate probability (she might go tomorrow) advisability (she ought not go tomorrow), or conditionality (she would have gone yesterday). Modality is often conveyed through the modal auxiliary verbs: *might, may,* and *must, can* and *could, will* and *would, shall* and *should, ought.* Modality can be conveyed in many other ways, however, as the following list suggests:

Conditionals: *if, unless*

Idioms: *have to, need to, ought to, have got to, had better, need to*

Adverbials: *probably, certainly, most assuredly*

Verbs: *appear, assume, doubt, guess, looks like, suggest, think, insist, command, request, ask*

All modals convey information about the level of obligation or certainty that speakers or writers associate with the content of what they are saying. If you are interested in tracking the degree of certainty with which interlocutors assess their claims, you may want to use modals as a unit of analysis.

Units in Conversation

In addition to the basic units that characterize all verbal data previously described, specific kinds of verbal data have additional regularities that can be exploited as units of analysis. In this section, we look at regularities in conversation that suggest a variety of units of analysis.

Time

All oral interactions, conversation preeminent among them, occur in *time.* Things said can be located temporarily both in absolute terms (2 P.M. on October 2, 2003) and in relative terms (5:21 minutes into a meeting). If you suspect that the phenomenon you are studying in oral interactions develops over time, you might well consider using time as at least one of your units of analysis.

Written interactions do, of course, occur in time; but a variety of time frames exist for their location: the time of their composing; the time of their publication; the time of the reception by a specific reader or readership. Time can be highly relevant to understanding text-based interactions between writers and speakers, but using time as a unit of analysis requires greater care in defining a temporal frame.

Time becomes particularly tricky in studying electronic interactions. Very often knowing when an e-mail was composed as well as when it was received is important to tracking the diffusion of messages across an organization. Time can also be highly important in tracking the versions of texts: A text read on January 9 might have the same name as one read on January 23, but the content might have been significantly changed.

Speakers

All conversation occurs between *speakers* and one of the most obvious ways to analyze conversation is to look at the contributions made by each speaker: How much does a speaker talk relative to another speaker? What kinds of things does he or she talk about? If you are interested in tracking a phenomenon associated with individuals in conversation, you may want to use speaker as a unit of analysis.

Turns

Conversation is made up of *turns*. For the most part, only one speaker talks at a time, although there is often some overlap at the edges. Much can be learned from looking at the turns in a conversation, particularly by speaker. How turns are allocated among possible speakers tells a great deal about relative power in a conversation: Who speaks most often? Whose turns are longest? Whose turn initiates new topics? If you are interested in phenomena of power, you may well want to look at the turn as a unit of your analysis.

Exchanges

Conversation does not take place through the random accumulation of speakers' turns. Instead it is organized by its participants into *exchanges*. An exchange can be thought of as a joint project undertaken by two or more speakers, through language. It is made up of the following components:

Initiation: the first speaker proposes a "joint project"

Response: the speaker responds to the proposal

Follow-up: the speaker acknowledges the response

There exist a variety of kinds of joint projects, with routinized initiations that call for expected responses. A question, for example,

Speaker 1: What time is it?

generally receives a reply that contains the information requested:

Speaker 2: Six-thirty

and that is followed up by some acknowledgement:

Speaker 1: Thanks.

Other routinized exchange include greetings:

Kate: Hi.
Ron: Hi.

and invitations:

June: Can you come to my party Saturday night?
Nance: Sure
June: Great!

There are many more.

While initiations in exchanges called for a certain preferred response, interlocutors need not give the preferred response. In fact, interlocutors have four options when faced with a conversational proposal in the form of an initiation:

Compliance: Interlocutor takes up the proposed project

Alteration: Interlocutor proposes an altered project

Declination: Interlocutor declines the proposed project

Withdrawal: Interlocutor withdraws from considering the proposed project

The options are roughly ordered in terms of the first speaker's preferences. They hope the interlocutor will comply, but if not, perhaps propose an alternative:

Don: How about dinner on Saturday?

Jen: Sorry. Can't. But what about tonight?

If no alternative is possible, the speaker hopes at least to get a declination that includes a reason for declining:

Don: How about dinner on Saturday?

Jen: Sorry. Can't. I'm going out of town to see my mom this weekend.

From the speaker's point of view, the worst response is a withdrawal:

Don: How about dinner on Saturday?

Jen: You've got to be joking.

Lots of information can thus be gained by looking at the exchange as a unit of analysis. If interlocutors routinely give dispreferred responses rather than preferred responses, for example, it is a sign of a lack of cooperation.

The nature of exchange structures can also shift significantly with context. With question-answer exchanges for example, the speaker is not supposed to know the information being requested. In school, however, teachers routinely ask for information they already know and then use their follow-up turn to evaluate the student's answer:

Teacher: Who knows the capital of New York?

Jean: New York City

Teacher: Good guess, Jean, but not quite right. Johnny?

Johnny: Albany?

Teacher: Good!

This IRE (Initiation-Response-Evaluation) exchange is so closely tied to the context of school that even adults long out of school will feel like they are in school if subjected to this exchange structure. Other contexts appear to have their own specific exchange structures as well. Thus, if you are interested in looking for variations in context, such as from teacher-directed discourse to peer-to-peer collaboration—the exchange structure may be your best unit of analysis.

Units in Text

Written texts have a variety of characteristics, some associated with conventions of publication, others with conventions of typography, and still others associated with the rhetorical interactions with readers at a distance. All can serve useful purposes as units of analysis for textual data.

Text

Perhaps the most obvious unit for analyzing textual data is the text itself. Unlike the stream of conversational data that must often be bounded in some arbitrary fashion for the purposes of analysis, written texts often have well-established boundaries. In a classroom, for example, students generally write and bind (with staples or paperclips) individual texts separately: The boundaries of individual student "papers" are seldom hard to determine. In published formats, conventions exist for separating individual texts: the chapters of an edited volume, the articles in a magazine or journal, the stories in a newspaper.

From the writer's point of view, many phenomena occur at the level of the text: the quality of the text, the genre of the text, the implied audience for the text. From the reader's point of view, texts also have a variety of characteristics that can be examined: their persuasiveness, their familiarity, their importance, and so on. If you are concerned with any of these or similar phenomenon, from either the writer's or the reader's point of view, you may find the text itself a good unit of analysis with textual data.

Date of Publication

Published texts have convention dates of publication that can be used as units of analysis. You might wish to select all texts published in a certain year. Or you might want to compare the characteristics of texts published in one year with those published in another year. If you suspect that your phenomenon shifts over time or you want to limit your selection of texts to a certain slice of the historical record, you may want to use publication date as a unit of analysis.

Publication Venue

Texts that are published as part of larger compilations—newspapers, journals, magazines, and so on—can be selected or analyzed by publication venue. You might want to select all the advertisements in *Wired* magazine, for example; or you might want to try to analyze the style of *Time* magazine. If you are concerned with a phenomenon associated with the kind of readership or affinity grounds that such publication venues represent, you may want to use publication venue as your unit of analysis.

Organization

Texts that are produced within a specific organization often provide evidence of the culture of that organization. You might want to select all the texts in the archives of a specific corporation, for example, or contrast two different corporations. If you are interested in a phenomenon associated with specific cultural contexts, you may want to choose the organization as the unit of analysis.

Author

The author of a text is often an important unit of analysis. When you use author as the unit of analysis, you look not at specific texts by an author, but at a body of work by that author. In a class, for example, rather than looking at one paper from each student, you look at a portfolio of work produced by that student. Or, with published texts, you might want to look at all the speeches made by a given candidate.

A lot of phenomena of interest are associated with authorship: the author's style; the impact of contextual and/or biographical factors on the individual; the development of the author over time. If you are interested in focusing on the phenomenon of the individual, you may want to use author as your unit of analysis.

Sentences and Paragraphs, Pages and Lines

Texts are structured by their layout with a variety of characteristics, any of which can be used as a unit of analysis. As units they can serve useful purposes as ways of selecting data when the phenomenon of interest is assumed to be regularly distributed through the text and you simply need some way of selecting part of the data.

You might choose, for instance, every third sentence, every fifth paragraph, every other page, or the first 10 lines of each section. When you are looking for a way of analyzing the distribution of meaning in a text, sentences, paragraphs, pages, and lines are not useful as units of analysis because they are arbitrarily related to meaning. But they can be quite handy as a way of making a stratified or random selection of textual data.

Sections

Longer texts are often divided into sections, each with its own label. You can use the section as the unit of analysis when you want to look at kinds of rhetorical moves that tend to happen in certain places. You might, for example, look at the opening section of research articles to examine citation patterns since these openings often contain reviews of the literature. Or, looking for the same phenomenon, you might examine all sections in which citations are made. Opening sections are also good places for looking at phenomena related to the voice of a piece, or the relationship defined between author, reader, and context.

Other times, you will want to skip opening sections and choose text from middle sections. Letters, for example, tend to have routinized openings that precede getting to the real issues. Using sections as a unit of analysis is closely related to genre issues discussed in the next section, but require less preliminary analysis to determine the rhetorical function of a piece of text.

Genre Components

Most texts belong to families of texts we call genres. While genres are not rigid, texts in certain genres do tend to share common features and common structures. Genres represent a typified response to a typified rhetorical situation. They thus exhibit many typified features: typified moves, typified relationships to audience, typified reading patterns, typified publication venues.

You can use the whole genre as a unit of analysis—looking at all letters to the editor, for example. Or you can use specific information you have about a genre to select or analyze specific genre-related features—the abstracts of research articles, the response of readers to scientific articles, and so on.

Metadiscourse

Metadiscourse is the part of discourse that talks *about* the discourse: the *meta*discourse. If you can imagine that a text has a primary channel in which information is conveyed, the metadiscourse forms a background channel through which the writer talks to the readers to tell them how to understand and interpret the text.

There are two primary kinds of metadiscourse. Textual metadiscourse directs the reader in understanding the text. Textual connectives such as *first, next,* and *however* help readers recognize how the text is organized. Illocution markers like *in summary, we suggest,* and *our point is* point to the kind of work the writer is trying to do. Narrators such *as according to, many people believe that,* and *so-and-so argues that* let readers know to whom to attribute a claim. Textual metadiscourse is directly related to the rhetorical awareness exhibited in the text, and can be used as a unit of analysis when you are concerned with rhetorical sophistication.

A second kind of metadiscourse is interpersonal, and serves to develop a relationship between writer and reader. Validity markers such as hedges (*might, perhaps*), emphatics (*clearly, obviously*), and narrators (*according to*) give the reader guidance on how much face value to give to the claim with which they are associated. Other attitude markers like *surprisingly* and *unfortunately,* communicate the writer's attitude toward the situation and invite the reader to share the same stance. Commentaries such as *as we'll see in the following section* and *readers are invited to peruse the appendix* are more extended directions to the reader. Interpersonal metadiscourse is directly related by the degree to which a text shows evidence of audience awareness. Interpersonal metadiscourse can vary by genre, by rhetorical sophistication, and by the degree of comfort a writer has with the audience addressed. If you are interested in a phenomenon related to audience, you may wish to look at interpersonal metadiscourse as a unit of analysis.

Units in Interviews

Interviews are a kind of conversation, and as such share all the features discussed in the earlier section on that topic. Interviews are, however, more structured than ordinary conversation and this structure provides us with further possibilities as units of analysis.

Response

Often implicitly, researchers select the *response* as their unit of analysis. That is, they look only at what is said in response to interview questions rather than at the interview as a whole. Such a move often helps to focus on the situation or person of interest, but it should never be done without considering the extent to which these responses have been shaped by conversational imperatives set up by the interviewer's questions.

Question

Interviews are often structured according to an interview schedule—that is, with certain fixed *questions* that are asked of all those interviewed or are asked repeatedly of the same person over time. In such situations, it is possible to use the question as a unit of analysis: to look at all responses to the same question. Since questions often direct respondents to particular topics, this unit of analysis will help to focus on phenomena related to the topic.

No guarantee exists, however, that the same topic will not have come up elsewhere in an interview. Thus, if you are concerned about being comprehensive, you may want to begin with the answers to certain questions and then move outward to look for the same topics elsewhere in the interview transcript.

Units in Electronic Interactions

On the surface, the stream of language found in electronic interactions may appear to be no different than other verbal data. Since we are in a relatively early stage for the development of e-mail, chats, webs, and other electronic forms of communication, it is difficult to be thorough in its treatment. It is well known, however, that some electronic interactions have characteristics that we have treated earlier as characteristic of conversation and characteristics that we have treated earlier as characteristic of text. In addition, there appear to be features that are specific to or more important in the context of electronic interactions. We describe these in the following sections as possible units for analysis.

Machine

In electronic interactions that occur in real time over networks, substantial differences can exist in the order of the stream of verbal data that appears on the *machine* of any given participant. In chats, for example, one machine will show a contribution being written in advance of it being posted and appearing on the machines of other electronic interlocutors. In fact, a text that is being written on one machine may never be posted. If you want to describe the experience of this writer, however, the text drafted but never posted—or drafted but then revised—may be quite important to you.

As well, because of bandwidth issues, different posts may appear on machines in different locations at different times. A message posted at Time 2 on a machine connected more remotely may appear on my machine after a message posted at Time 1 by a machine connected less remotely. The ordering of real time interactions, can, therefore, be different at different machines. Most researchers do not consider the effect of the machine, but in some situations, especially those where bandwidth is not adequate to manage the verbal stream, machine can be an important unit of analysis.

Version

The *version* of a text—the specific draft that it represents—has always been an issue with texts. Shakespeare's plays come in various versions, for example, and scholars have developed a way of analyzing them. In electronic interactions, versioning may be an even more important issue. Web pages can change from day to day; e-mail attachments may be revised hourly as they move from one interlocutor to another across a network. Controlling versions has become a serious issue in organizations that depend upon texts (including the special texts we know as "the code" in software development), and few good ways exist for looking at an electronic text and knowing whether it represents the same or a different version of another electronic text. Such differences can, however, be very important.

If you are studying electronic texts, you may wish to collect all versions of a specific text and analyze the changes. You may only wish to look at final versions. In any case, if you are dealing with electronic texts, some attention to the version as a unit of analysis is probably called for.

Application

Word processing may be the default application we think of for electronic texts, but a wide variety of computer applications create electronic texts, and if we are looking at issues related to technology, we may want to choose *application* as a unit of analysis. Because of the growing importance of electronic interactions in our culture, researchers using verbal data will increasingly be faced with analyzing verbal data that seems quite different from our prototypical conceptions of oral and written interactions. Application is the unit of analysis that will direct our attention to these differences.

One reason to consider application is that the features of a given stream of verbal data can vary enormously from application to application. The verbal stream in word processing has many of the features we associate with written texts (paragraphs, lines, sections, etc.) but the verbal stream in a spreadsheet application is organized with quite different units (cells, sheets, workbooks). In fact, in many applications, the whole notion of a *stream* of verbal data breaks down to be replaced by a spatial array. When we look at the myriad of verbal arrangements that make up a personal organizer, for example, we cannot recover in any way the temporal order in which such texts have been created or may be read. If you are dealing with verbal data that comes from a variety of applications, you would do well to consider application as one of your units of analysis.

3.1 Test Your Understanding

Within each group here and downloadable from the course website, match the unit in the first column with the kind of phenomenon it can be used to study in the second column.

Group 1

1	application in electronic interactions	r	the certainty or obligation of claims
2	text in written interactions	j	the domains of knowledge a writer or speaker refers to
3	t-units in language	y	the audience for written discourse
4	modals in language	x	rhetorical awareness in text
5	textual metadiscourse in written interactions	a	the moves a writer or speaker makes
6	nominals in language	v	The features associated with a given electronic text

Group 2

7	responses in interviews	u	the order of turns in electronic interactions
8	version in electronic interactions	k	frequency of textual phenomenon
9	author in written interactions	aa	the complexity and depth of ideas
10	sentences, paragraphs, pages, and lines in written interactions	c	the perceptions, feelings, beliefs of an interviewee
11	topical chains in language	d	phenomenon associated with the individual in text
12	machine in electronic interactions	b	the revisions in an electronic document

Group 3

13	exchanges in conversation	l	the schemata a writer or speaker uses
14	interpersonal metadiscourse in written interactions	q	relative power among speakers
15	verbals in language	s	typified action in writing
16	turns in conversation	e	context of interaction
17	date of publication in written interactions	m	the function of textual components
18	genre in written interactions	z	audience awareness in text
19	sections in written interactions	i	changes in text over time

3.1 **Test Your Understanding (continued)**

Group 4

20	time in conversation	h	cultural and organizational contexts for text
21	publication venue in written interactions	g	the common ground and/or coordination between participants
22	personal pronouns in language	o	the claims a writer or speaker makes
23	words in language	f	contrasts among interlocutors over time
24	clauses in language	t	the frequency of a phenomenon in language
25	indexicals in language	w	references to the human world

For discussion: How can you see the phenomenon at work in each unit?

Shaping the Text

Once you have chosen the appropriate unit for your analysis, you will need to apply it to your data in preparation for analysis. Essentially, this will involve three steps: shaping the text in Word, moving the text from Word to Excel, and then labeling the text once in Excel.

The goal of shaping the text within Microsoft Word is to produce a file where each segment of data is separated from the next by a single carriage return. Such data will be easy to move into Excel for further manipulation.

Inserting the Segmentation

The segmentation itself is perhaps the easiest task. Place your cursor at the break between one segment and the next and hit Return.

Removing Unwanted Carriage Returns

Before you segment the data, you will often need to clean up the data by removing extraneous carriage returns that could be mistaken for segmentation breaks. Particularly if you have copied electronic interactions to a file, you may find unwanted carriage returns at the end of each line. In texts, you may find unwanted blanks lines (two carriage returns) between each paragraph.

Removing unwanted carriage returns by hand can be tedious in the extreme. In Word, however, you can create a macro to do the task, assign it to a keyboard shortcut, and then apply it repeatedly with far less tedium. Basically, you are linking three separate commands together into a sequence that can then be repeated as a single command. The sequence that will remove a carriage return immediately preceding a line break is:

Backspace delete + insert space + move to beginning of next line

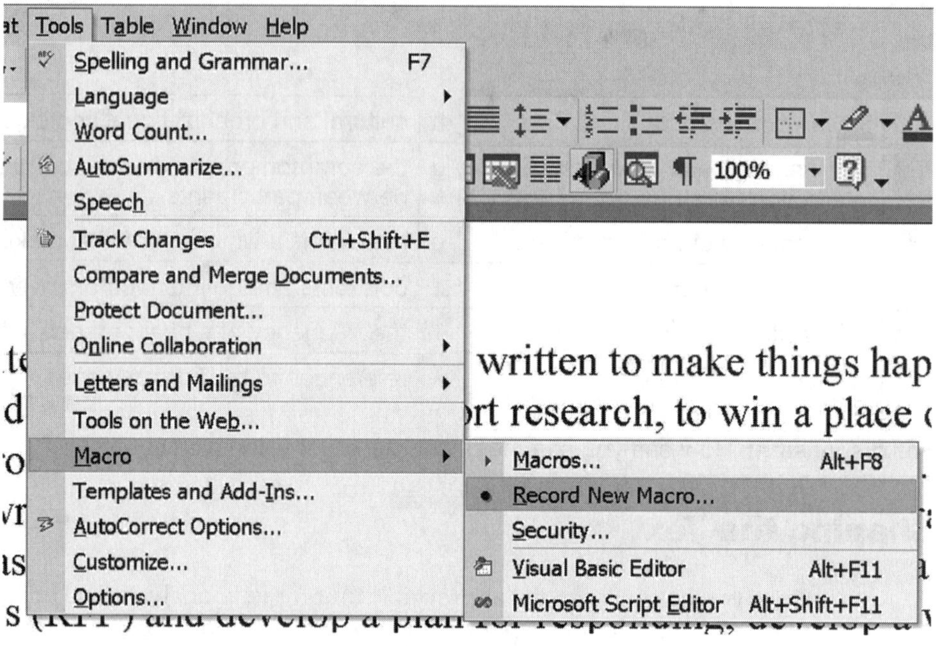

Figure 3.2   Invoking the Record New macro command in Word.

To link this sequence of commands into a single macro, invoke the Record New Macro option under Macro on the Tools menu as shown in Figure 3.2.

Give the macro a name you will remember and then click on the keyboard icon (shown in Figure 3.3) to assign it to a keyboard sequence.

Now type the keyboard sequence you wish to use and click the Assign button as shown in Figure 3.4. I usually assign my macros to the keyboard sequence cre-

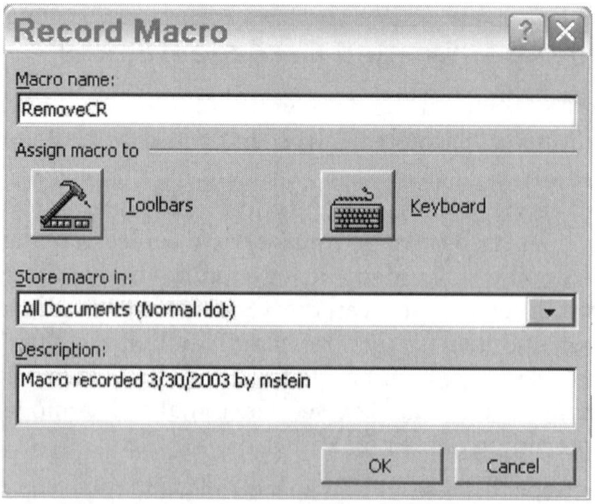

Figure 3.3   Naming the macro.

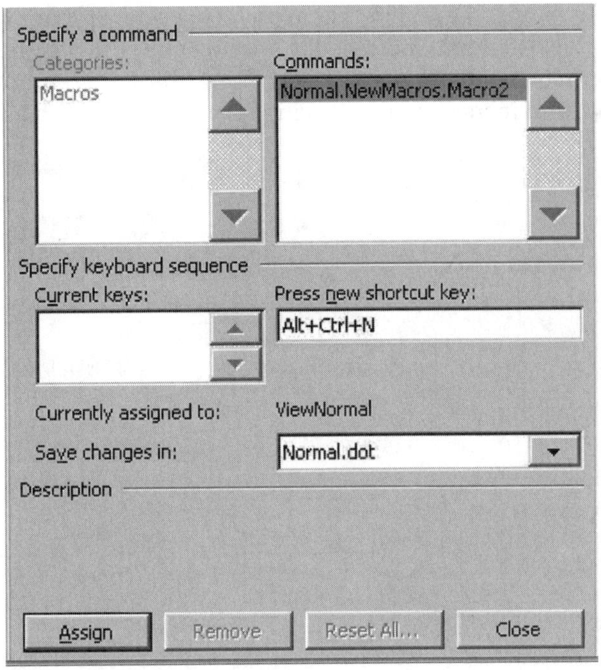

Figure 3.4 Assigning the macro to a keyboard shortcut.

ated by holding down both the Ctrl and the Alt keys while typing N. This sequence is not likely to be confused with any other commands, and by using the same one all the time, I save myself confusion.

Finally, once you return to the file in which you are working, key in the sequence of the three commands described (or whatever sequence you wish to use as a macro) and click on the square Stop Recording button in the small window that has appeared on your screen as shown in Figure 3.5.

Once you have recorded the macro you want, you can invoke it as many times as you want by typing in the keyboard sequence (such as Control + Option + N) you assigned it.

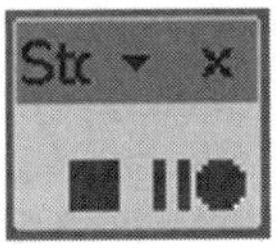

Figure 3.5 Recording the macro.

Creating a Segmenting Style

A file full of text segmented using paragraph breaks can be difficult to read, a problem that can be remedied by applying stylistic formatting to shape the text into a more readable form. For example, it is often helpful to increase the spacing after each segment in order to distinguish these breaks from simple text wrapping.

To create a new style, begin by formatting a paragraph the way you want. For example, we might increase the spacing after the paragraph to 6 points by placing the cursor in the paragraph, invoking the Paragraph command on the Format menu, and increasing the spacing after the paragraph as shown in Figure 3.6.

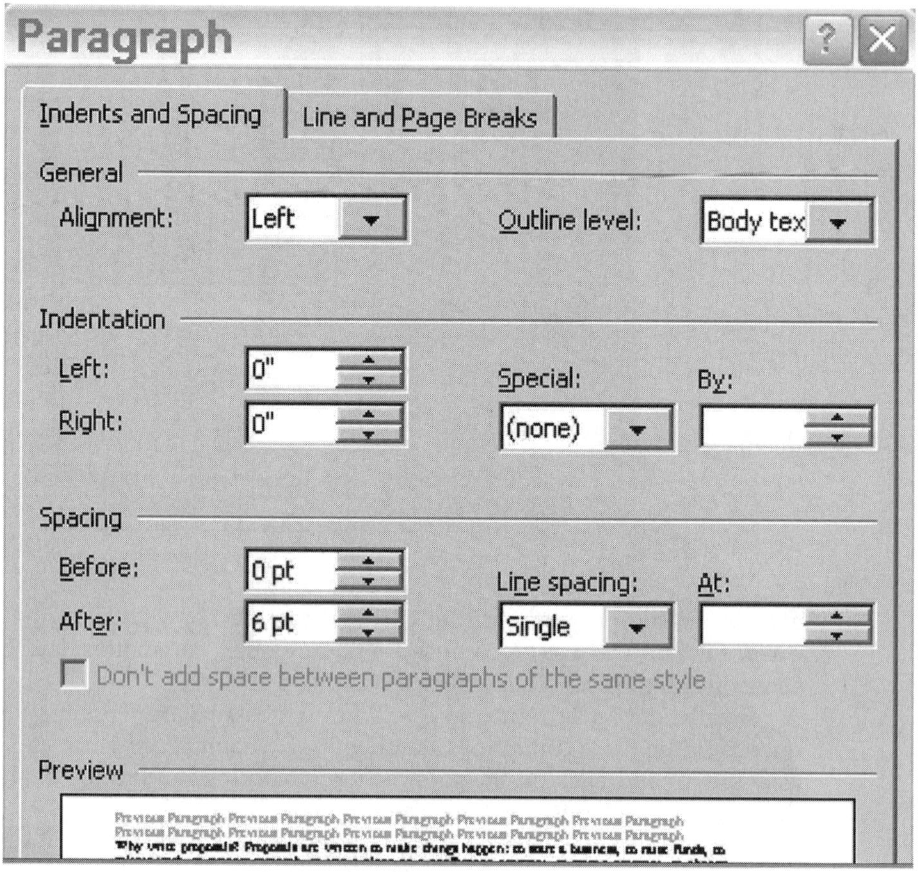

Figure 3.6   Increasing paragraph spacing.

To make this formatting change part of a new style, type a name for the new style (such as "Segment") in the style box usually located in the left-hand corner of the Formatting toolbar as shown in Figure 3.7.

To apply this style to other segments, select them and then choose the new style from the drop-down menu in the style box.

One of the benefits of creating a new style is that it can be easily changed in one place and these changes will be applied to every instance of the style in your file. So, for example, if we decided we wanted to indent each segment, we could indent one segment and then ask Word to update the Segment style so all of them were indented. To do this, click on the style name in the Style box on the Formatting menu bar and hit Return. In the dialogue box shown in Figure 3.8, click Update. Word will automatically apply the new style changes to every segment in your file.

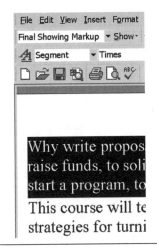

Figure 3.7 Creating a new style "Segment."

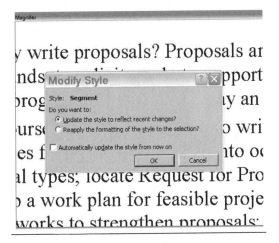

Figure 3.8 Updating a style.

Shaping Conversational Data

Shaping conversational data in preparation for moving it to Excel poses some special challenges. This data often takes the following form with a tab separating the speaker from the actual conversational snippet:

> P: okay . . . ah . . . in terms of your overall plan . . . then . . . where do you move from here . . . after you finish extracting information . . .
>
> J: which is going to be a chore . . . considering . . .
>
> P: it's going to take a while right . . .

Ideally, in Excel, you will want the speaker identification (P or J) in one column and the actual conversation in an adjacent column. To shape the text to meet this goal, use a hanging indent under the Paragraph command on the Format menu to move the conversation to the right:

> P: okay . . . ah . . . in terms of your overall plan . . . then . . . where do you move from here . . . after you finish extracting information . . .
>
> J: which is going to be a chore . . . considering . . .
>
> P: it's going to take a while right . . .

Now convert the text to a table by selecting it and invoking the Convert Text to Table command under the Table menu as shown in Figure 3.9.

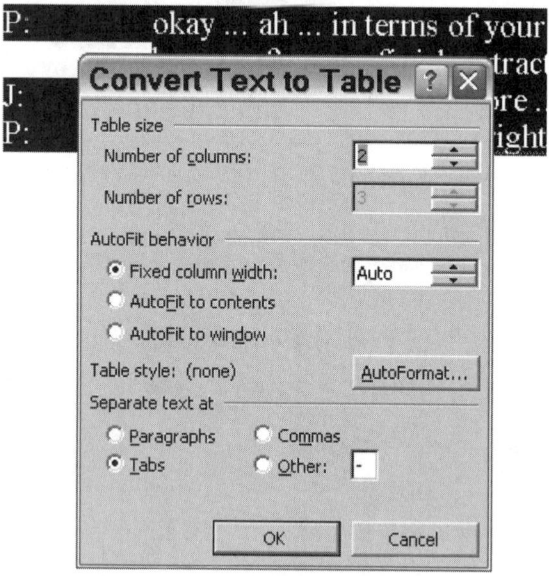

Figure 3.9   Converting text to table.

The result should be a 2-column table with each segment in a separate row:

P:	okay . . . ah . . . in terms of your overall plan . . . then . . . where do you move from here . . . after you finish extracting information . . .
J:	which is going to be a chore . . . considering . . .
P:	it's going to take a while right . . .

You can manipulate the width of each column by clicking on it and then moving your cursor over the border you want to move and dragging to the desired width.

Identifying Selections

If you plan to selectively code the data for a feature such as nominals or verbals, you should use formatting in Word to identify those features for later analysis. Perhaps the easiest way to do this is to underline the selected text:

P: okay . . . ah . . . in terms of <u>your overall</u> plan . . . then . . . where do <u>you</u>
move from here . . . after <u>you</u> finish extracting <u>information</u> . . .

J: which is going to be <u>a chore</u> . . . considering . . .

P: <u>it</u>'s going to take a while right . . .

When you move this text into Excel, this formatting will be preserved and help to direct attention during coding.

Alternatively, you may want to more explicitly pull the feature being selected from the full context of the segment. In this case, you should convert your text to a table in Word and add a second column next to the data column, into which you cut and paste the featured text:

P:	okay . . . ah . . . in terms of *your overall plan* . . . then . . .	your overall plan
J:	where do *you* move from here . . .	you
P:	after *you* finish . . .	you
	extracting *information*	information
J:	which is going to be a chore . . . considering . . .	a chore
P:	*it*'s going to take a while right . . .	it

You will need to add lines for each instance of the feature as we have done. This process is laborious, but may be necessary when underlining alone is not sufficient to distinguish the feature from its surrounding context.

Moving the Text

Once the text has been shaped appropriately in Word, you are ready to copy and paste it into the data workbook you set up in the last chapter. Open the workbook and click on an empty worksheet. Select and copy the data to be moved in Word and paste it into the worksheet, starting with Column B, leaving Column A free for the labels you will insert in the final step of this process. You should now have each segment on a separate line in Excel. If you have conversational data, the speaker identification should be in the first column and the conversation itself in the second column as shown in Figure 3.10.

Labeling the Data

After segments of verbal data are moved into Excel, you should label them to give each one a unique identity. Minimally, this means numbering each segment in the worksheet beginning with 1 and continuing until all the data is numbered. You will probably also want to label the data for its source and, if there are speakers, for its speakers.

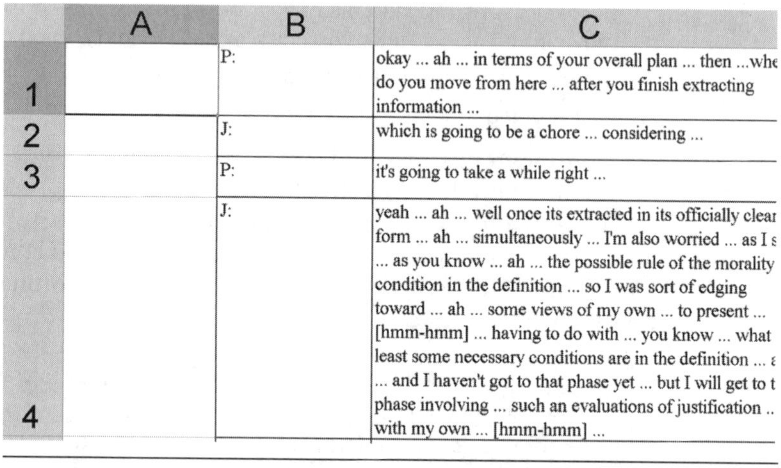

	A	B	C
1		P:	okay ... ah ... in terms of your overall plan ... then ...whe do you move from here ... after you finish extracting information ...
2		J:	which is going to be a chore ... considering ...
3		P:	it's going to take a while right ...
4		J:	yeah ... ah ... well once its extracted in its officially clear form ... ah ... simultaneously ... I'm also worried ... as I s ... as you know ... ah ... the possible rule of the morality condition in the definition ... so I was sort of edging toward ... ah ... some views of my own ... to present ... [hmm-hmm] ... having to do with ... you know ... what least some necessary conditions are in the definition ... ε ... and I haven't got to that phase yet ... but I will get to t phase involving ... such an evaluations of justification .. with my own ... [hmm-hmm] ...

Figure 3.10   Conversation data moved from Word to Excel.

Numbering Segments

To number the segments, in Column A, insert numbers starting with 1 and continuing for three or four segments. Next, select these cells and drag down to fill the column next to the data as shown in Figure 3.11.

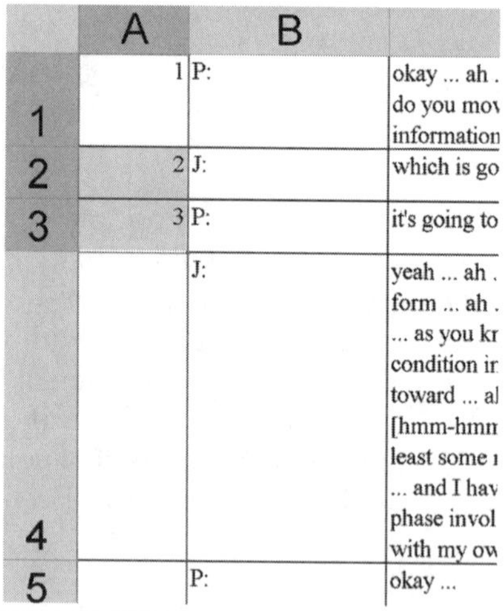

	A	B
1	1	P:	okay ... ah . do you mo information
2	2	J:	which is go
3	3	P:	it's going to
4		J:	yeah ... ah . form ... ah . ... as you kr condition ir toward ... al [hmm-hmn least some ı ... and I hav phase invol with my ow
5		P:	okay ...

Figure 3.11   Dragging down to number segments.

Labeling Segments

To label the segments with a label to indicate the source of the data or other relevant attribute (such as speaker), select the column where you want the label to appear and invoke the Column command on the Insert menu. This will insert a new column. Now type the label next to the first segment in the worksheet. Next, copy the label and select the rest of the cells in the column that have data and issue the paste command. Excel will copy the label next to each of the segments.

Numbering and labeling segments in this way will insure that each segment of data has a unique identity in analysis. Later on, you will always be able to tell the context from which a segment came through this identifying info.

3.2 Try It Out

In Word, segment the following text, downloadable from the course website, by t-units, move it into Excel, and label the segments. Compare your results with others in your class.

> The language people speak or write becomes research data only when we transpose it from the activity in which it originally functioned to the activity in which we are analysing it. This displacement depends on such processes as task-construction, interviewing, transcription, selection of materials, etc., in which the researcher's efforts shape the data. Because linguistic and cultural meaning, which is what we are ultimately trying to analyse, is always highly context-dependent, researcher-controlled selection, presentation, and recon- textualisation of verbal data is a critical determinant of the information content of the data. Data is only analysable to the extent that we have made it a part of our meaning-world, and to that extent it is therefore always also data about us. Selection of discourse samples is not governed by random sampling. Dis- course events do not represent a homogeneous population of isolates which can be sampled in the statistical sense. Every discourse event is unique. Dis- course events are aggregated by the researcher for particular purposes and by stated criteria. There are as many possible principles of aggregation as there are culturally meaningful dimensions of meaning for the kind of dis- course being studied. (Lemke, 1998).

For discussion: What issues did you have to resolve to do this segmenting?

Issues in Segmenting

As you segment verbal data, a number of issues will arise that require special han- dling. In closing this chapter, we call your attention to some of these.

Pronouns

Pronouns pose more difficulties in interpretation than the noun phrases they refer to. Many references are vague; others refer to persons or things outside of rather than in the text. And, of course, anytime you ask people to take the additional step of deciding what a pronoun refers to before they decide how to code it, there will be uncontrollable variation.

To manage this referential complexity, you can take one of two approaches as you segment the data. The first is simply to remove pronouns from coding if your unit of analysis would otherwise indicate that they should be coded. So, for example, if you are planning to code all nominals, you might decide not to code any nominal that was a pronoun. While such a decision might seem to eliminate a lot of data, if the elimination is spread proportionately through your coding categories, the overall patterns will be preserved.

Sometimes, however, you will not be able to eliminate the pronouns because they contain important information about the phenomenon of interest. If, for example, you are looking at references to human agents, you may not want to eliminate pronouns because they disproportionately contain a lot of information about agency in verbal data.

In this case, you can preprocess the verbal data to insert the noun to which the pronoun refers. So, for example, if we take the pronoun "he" to refer to Harry, we could insert as follows:

He [Harry] was taking his dog for a walk.

Resolving pronominal reference in advance of coding will allow you to code this data, but is inherently tricky. It may be best to resolve only those references about which there is no ambiguity and eliminate the rest.

Back-channeling

In much conversational data, the amount of back-channeling is tremendous. Ok's and Uh-huh's are usually frequently repeated and sometimes irrelevant to the phenomenon of interest. If you are interested in the content of the utterances, for example, back channel clues could be eliminated before coding. If you are interested in strength of cooperation, on the other hand, back-channeling may be very important.

PROJECT: SEGMENTING YOUR DATA

Segment a sample of your data. A sample of segmented data is available at the course website.

Begin by selecting a unit of analysis appropriate to the phenomenon on which you wish to focus. Next take a small selection of your data from a data worksheet in which you think this phenomenon is evident. Segment the data with your chosen unit of analysis. Then, shaping the segmented data in Word, move it to Excel and label the segments. Finally, check that the unit works for you:

■ Are the segments where more than one thing is going on relative to your issues of interest? If so, redo your segmentation with a smaller unit of analysis.

■ Are there segments where the phenomenon appears to go across segment boundaries? If so, redo your segmentation with a larger unit of analysis.

On a second worksheet labeled Segmentation, write up a short explanation of your choice of unit of analysis, its relationship to the phenomenon that interests you, and your reasons for rejecting other units of analysis that might also have been appropriate.

For Further Reading

Clark, H. (1996). *Using Language.* Cambridge, MA: Cambridge University Press.

Heritage, J. (1984). *Garfinkel and Ethnomethodology.* Cambridge: Polity Press.

Kolln, M., and R. Funk (1998). *Understanding English Grammar.* Boston: Allyn and Bacon.

Lemke, J. L. (1998). *Analysing verbal data: Principles, methods, and problems.* In K. Tobin and B. Fraser (eds.), *International Handbook of Science Education* (pp. 1,175–1,189). London: Kluwer Academic Publishers.

McCarthy, M. (1996). *Discourse Analysis for Language Teachers.* Cambridge, MA: Cambridge University Press.

Mehan, H. (1979). *Learning lessons: Social organization in the classroom.* Cambridge: Harvard University Press.

CHAPTER 4

Coding the Data

In this chapter, you will code the data you segmented in the previous chapter. After you devise an initial start list of codes, you will use an iterative process to move back and forth between sample data and coding scheme to develop a coding scheme that best tracks the phenomenon in which you are interested.

Coding Schemes

The ultimate goal of coding verbal data is to label segments of verbal data according to the phenomenon in which you are interested. Each segment should be assigned to one and only one code. The way that the segments are assigned to codes is governed by a coding scheme.

A coding scheme should articulate clearly the procedures you have used to code your data. It serves two functions. In the next stage of analysis, it will serve as a set of directions to a second coder. Later on, when you publish your study, it will let your reader know how you have defined your categories and how you have assigned data to them.

A sample coding scheme can be found in Figure 4.1. As you can see, it is written as a set of directions to a coder and includes the following:

1. The name of the *dimension* being coded for. In Figure 4.1, the name of the dimension being coded for is the World of Discourse. The name of the dimension should be clearly identified at the top of the coding scheme.
2. The names of the *coding categories*. In Figure 4.1, these include Rhetorical Process, Domain Content, and Narrated Cases, and are clearly labeled in bold type.

Coding the World of Discourse

Code as **Rhetorical Process** any t-unit that refers to the worlds in which people make claims as authors. This includes referring to:

- the texts, or parts of texts, in which claims are made: "the book," "the introduction";
- the authors of claims, including the students and teacher as makers of claims: "Childress," "I," "you";
- nominals that characterize actions taken by authors as claim makers: "question begging";
- descriptions of the interactions among authors as claim makers: "discussions," "disagreements";
- the requirements or directions for the assignment: "a paper in two sections";
- general categories of claims that can be made by authors: "a definition," "a justification," "a reason," "a question"; and/or
- any consideration or product relevant to the generation of claims: "my notes."

Code as **Domain Content** any t-unit that refers to the world of truths about paternalism. These truths have an eternal flavor to them: They are said to be true independent of any claim. This will include t-units referring to:

- philosophical concepts related to paternalism: "paternalism," "respect for persons";
- terms for the standard components of paternalism taken in an abstract way: "agent," "actions," features," "case";
- relationships between these concepts or components: "connection"; and/or
- characteristics, either positive or negative, of these concepts or components: "principle."

Code as **Narrated Case** any t-unit that refers to particular worlds in which (paternalistic) narratives take place that are taken to exist independently of domain concepts. These will include:

- specific people or actions that are taken to exist independently of the concepts in the domain but that may potentially be characterized with respect to these concepts;
- general categories of people or actions that are taken to exist independently of the concepts in the domain but that may potentially be characterized with respect to these concepts;
- characteristics of specific or general people or actions that are taken to exist independently of the concepts in the domain but that may potentially be characterized with respect to these concepts; and/or
- "you" or "I" when cast in a role involving an action that is taken to exist independently of the concepts in the domain but that may potentially be characterized with respect to these concepts.

Figure 4.1 Sample procedural coding scheme.

3. The *unit* of analysis to which the codes are to be applied. In Figure 4.1, the unit mentioned as being coded is the t-unit.
4. A *definition* for each coding category. In Figure 4.1, the definition for Rhetorical Process is given as "the worlds in which people make claims as authors."
5. An enumeration of the kinds of *cases* that the coding category includes. In Figure 4.1, Rhetorical Process includes cases referring to texts as well as cases referring to authors.
6. One or more *examples* of each case. Examples of authors in Figure 4.1 include "Childress," "I" and "you."

Getting Ready To Code

Developing a coding scheme involves an iterative process of moving back and forth between the developing scheme and a sample of the data to be coded.

Selecting a Sample

Select a part of the stream of verbal data that can be easily coded in one sitting that at the same time gives you enough data to see regularities in the phenomenon. Give some care to deciding how to select this initial sample. You want to maximize the amount of variation in the phenomenon being investigated. In most cases, this means selecting some data from both sides of any comparisons you have built into your design. On each side of the comparison, try to select a part of the stream of verbal data that represents the best case for the phenomenon: On the one side of the comparison, choose the part of the data in which the phenomenon is most obvious; on the other side, choose the part of the data in which you expect the phenomenon to be most absent or most different. Maximizing contrast through best case selection at this early stage will help you to sharpen your focus on the phenomenon and refine the coding scheme in a way that will distinguish among its variations.

How much data should you select? Generally, select somewhere between 200 and 500 segments if they are shorter units (clauses, t-units, etc.) and significantly fewer if you are working with longer units (exchanges, topical units), maybe 50–100. Overall, you want to balance the amount to be read (10 pages seems about the most that someone can code initially), the number of segments to be coded, and the range of the phenomenon to be considered. Put each part of your contrasting sample into separate worksheets in your data workbook.

In the example to be used in this chapter, as shown in Figure 4.2, we begin with the data after it is segmented and moved to a spreadsheet. In this case, the data are taken from a screen capture of desktop activity and focused on the way that texts are used and transformed during this activity. The data has been segmented using user action as the unit of analysis. The data recorded for each segment of user action consists of the time when the action was initiated (Column B), the contents of the text that was acted on during the action (Column E), the label

	A	B	C	D	E	F
1	**Segment**	**Time in 60 seconds**	**Text**	**Label**	**Text**	**How acted on**
9	8	001.31	5	have you heard of this	I've been searching on sources for enculturation in professional writing and have come across a german journal more than a few times. It is called Die Unterrichtspraxis. Have you heard of this journal? Jason	read
10	9	001.39	6	heard of this	I'm afraid I haven't.	reply
					sources for enculturation in professional writing and	

Figure 4.2 Sample data before coding begins.

for that text (Column D), and the analyst's informal note about how that text was acted on (Column F). Finally, each segment has been assigned a unique identifying number (Column A).

Managing Coding

To manage the coding, always store your code in the same data workbook as the coded data. When you return to the data after days, months, or even years, this practice will alleviate the need to hunt for the scheme underlying an analysis. It will also enable you to keep track of which version of a coding scheme was used with which set of coded data. Otherwise, proliferating coding schemes and multiple copies of data sets can make your life unbearable.

Storing the coding scheme in the data workbook can make the logistics of using the scheme hard to handle, however. You will find yourself repeatedly clicking tabs at the bottom of the workbook to go back and forth between the data and coding scheme. A better solution is to be able to see both worksheets at the same time as shown in Figure 4.3. To do so, move the relevant coding scheme worksheet out of the data workbook and into a new workbook using the Edit/Move or Copy command. Then you can arrange the two workbook windows to best suit your work. Just remember to move the coding scheme worksheet back into the data workbook before you save and close your work for the day!

	A	E	F	G
1	**Segment**	**Text**	**How acted on**	**Tool**
9	8	I've been searching on enculturation in profes and have come acros journal more than a fe called Die Unterrichtsp heard of this journal?		Eudora Pro
10	9	I'm afraid I haven't.		Eudora Pro
11	10	I've been searching on enculturation in profes and have come acros journal more than a fe called Die Unterrichtsp heard of this journal?		Eudora Pro

(Overlapping window "Book3")

	A
1	**Tool**
2	Eudora Pro
3	Palm Desktop
4	Netscape
5	Word
6	Excel
7	Off-line

Figure 4.3   Viewing data and coding scheme simultaneously.

Generating a Coding Scheme

Two methods exist for generating a coding scheme. In the first, you begin with existing categories. The anchoring literature (see Chapter 1) may have already suggested the categories in which the phenomenon should fall. Or your work on the analytic design may have already suggested the ways in which the built-in comparisons in your data set should be different. And finally, especially if you have mucked around in a site, you may have strong intuitions about what to look for. All three of these sources—literature, built-in comparisons, and intuition—should be consulted to create a "start list" of possible categories that may be relevant to coding. You will, of course, need to extend and modify this start list as you go along in order to mold your categories more appropriately to the data.

The second method for generating a coding scheme does not begin with a start list of preexisting categories. Instead, you look at the initial data set and let it speak to you. That is, you let each segment of the data suggest appropriate categories to describe what's happening with the phenomenon of interest. Such categories are more grounded in the data than those gleaned from external sources like the literature, but cannot help but be influenced by the knowledge and experience you bring to the analysis. For this reason, the difference be-tween these two methods, the start list approach and the grounded approach, lies not so much in the presence or absence of influences external to the data it-self, but in the degree to which the analyst has tried to articulate these outside influences.

The process of developing a coding scheme, whether it begins with a start list or not, involves the same process. Take each segment in your initial data sample and try to assign it one of the codes in your scheme. As long as such an assignment can be made, coding continues. You should assign each segment of data to one and only one category in the coding scheme. As shown in Figure 4.3, for example, each segment of the sample data has been coded for "Tool." Segments 8, 9, and 10 all fit under the category of "Eudora Pro" since they are user actions taken in the e-mail tool by that name.

Assigning codes within Excel is relatively easy with Excel's auto-completion. As soon as you type the first few letters of a code you have used previously, Excel will automatically suggest that completion. To select it, hit Return. To use auto-completion effectively, it is best to use codes that are distinct in their first few letters.

Revising a Coding Scheme

When you encounter a segment that is not covered in the coding scheme, you need to revise your scheme. The process of revising your coding scheme should accomplish two purposes. First, it helps you to come up with a set of coding categories that best reveal the distinctions you consider important in tracking the phenomenon of interest. Second, and almost as important, the process should help you to better understand the phenomenon of interest—what is it that you are coding for? In the next few sections we talk about the further development of coding schemes to reflect this growing understanding.

Adding a Category

Adding to a coding scheme requires you to add a new category to cover a new variation in the phenomenon. As shown in Figure 4.4, for example, when the coder reached Segment 21 in our example, she realized that the user action, "Go to Daily Calendar" was not completed using the e-mail tool Eudora Pro but was executed using the Palm Desktop tool. So she added a new code "Palm Desktop" to cover the case. Applying codes and generating new codes as needed continues until the sample of data taken for initial coding has been coded.

Breaking a Category Apart

Refining a coding scheme is a bit more complex. In refining a scheme, you often take an existing code and break it apart into two or more new codes. Such breaking apart is required when you realize you have been lumping together phenomenon that need to be distinguished. For example, suppose the coder has reached Segment 319 in which the user checks off the task "scope out Palm Project (Feb 1)." This user action has occurred in the Palm Desktop and the coder could easily assign it the Palm Desktop code as she has done for the view Daily

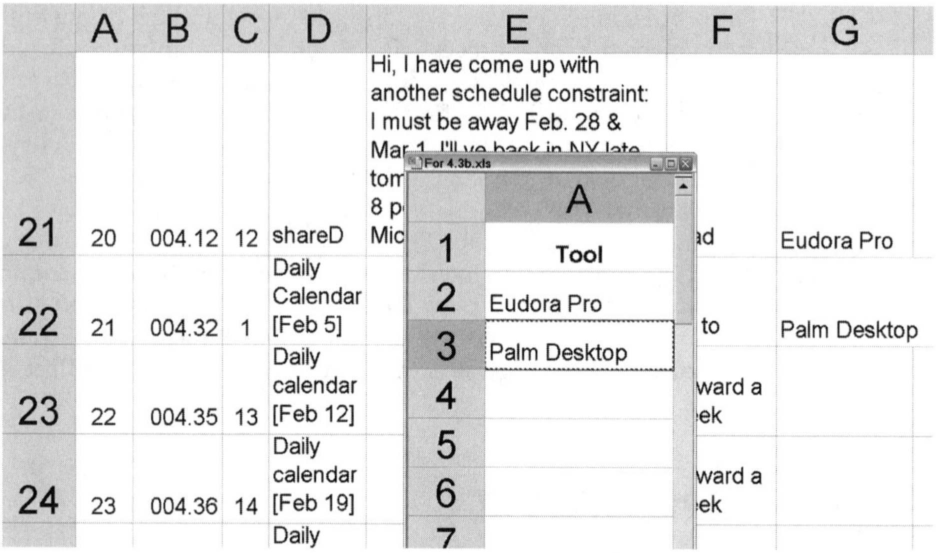

Figure 4.4 Adding a code to a coding scheme.

Calendar action in segment 318 before it. The coder realizes, however, that the Palm Desktop should be treated as a bundle of tools rather than a single tool: first, a Calendar tool in which users can see and schedule events on a calendar, but also a Task List tool where users can create and manage a To Do list.

Once you decide to break apart an existing code into components, two distinct actions must be taken. First, you must edit your code book to remove the current category and replace it with codes for the new categories. Second, you must review all data coded thus far and replace their codes with one of the new codes. Thus, if our coder decided to split the Palm Desktop tool into its components, she would need to add codes for Calendar and Task List to her coding scheme (as well as other codes for additional functionalities in the Palm Desktop such as Address Book), and then review the 318 segments coded thus far to replace all instances of the code Palm Desktop with one of the new codes.

Be careful about how you split categories into subcomponents. Make sure that the new distinctions you are entering into your coding scheme are both relevant to your phenomenon of interest and at the same level as the remainder of your coding scheme. If your new categories do not seem to go with your existing categories, but nevertheless seem to be going in the right direction, you may decide to revise your entire scheme in this new direction.

For example, once our coder splits the application Palm Desktop into multiple tools like Calendar and Task List, she may begin to wonder whether the remaining codes in her coding scheme, all of which are defined at the level of the application, may also be at the wrong level. In Eudora Pro, for example, she may realize that in addition to the tools for reading and archiving mail, there is also an

Address Book. Why should the Palm Desktop Address Book have its own code while the Eudora Address Book does not?

If you decide to revise your entire coding scheme, you will need to start over and recode your entire data set codes thus far. Rather than deleting the existing codes immediately, you may wish to try out the new coding scheme in a second column in your worksheet and compare the two. Which one better gets at what you're interested in? It is not at all uncommon for a coder to decide that the first scheme is better than the more detailed scheme. If this is the case, then keeping rather than deleting the column with the first coding will save a great deal of reconstructive work.

Adding Another Dimension

Occasionally, as you work to refine a coding scheme, you will realize that you have combined categories for two distinct phenomena into a single coding scheme. One clue that this has happened is a repeated desire to apply two different codes to the same segment. As we have already said, a scheme should be so devised that only one code applies to each segment of data. If you find yourself repeatedly wanting to apply two codes to the same segment, it may indicate that you are dealing with two distinct dimensions of the phenomenon that ought to be coded separately.

A dimension of an analysis of verbal data is a range of variation, represented through a coding scheme, that represents a feature of the data and can stand as conceptually independent of other features. Each coding scheme should be associated with only one dimension of data variation that, in turn, should correspond to only one feature of the phenomenon of interest. When you realize you are dealing with two distinct dimensions of your data, you should separate them, develop a separate coding scheme for each one, and then apply each scheme to the data separately.

For example, when our coder wondered why the Palm Desktop Address Book should have its own code while the Eudora Address Book does not, she could have begun to think about separating her analysis into two distinct dimensions. She might realize that the code Address Book did not so much represent a different kind of Tool as a distinct kind of Structure. Structures like address books, she might think, have the similarities no matter what Tool they are embedded in: They have names of people, they have phone numbers, addresses, etc. For this reason, rather than revise the coding scheme for tool, then, our coder could instead create a new dimension for coding called "Structure" and develop a coding scheme to track it. In this example, our coder would code the entire sample of data for Tool first and then return to do a second pass through the data on this new dimension of Structure.

4.1 Test Your Understanding

In the table below and downloadable from the course website, match the following coding situations with ways of dealing with them. Compare your answers with your classmates.

1. You find yourself placing multiple segments in succession into the same category.

2. You think a segment belongs in a certain category, but there's nothing in your definition to indicate this.

3. You worry that by coding the data for one phenomenon, you are overlooking another equally important phenomenon.

4. You realize that the same piece of data can be placed into two different categories because the categories can both be applicable at the same time.

5. You keep making a mistake, putting a certain kind of phrase in one category rather than another.

6. You realize that the same piece of data can be placed into two different categories because the first part of it fits the first category and the second part fits the second category.

7. You keep changing your mind about how to code the data each time you look at it.

8. You find yourself placing a larger percentage of your data into a miscellaneous category.

a. You add a case to the coding category.

b. You decide to change from a comprehensive coding scheme to a selective one and code only for the phenomenon of interest.

c. You decide you need a better understanding of the phenomenon that you are coding for with better definitions of each category.

d. You realize that you are coding data along two different dimensions, so you develop two coding schemes and code for each dimension separately.

e. You realize that you are interested in coding for two different phenomena, so you develop two coding schemes and code for each dimension separately.

f. You add an example to the category.

g. You decide you have not segmented your data finely enough. You go back and resegment using a smaller unit of analysis.

h. You decide you have segmented your data too finely, and go back and resegment using a larger unit of analysis.

For discussion: If you and your classmates saw alternative strategies for dealing with a situation, how would you decide among them?

Techniques for Inspecting Coding

As you develop a coding scheme during the iterative back and forth between data and scheme, you will often want to look at all the data you have assigned a given code. Several techniques can be used to accomplish this in Excel.

	A	B	C	D	E	F
1	**Segment**	**Time in 60 seconds**	**Text**	**Label**	**Text**	**How acted on**
342	322	42.57	81	Task List [Palm]		view
343	323	42.59	81	Task List [Palm]		move
344	324	43	81	Task List [Palm]		enlarge
346	326	43.17	81	Task List [Palm]		view
405	385	119.17	81	Task List [Palm]		open
				Task List		

Figure 4.5   An Autofilter turned on in Column C showing all data coded as Text 81.

Filtering

Perhaps the most important is filtering. When you ask Excel to filter your data, you ask it to show you data that meets certain criterion and hide the rest. With an autofilter, you may choose to look at the data that matches any given code in a column. In Figure 4.5, for example, an autofilter has been activated in Column C showing all data that has been coded as referring to Text 81.

To use an autofilter, select the column containing the coding (Column C in this case). Next select the Autofilter command under Filter under Data in the toolbar. A down arrow like that shown in Figure 4.5 will now appear at the top of the column. Finally, click on the down arrow and drag to select the particular code you want to inspect (in this case 81). To turn the autofilter off, return to the Autofilter command under Filter under Data in the toolbar and deselect it.

Sorting

You can also inspect the results of a coding scheme by sorting the data according to coding category. With sorting, you ask Excel to reorganize the data so that all data with a certain code is clustered together.

To sort data, select the rows to be sorted and then select the Sort command under Data on the toolbar. A dialogue box will pop up like that shown in Figure 4.6. Choose the heading of the column by which you wish to sort and then select OK. Excel will then group the data by values in that column.

Unlike filtering, sorting changes the actual order of data in a spreadsheet. Since you probably wish to preserve your coding sheet with the order of data intact, you will want to make a copy of it before you sort. Of course, to unsort data just sorted, you can use the Undo command under Edit on the toolbar.

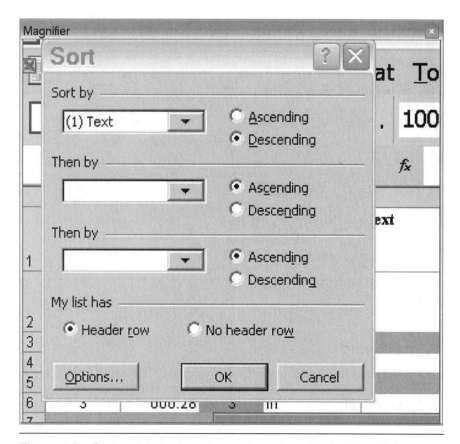

Figure 4.6   Sorting data by the values in the column labeled Text (Column C).

Techniques for Automated Coding

In coding, you may be able to use some form of automated coding. By looking for and matching selected patterns, many applications, including Word and Excel can find exact matches for a member of an enumerated category.

In Word, this is accomplished by the Find and Replace command under Edit on the toolbar. As shown in Figure 4.7, by searching in a text for a specific word such as the definition pronoun *the* and replacing them all with something easier to find (such as ****the***), not only will Word make these replacements, but it will also report how many replacements it made.

Excel has even more powerful pattern-matching functions for automated coding. In Figure 4.8, we have an example where the clauses shown in Column E have been automatically coded for the presence or absence of various modals such as *can, may,* and *could.* Column F, for example, records 1 if *can* is present and 0 if it is absent. At the top of the column, in Row 2, we see a total of 18 turns containing *can.*

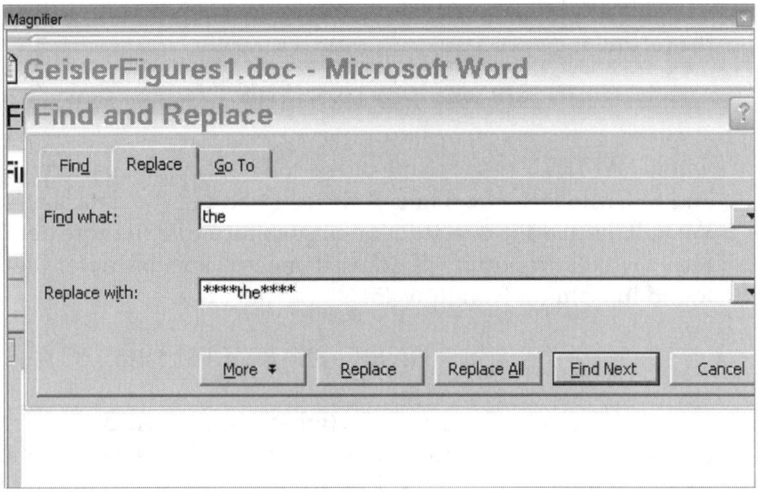

Figure 4.7   Global Find and Replace for automatic coding.

Figure 4.8   Automated coding.

This kind of automated pattern matching is accomplished through the use of the formula

=IF(ISERR(SEARCH(PATTERN,SEGMENT)),0,1)

where PATTERN is the name of the cell holding the pattern you are searching for and SEGMENT is the name of the cell holding the data that you want to search. We will discuss the construction of such formulas in more detail in a later chapter. Here, what's important is what it means. For example, the following formula found in Column F on Row 45:

=IF(ISERR(SEARCH(F$1,$E45)),0,1)

searches for the pattern in F1 (which is the word *can*) in the cell E45 ("Of course, I can't"). Because it finds can in the word "can't", the formula returns 1. Otherwise, it would return 0, as you see in many of the other cells in Column F.

You can use this formula whenever you want to do automatic coding in Excel. To use it, you must place the pattern you want to use in Row 1 and the text to be searched in Column E. In the formula, replace F with the name of the column in which you want to code for the pattern. Replace 43 with the number of the first row of data. Then type in the resulting formula. For example, if I wanted to code *me* in column F and the first row of data was on Row 4, I would type *me* into F1 and the following formula into cell F4:

=IF(ISERR(SEARCH(F$1,$E4)),0,1)

Next, I would select this cell and drag it down to fill the rest of Column C until the last line of data. At the top, in cell F2, the following simple formula provides me with the total 22:

=SUM(F4:F395)

4.2 Try It Out

In the workbook Automated.xls, downloadable at the course website, is an example of a sample of conversational data with an automatic coding for the word *me* in Column E. In Column F, use an automated coding procedure to code for the word *we*. Begin by copying the formula in E4 to F4 and then edit it as described in the previous section.

For discussion: Under what circumstances could you imagine using automatic coding with your data? What is it good for? In what ways is it limited?

Some Complex Coding Situations

In most situations, coding data is relatively straightforward. Each segment of data is placed in one and only one category, taking a comprehensive approach to analysis. Two more complex situations can arise, however, where your procedures and coding scheme can become more complex. These are addressed in the following sections.

Selective Coding

So far, we have been discussing the comprehensive approach to coding verbal data analysis. As we have seen, this requires you to place each segment of the verbal stream into a category. In a more selective approach, the entire stream is not coded, however. Instead, units from that stream are first selected and then coded.

In order to preserve the context for coding the selected units, it is important to keep them together with the stream of data from which they come. The easiest way to do this is to segment the data into some reasonable unit, place those segments in one column and place the units contained in that segment in a second column. If a segment contains more than one unit, multiple lines are used, one for each unit, and the contextualizing segment is repeated for each one.

For example, if we wanted to code all nominals as shown in the selective analysis in Figure 4.9, we would first segment the data into some reasonable unit like the t-unit to create the context as we have done in Column E. Next we would pull out the nominals in that t-unit and place them in the adjoining column as we have done in Column F. Then we could go on to code each of these nominals while still having ready access to the context from which they were drawn.

	A	B	D	E	F
1	Nominal	T-Unit #	Speaker	Text	nominal
2		346			
3					
4	1		1 Cheryl	I mean...	I
5	2		2 Lee	Jesus.	Jesus
6	3		3 Cheryl	See I :	I
7	4		4 Cheryl	see where	
8	5		5 Cheryl	this little thing is?	this little thing
9	6		6 Cheryl	It looks to me	It
10	7		6 Cheryl	It looks to me	me
11			7 Cheryl	like it got wiped out.	it
12			8 Cheryl	That's where	that
13			9 Cheryl	I wrote it.	I
14			10 Cheryl	I wrote it.	it

Figure 4.9 Selective coding for nominals using the t-unit as context.

If a segment you are preparing for selective coding contains more than one unit, you should use multiple lines, one for each unit, and repeat the contextualizing segment for each one. We have done this, for example, in Figure 4.9 with t-unit 6, which has two nominals, *it* and *me*. As you can see, they are placed on separate lines in the worksheet and the contextualizing information (t-unit 6) is placed next to both of them. The same procedure has been followed for t-unit 9. Notice that all the nominals have been separately numbered in Column A using a different sequence than the numbering of the t-units in Column B. This will then allow you to keep their identity distinct in your analysis despite their common contextualizing segment.

Nested Coding

A second complex coding situation can arise when you want to nest one coding scheme within another. Suppose, for example, you code the conversational turns of a tutor in a writing center using a coding scheme that includes "responds to text," "discusses assignment," and "talks about other things." You then want to go on to look more closely at those turns that "respond to text," to decide whether they were facilitative or directive. You would then be using nested coding schemes in which the second dimension (facilitative versus directive) was applied selectively only to data that had been placed in a specific category as a result of the first coding scheme.

To prepare for nested coding of data once the first coding is complete, block out the cells for which no further coding is needed, as shown in Figure 4.10. Here,

	A	C	D	E	F
122	117	John	The way I had seen this personal communications device	Proposal	
123	118	John	was it	Response	
124	119	John	actually belongs to the DCR table, not to the person.	Proposal	
125	120	Ed	Right.	Question	
126	121	John	Th-at it would be here	Question	
127	122	John	and then really when you plug in your portable,	Response	
128	123	John	you're really only accessing applications	Response	
129	124	John	and you really only access the hard disk.	Question	

Figure 4.10   Preparing for nested coding.

we are preparing to further code just those turns that were coded as "Questions" using the first coding scheme in Column E. We will then be able to go on and use a second nested coding scheme in Column F. The dark shading in cells in Column F tells us that those particular segments are not to be coded, but by keeping them in the worksheet while we code, we have access to the full context of the surrounding turns.

Enumerative Coding Schemes

The kind of coding schemes we have been talking about so far in this chapter can be thought of as *procedural*. They provide decision rules that will allow us to place each segment into the category intended by the researcher.

A second kind of coding scheme exists that is *enumerative* rather than procedural. Instead of providing cases and examples of those cases, a complete enumeration is provided. In Figure 4.11, for example, a complete enumeration is provided of the text codes used in the study of desktop activity. Each distinct

	A	B	C	D
1	#	**Structure**	**Header**	**Text**
2				
3	1	calendar	Daily Calendar [Feb 5]	
4	2	Out box	Out	
5	3	In Box	In	
6	4		Activity Theory Refs	see email "activity theory refs" in research folder
7	5	email	have you heard of this	I've been searching on sources for enculturation in professional writing and have come across a german journal more than a few times. It is called Die Unterrichtspraxis. Have you heard of this journal? Jason
8	6	email	have you heard of this	I'm afraid I haven't.
9	7	email	Fabric.com: A "We Love You" Sale	Good Friday Morning. I hope this note finds you well and ready to enjoy a pleasant and relaxing weekend.

Figure 4.11 Example of an enumerative coding scheme.

text that was accessed during the desktop session is listed here and assigned its own number. In the data itself then, these numeric codes have been used to code the data for the dimension of Text as shown in Column C in Figure 4.2 and following.

Generally, a procedural coding scheme is preferred to an enumerative scheme because neither your second coders nor your readers can hold in their minds and make meaning of long lists. A few important exceptions exist. First, if the dimension shows relatively small variation along recognizable categories, an enumerative list can suffice. Second, if the concept underlying the dimension is hard to grasp, perhaps because the distinction is part of the culture being studied but not part of the culture of your second coder or your readers, an enumeration may be the best way to communicate the fuzzy set.

PROJECT: CODING YOUR DATA

Code a sample of your data. A sample of coded data is available at the course website.

Select an initial sample of data, making sure to include maximum variation on the phenomenon that interests you. Then develop a coding scheme that does justice to the variations you find there. If possible, begin with a start list based on the literature, the built-in contrasts, or your intuitions. Be sure to develop the scheme fully as a procedure or enumerative scheme so that another coder can use it. Try out automated coding if you can.

Make sure to save the coding scheme in the same workbook as your initial sample of data.

For Further Reading

Coffey, A., and P. Atkinson (1996). "Concepts and Coding," in *Making Sense of Qualitative Data: Complementary Research Strategies* (pp. 26–53). Thousand Oaks, CA: Sage.

Kelle, U. (2000). Computer-assisted Analysis: Coding and Indexing. In M. W. Bauer and G. Gaskell, *Qualitative Researching with Text, Image, and Sound* (pp. 282–298). Thousand Oaks, CA: Sage.

Kronberger, N., and W. Wagner (2000). "Keywords in Context: Statistical Analysis of Text Features." In M. W. Bauer and G. Gaskell, *Qualitative Researching with Text, Image, and Sound* (pp. 299–317). Thousand Oaks, CA: Sage.

Miles, M. B., and A. M. Huberman. (1994). "Codes and Coding," in *Qualitative Data Analysis: An Expanded Sourcebook* (pp. 55–65). Thousand Oaks, CA: Sage.

CHAPTER 5

Achieving Reliability

In this chapter, you will revise your coding scheme with the help of a second person in order to achieve reliability. After you get a second coding of your data set, you will calculate the agreement between coders, using formulas for both simple and corrected agreement. You will then inspect the disagreements between coders and refine your analytic procedures to reduce them. This process is repeated until an adequate level of agreement has been reached.

Reliability

Perhaps no issue is more contentious in the analysis of verbal data than reliability. In general, reliability refers to the degree of consistency with which instances are assigned to the same category. In the classic positivist tradition, a "scientific" analysis was expected to be reliable. That is, the phenomenon was expected to be stable and the analytic procedures so explicit than any reasonably qualified person would get the same results. As we noted in the preface, language phenomena pose a strong challenge to this positivist goal because meaning-making is context-bound. The extent to which two people looking at the same verbal phenomena will make the same interpretation depends upon the extent to which the context of interpretation overlaps with the context of production.

The conditions for overlap are not fixed, however. As the diagram in Figure 5.1 suggests, some phenomena are more transparent than others. With a relatively transparent phenomenon, the limits of interpretation extend far from the context of production, nearly reaching to the boundaries of the context in which you hope your analysis to be interpreted. With an opaque phenomenon, on the other hand,

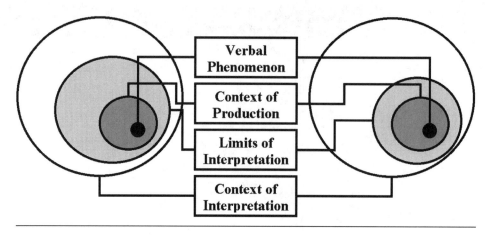

Figure 5.1   Transparent and opaque phenomena.

the limits of interpretation are wrapped tightly around the context of production and few if any outside that context are able to interpret what's going on.

For example, if we are coding for the phenomenon of *author mentions*—how often and when an interviewee mentions the names of the authors she is reading, we might expect the phenomenon to be relatively transparent. That is, in the context in which such an analysis might be expected to be interpreted, what is and is not an *author mention* would not seem to be problematic:

> P: at what point did you stop on . . . Friday I guess it was . . . yeah Friday
>
> V: can't even remember ... [ ] seemed like years ago ... I should write down like ...
>
> P: well it's not important that I get precisely ... what you were doing ...
>
> V: I don't remember what I was doing ...
>
> P: but just tell me about what you were doing ...
>
> V: I think I was reading this ... um ... I was reading over *Gerald Dworkin* ... [flipping pages]

In this example, even if we are not familiar with the context, most of us can recognize that the phrase "Gerald Dworkin" refers to the author of a text the interviewee was reading.

With other verbal phenomena, interpretation is far harder for those outside the context of production. If, for example, we were coding indexicals for what they refer to, most of us would be hard pressed to interpret the *this*'s, *here*'s, and *now* in the following conversational turn:

> J: But I think that it would be good for us to really imagine what *this* could be because there are a number of issues that come up down *here:* to the new goal : where am I? Oh, I'm *here.* I just went off the screen. I think I had: *this* is deriving from the last : you know, was the revised goal of the DCR the same as the first one. And *this* is the one *here:* network support. See, I'm not sure. What about the dominance? What about the dominance in the computer right *now?*

In this example, interpretation is complicated by the usual opacity of topical information ("it would be good for us to really imagine what *this* could be") and the temporal positioning of the conversation ("What about the dominance in the computer right *now?*"). Interpretation is further complicated by the fact that J is looking at a computer screen ("where am I? Oh, I'm *here*. I just went off the screen.") and looking at a file containing text from which he may or may not be reading ("*this* is deriving from the last: you know, was the revised goal of the DCR the same as the first one. And *this* is the one *here*: network support.").

When phenomena are relatively transparent, when the context of production overlaps with the context of interpretation, we can expect it to be relatively easy to achieve reliability. That is, from one time to the next, from one coder to the next, judgments will remain relatively constant with respect to the phenomenon of interest (is this an *author mention?*). When phenomena are more opaque, when the context of production overlaps little with the context of interpretation, we can expect reliability to be harder, if not impossible, to achieve. In some cases, only the participant herself may be in a position to make a judgment (is this speaker *deliberately lying?*). Verbal phenomena, then, may range along a continuum of interpretation, with some phenomena being relatively opaque and some being relatively transparent, and a great many lying somewhere in between.

In this chapter, we will describe methods aimed at achieving as reliable an analysis of this range of verbal data as possible. Our position here is that reliability is important not because we expect verbal phenomena to be wholly interpretable outside of its context of production (we do not) but because reliability is our key tool in insuring that we have been clear in the definition of our analytic constructs and that we have been explicit in our analytic procedures. As you will see, working with a second coder is an excellent way to understand the extent to which specific phenomenons are context-bound and the best way to develop methods for communicating an interpretation of that phenomenon outside the context of production.

Fundamentally, we believe that analysis is a rhetorical act of persuasion: We must persuade our intended readers that the pattern of phenomenon is as we claim. If a phenomenon is wholly opaque outside its context of production, this rhetorical effort is hopeless. We can never expect to communicate an interpretation of what is going on to those who were not there. Happily, intended readers are more resilient in their powers of interpretation than that. Working to achieve reliability will help you to develop the means to help you and your readers to understand what you mean.

Managing the Second Coding

Plan to give a second coder no more data than can be coded in an easy sitting of 1 to $1\frac{1}{2}$ hours. Coding is intense work; coders are often trying to do their best, so it makes sense to give them the most comfortable and least distracting circumstances possible.

	A	Time in 60 seconds	Text	Header	**E** Text
1	#	**Time in 60 seconds**	**Text**	**Header**	**Text**
2	1	000.00	1	Daily Calendar [Feb 5]	
3	2	000.15	2	Out	
4	3	000.28	3	In	
5	4	001.04	3	In	
6	5	001.07	4	Activity Theory Refs	see email "activity theory refs" in research folder
7	6	001.09	4	Activity Theory Refs	see file "activity theory refs" in scholarship folder
8	7	001.26	4	Activity Theory Refs	see email "activity theory refs" in research folder

Figure 5.2   Hiding irrelevant columns in preparation for second coding.

Preparing the Data

To prepare data for a second coder, you need to organize your data sheets in a way that is easy to use and at the same time gives them no hints about how the segments have been coded previously. As shown in Figure 5.2, you can hide irrelevant columns by selecting the column and using the Column/Hide command under the Format menu. (To see these columns later on use the Column/Unhide command.) To insure that your second coder cannot view the results of your first coding, hide that column as well.

Because pages and pages of similarly formatted rows make concentration hard, you should consider using fill color to break up rows into manageable chunks. For example, you might alternate every other line in gray fill. To apply this formatting to the rest of your data, select the rows with the format you wish to use, click on the format painter symbol on the toolbar as shown in Figure 5.3, and then select the remaining rows you wish to format. The formatting will be applied to the rest of your data.

You will need to decide whether your coder will work on line or in paper format. If your coder is comfortable working electronically, do so. This will save you time in later entering their coding by hand. It will also make coding easier for them because they will be able to take advantage of auto-completion rather than having to write out the name of the entire code. Many coders, however, will feel more comfortable working on paper. If this is the case, you should print the data to be coded.

The coder ought to be able to see the column headers on the data sheet at all times. If you are working electronically, this can be accomplished by splitting the

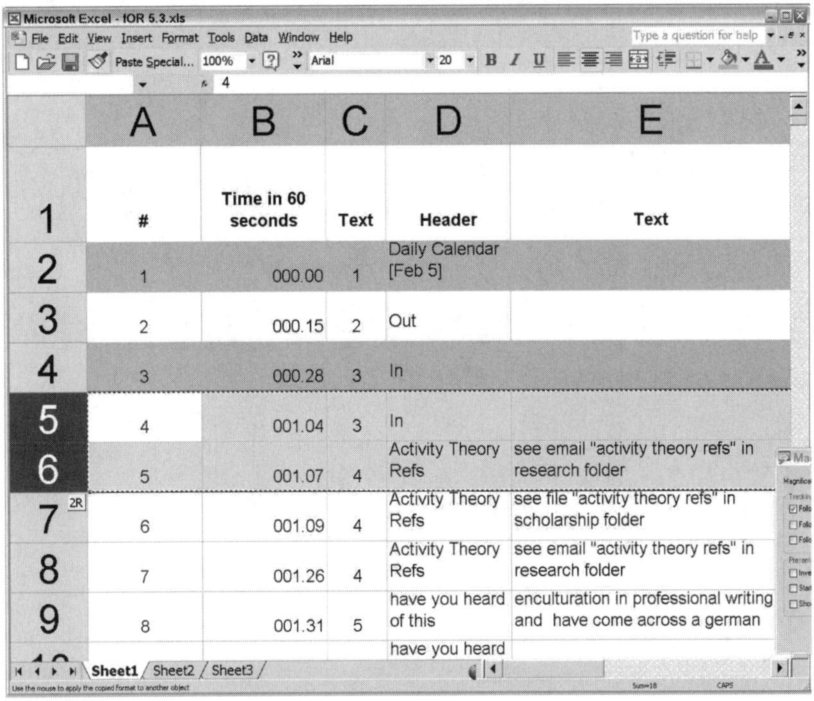

Figure 5.3   Using format painter to break up the spreadsheet for readability.

window in two, arranging the top pane so the column header is visible, and then issuing the Freeze Panes command under the Window menu as shown in Figure 5.4. (You can split the window into panes and adjust their size by dragging the black bar in the scroll bar).

If you are using a printout, you can set the rows to repeat at the top of each page in the Sheet tab of the Page Setup command under the File window as shown in Figure 5.5. Just click on the spreadsheet icon to the right of the field and then select the row or rows you want to include at the top of each printed page.

No matter whether your second coder is working on-line or on paper, you should print out the coding scheme. Make sure it is formatted for each use, with names of codes in bold, cases indented and bulleted (see Figure 4.1 in Chapter 4 for an example). Ideally a coding scheme is one page long; it should never exceed two pages.

Handling the Session

Begin the coding session by spending about 15 minutes familiarizing the coder with the coding scheme, the data, and the coding task. Concerning the data, make sure they understand how the data has been segmented and where they are to record their coding decisions. Concerning the coding scheme, make sure they know what the categories mean and how to apply them. One of the best ways to

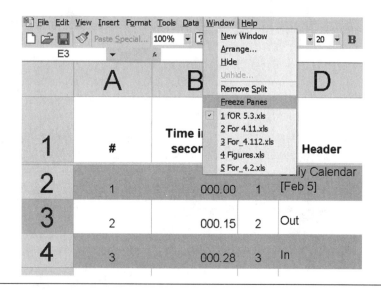

Figure 5.4   Freezing panes so that column headers are always visible.

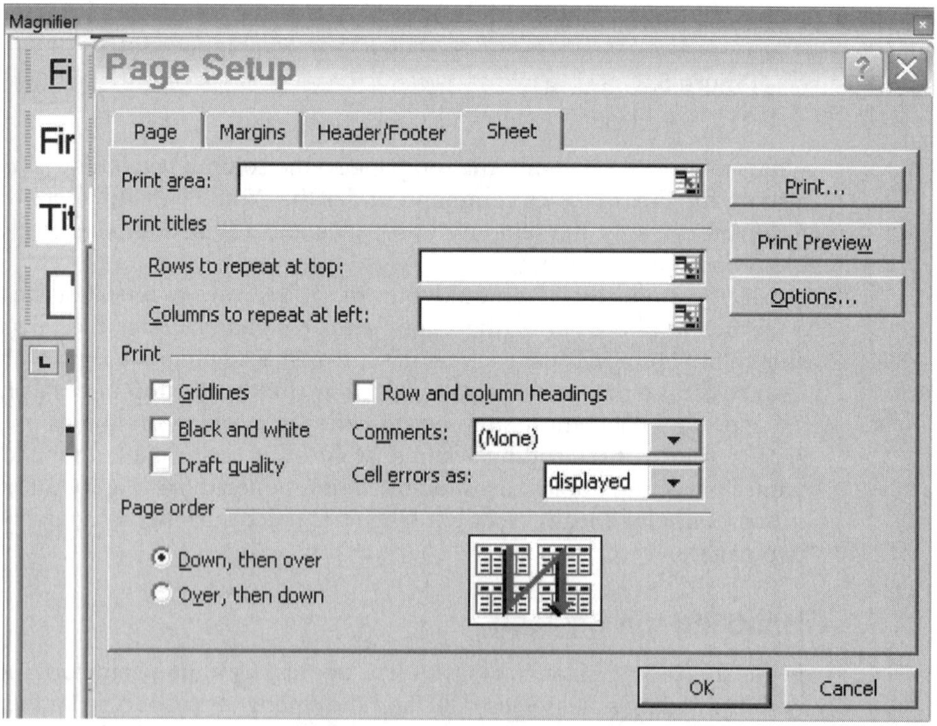

Figure 5.5   Setting the rows to repeat at the top of each page.

do this is to prepare a very small data set, formatted in the same way as the data to be coded, and ask them to try to apply the scheme. As they do so, you can then work through any questions they have about procedure.

Avoid using this training period to give the coder information about coding that is not included in the coding scheme itself. Of course, you never let them know what kinds of patterns you expect to see in the data (for example, that you expect turns by one speaker to have more X than by another speaker). But even further, be sure not to communicate to them any additional information about how to decide how to apply the codes. After all, you are trying to find out how well your coding scheme can communicate—both to coders and to your eventual readers—the nature and variation in the data.

Calculating Agreement

Once a second coder has completed coding the sample data set, you need to calculate the level of agreement between the two codings. This should be done in two ways. First, you should calculate simple agreement that is a straightforward measure of agreement. Second, you should also calculate corrected agreement that, as we will see, is the simple agreement with a correction for agreement by chance.

Calculating Simple Agreement

Simple agreement is defined as the percentage of decisions that are agreements. It is calculated as

# of agreements / # of coding decisions

An example showing the calculation of simple agreement is shown in Figure 5.6. Column A contains the first coding; Column B the second coding; and Column C the agreement where 1 if used for agreement and 0 for disagreement. At the bottom of the column, we find the total number of agreements (14), the total number of coding decisions (16), and simple agreement (14/16 or .88).

 In Excel, you can create a formula that will automatically check whether the value in Column A is the same as the value in Column B. For the spreadsheet shown in Figure 5.6, the following formula was created in C2 and dragged down to fill the column to Row 16:

= IF(A2=B2,1,0)

In this formula, we tell Excel to check whether A2 (the code assigned by the first coder) is the same as B2 (the code assigned by the second coder):

A2=B2

If this is true, we tell Excel to record a 1 for 1 agreement

IF(match,1)

If there is no match, we tell Excel to record a 0 for no agreement

	A	B	C
1	business	business	1
2	user	user	1
3	business	business	1
4	system	team	0
5	system	system	1
6	system	team	0
7	team	team	1
8	system	system	1
9	business	business	1
10	user	user	1
11	system	system	1
12	user	user	1
13	user	user	1
14	user	user	1
15	user	user	1
16	system	system	1
17			
18		# of agreements	14
19		# of decisions	16
20		simple agreement	0.88

Figure 5.6   Calculating simple agreement.

IF(no match, ,0)

Once you have determined whether there is agreement or disagreement on each segment, you can use another formula to sum up the column of 1's and 0's you have created. In Figure 5.6, the following formula in C18 has given us the sum of 14 agreements:

=SUM(C2:C16)

With this formula, we tell Excel to add up the values in the cells from C2 through C16. We can use a similar formula to tell us how many decisions there have been. In Figure 5.6, the following formula in C19 has given us the count of 16 decisions:

=COUNT(C2:C16)

Finally, we can use a third formula to calculate the simple agreement. In Figure 5.6, the following formula in C20 has given us the simple agreement of .88:

=C18/C19

With this formula, we tell Excel to divide the number of agreements (in C18) by the number of decisions (in C19).

5.1　Try It Out

Calculate the simple agreement for the data downloadable at the course website.

1. Begin by creating a formula that will check for agreement between the two columns of coded data.
2. Then use a second formula to sum up the number of agreements.
3. Use a third formula to count the number of decisions.
4. Finally, create a fifth formula to calculate the simple agreement.

For discussion: Are you satisfied with this level of reliability?

Calculating Corrected Agreement Using Cohen's Kappa

Simple agreement is an intuitive measure of reliability. It tells us how many times two coders agreed as a percentage of the number of times they could have agreed. The trouble with using simple reliability alone is that the fewer the coding categories, the more likely it is that the two coders have agreed simply by chance. The method for correcting for agreement simply by chance involves using Cohen's kappa.

To understand the impact of chance on levels of agreement, imagine that I give you a coding scheme that has only two categories. The chances that we would pick the same category in any given coding decision are rather high, 1 out of 2. If, on the other hand, we are using a coding scheme that has 10 categories, the chance of accidental agreement is a lot lower, 1 out of 10. Thus achieving an agreement level of 90% with a 2-category scheme is a lot easier than achieving that same level of agreement with a 10-category scheme. Using Cohen's kappa to adjust the level of agreement is a way of acknowledging that fact.

In the rest of this section, we explain, in general, how this correction works. At the end of this section, we give you a quick way to calculate it.

Correcting simple agreement using Cohen's kappa begins with a table of agreements and disagreements like that shown in Figure 5.7. Down the side, in uppercase letters, we list the categories assigned by the first code. Across the top, in lowercase letters, we list the categories assigned by the second coder. In the table itself, we list the number of times each combination occurred. For example, the table shows that the number of times the first coder assigned "S" while the second coder assigned "c" was 2. The eighth column shows the row totals; the eighth row shows the column totals. Their intersection contains the grand total (16).

If the two coders had been in perfect agreement, all the values would be on the diagonal shown shaded in Figure 5.7. As we have noticed before, agreement was not perfect because of those two coding decisions where the first coder recorded "S" while the second coder recorded "c."

I. Agreement Data

	a	c	d	p	s	u	sum
A	0	0	0	0	0	0	0
C	0	1	0	0	0	0	1
D	0	0	3	0	0	0	3
P	0	0	0	0	0	0	0
S	0	2	0	0	4	0	6
U	0	0	0	0	0	6	6
sum	**0**	**3**	**3**	**0**	**4**	**6**	**16**

Figure 5.7   Table of agreements and disagreements.

Using this table, simple reliability can be calculated as the sum of the diagonals:

$$0 + 1 + 3 + 0 + 4 + 6 = 14$$

divide by the grand total of 16, or the value of .88 we calculated earlier.

Corrected agreement involves calculating a correction known as Cohen's kappa, named for the man who first developed the technique (Cohen, 1960). Cohen's kappa is determined by calculating the expected level of agreement for each coding category if the decisions were made simply by chance. The expected level of agreement for a category involves calculating what is known as the joint probability of that agreement.

To calculate joint probability of agreement for a specific category, we take the probability that the first coder chose a particular value—what's called its simple probability—and multiply it by the probability the second coder chose that same value. In our example, what is the joint probability of an agreement Dd just by chance? The first coder chose D 3 times out of 16 decisions so its simple probability is:

$$P(D) = 3 \text{ in } 16 \text{ or } .19$$

The second code chose d 3 times out of 16 decisions as well, so its simple probability is

$$P(d) = 3 \text{ in } 16 \text{ or } .19$$

The joint probability of D with d is the two simple probabilities multiplied together:

$$P(Dd) = P(D) * P(d)$$

or

$$P(Dd) = .19 * .19 = .035$$

To use the joint probability to calculate the expected frequency of a category, you multiply it by the total number of decisions made:

$$Dd_{expected} = P(Dd) * Grand\ Total$$

or

$$Dd_{expected} = .035 * 16 = .563$$

The expected frequency for the other agreement combinations (Aa, Cc, Pp, Ss, and Uu) are calculated in the same way and then all of them are added up to give a total value for the expected level of agreement by chance, known as q.

Aa	0
Cc	0.19
Dc	0.56
Pp	0
Ss	1.5
Uu	2.25
q	**4.5**

Using q, we can then calculate Cohen's kappa as

$$Kappa = (d - q)/(N - q)$$

where

$$d = number\ of\ actual\ agreements$$

$$q = sum\ of\ agreement\ by\ chance$$

$$N = number\ of\ decisions$$

For the data in Figure 5.7, then,

$$kappa = (14 - 4.5) / (16 - 4.5)$$

or

$$kappa = 9.5 / 11.5 = .83$$

If we were to report the reliability for this coding scheme, we could report "Agreement between coders was .88 or .83 corrected using Cohen's kappa."

Although you can calculate Cohen's kappa by hand, a number of calculators can be found on the World Wide Web that make the task infinitely easier. One of the best was developed by Joji Takamoto at the Joetsu University of Education in Niigata, Japan. It can be found at:

http://www.kokemus.kokugo.juen.ac.jp/service/kappa-e.html

Figure 5.8   Entering coding categories at *http://www.kokemus.kokugo.juen.ac.jp/service/kappa-e.html*

At this website, you begin, as shown in Figure 5.8, by listing your coding categories, separated by commas.

On the same page, you also enter the coding data, with the results of the two codings separated by a comma, one line per coding decision as shown in Figure 5.9. Make sure that there are no spaces at the end of your list or at the ends of your lines.

To get your coded data into this format from your Excel spreadsheet, copy the columns into Word and use the Table to Text command on the Table menu as shown in Figure 5.10, requesting that the text be separated with commas. The result will be data formatted appropriately for the website. Cut and paste it into the field shown in Figure 5.9 and click Compute.

As show in Figure 5.11, the site returns not only kappa (0.826086956521739) but also the simple agreement, labeled as Po (.875), and provides you with a table of agreements and disagreements.

Levels of simple agreement in the high 80s or 90s are the kinds of percentages to which you ultimately aim in developing your coding scheme. When you give a coding scheme to a second coder for the first time, it is not uncommon to find your levels of simple agreement in the 60s. At this point, you may wonder how you will ever refine your analytic procedures to get an acceptable level of agreement. The rest of this chapter addresses this issue.

Revising Your Analytic Procedures

Increasing the reliability of a coding scheme involves inspecting the disagreements between coders for each category, identifying probable causes, and then revising your analytic procedures to eliminate them.

Inspecting Your Disagreements

Begin by looking at your table of agreements and disagreements to identify the places in which there are disagreements. They often cluster in a number of

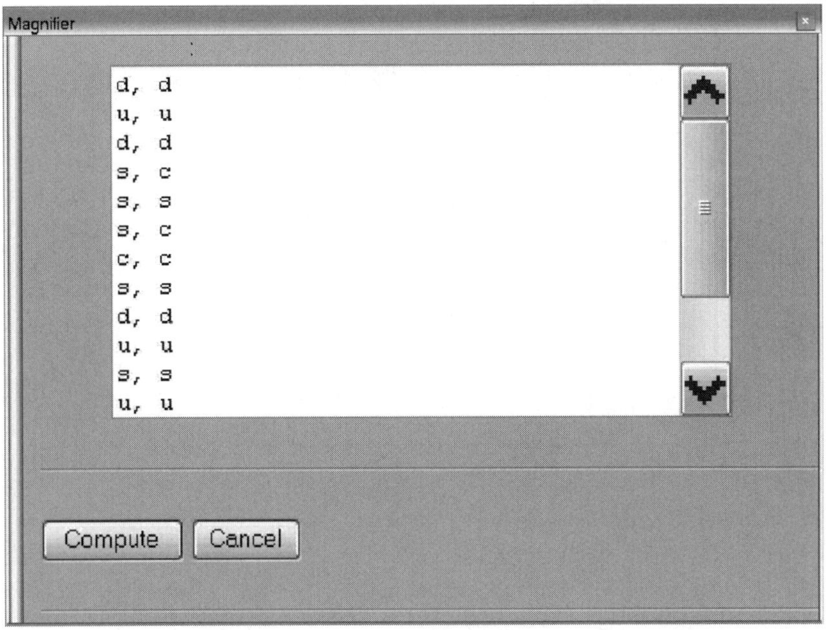

Figure 5.9   Entering coding data at *http://www.kokemus.kokugo.juen.ac.jp/service/kappa-e.html*

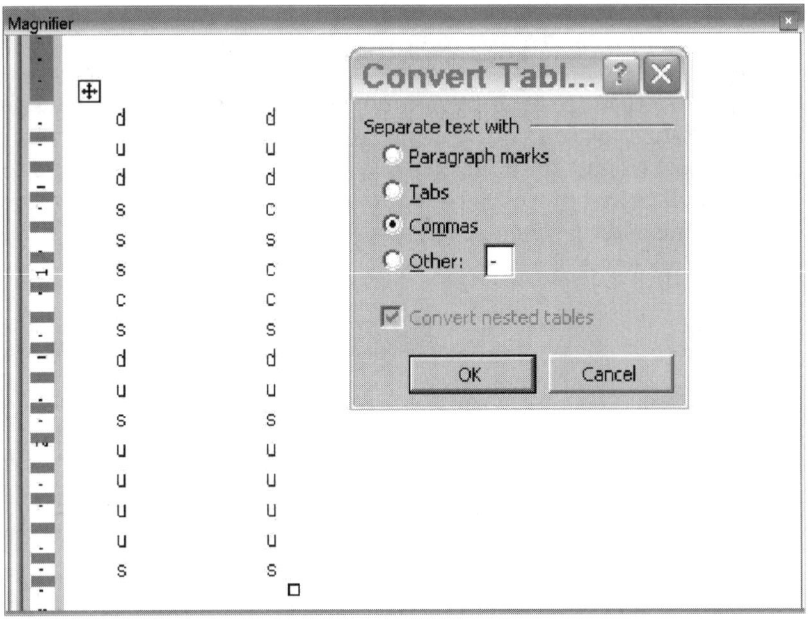

Figure 5.10   Converting Excel coding data to submit it to *http://www.kokemus.kokugo.juen.ac.jp/service/kappa-e.html*

Magnifier

	a	c	d	p	s	u	SUM
a	0	0	0	0	0	0	0
c	0	1	0	0	0	0	1
d	0	0	3	0	0	0	3
p	0	0	0	0	0	0	0
s	0	2	0	0	4	0	6
u	0	0	0	0	0	6	6
SUM	0	3	3	0	4	6	16

Kappa : 0.826086956521739
Po : 0.875
Pc : 0.28125
Se : 0.147642148991371
Z : 5.59519732112556

Figure 5.11   Results of computing Cohen's kappa at
http://www.kokemus.kokugo.juen.ac.jp/service/kappa-e.html

combinations. Then return to your coding sheet and use Autofilter to look at one combination at a time. For example, the table of agreements and disagreements in Figure 5.11 suggests that the combination sc accounts for all the disagreements.

Returning to the data sheet, as shown in Figure 5.12, we can filter Column D to show all data that was coded with "s" by the first coder. We could further filter to look at just those also coded as "c" by the second coder. Looking at the data and the coding scheme, we then try to understand the nature and cause of the disagreements.

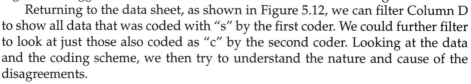

	A	B	C	D	E	F
1	1	TC	1	d ▼	d ▼	1
4	4	TC	1	s	c	0
5	5	TC	1	s	s	1
6	6	TC	1	s	c	0
8	8	TC	1	s	s	1
11	11	TC	1	s	s	1
16	16	TC	1	s	s	1
21						

Figure 5.12   Using Autofilter to inspect disagreements.

5.2 Test Your Understanding

A set of 20 data segments were coded using two different coding schemes. One had 10 categories (A–J) and the other had 5 categories (A–E). When the researcher went to check the reliability of each scheme using second coders, the simple agreement in both cases was pretty poor—the second coders agreed with her only 50% of the time.

Look at the table of agreements and disagreements and the corrected reliability for these two schemes given here and downloadable at the course website. Are both schemes equivalent in terms of their reliability, or is one more reliable than the other? Be prepared to explain your answer.

	a	b	c	d	e	f	g	h	i	j	
A	1										1
B		1				1			1		3
C					1						1
D											0
E				3	1						4
F								1	1		2
G							1				1
H		2						1			3
I							1	1	1		3
J									2		2
	1	3	0	0	4	2	2	3	3	2	20

Kappa: 0.422

	a	b	c	d	e	
A	1		1	1		3
B	1	2		1		4
C		2	1		1	4
D		1	1	1		3
E	1				5	6
	3	5	3	3	6	10

Kappa: 0.36

For discussion: Be prepared to explain your answer to your classmates.

Roger created a 4-category coding scheme and applied it to a 99-segment sample of data. When he checked the level of agreement with a second coder, he was happy to find that his simple reliability was high: 80%. But when he looked at the corrected agreement using Cohen's kappa, he was concerned. It was only .42. His table of agreements and disagreements looked like this:

	N	P	R	O	SUM
N	5	4	0	0	9
P	3	71	0	0	74
R	2	2	1	0	5
O	1	8	0	2	11
SUM	11	85	1	2	99

He is considering three different strategies to improve this reliability:

a. Revise the definition of category "N" to eliminate the second coder's confusion with category "P."
b. Revise the category "O" to eliminate the coder's confusion with categories "N" and "P."
c. Eliminate the category "O" altogether.

Modify his coding data (downloadable at the course website) in these three different ways; then recalculate his simple and corrected reliability. Based on your results, which of the three strategies do you recommend?

For discussion: What generalization can you make about the best strategies for improving reliability using the table of agreements and disagreements as a guide?

Revising the Coding Scheme

In the simplest cases, disagreements between coders arise from lack of clarity in the coding scheme. By adding cases and examples of those cases, we can often better indicate to a coder that certain kinds of data should go in one category rather than another. In the coding scheme found in Chapter 4, Figure 4.1, for example, coders were initially inconsistent in how they categorized t-units that contained phrases such as "definition" and "justification." After thinking about this for some time, I realized that such words signal attention to the discourse functions of a text and therefore should be coded as Rhetorical Process. The following case with examples under Rhetorical Process clarified this decision and eliminated this kind of confusion:

a. general categories of claims that can be made by authors: "a definition," "a justification," "a reason," "a question";

Occasionally, you will find that some verbal phenomenon consistently confuse your coders and need to be addressed explicitly. In the example coding scheme on Worlds of Discourse, for example, I found that t-units with "you" in them always confused coders. Sometimes they were coded as Rhetorical Process; sometimes as Narrated Cases. Looking at these disagreements, I realized that I needed to explicitly address a use of "you" that should be included in Narrated Cases, which I did with the following addition to the coding scheme under Narrated Case:

"you" or "I" when cast in a role involving an action that is taken to exist independently of the concepts in the domain but that may potentially be characterized with respect to these concepts.

Finally, coding schemes can be revised to add categories or refocus definitions of categories so that analytic constructs are better understood. This kind of move prompted me to add the category of Narrated Cases to my original scheme, which had only included Rhetorical Process and Domain Content on its start list.

Changing the Unit of Analysis

More complex revisions to analytic processes can be made by changing the unit of analysis. As described in Chapter 3, if the unit of analysis is inappropriate to the phenomenon of interest, coders will have great difficulty using a coding scheme. If the unit is too large, more than one category may apply. If the unit is too small, coders may not recognize the phenomenon as it is broken across segments. To remedy these problems, return to the original data in Word, resegment, recode, and then compare the results of a second coding.

Adding Another Dimension

As describe in Chapter 4, we often find ourselves placing too much into a single coding scheme, trying to ask a coder to look for things that are, in essence, quite different. It's as if we were to ask a coder to tell us, "Is it a yellow chick or a brown goat?" and then finding they do not know what to do with brown chicks. We could revise our coding scheme to include the following under the category Yellow Chick:

1. any brown chick

We might realize, however, that our scheme had conflated two different dimensions, color and animal type.

If you realize that you have conflated dimensions of the phenomenon into a single coding scheme, you need to break your one scheme into two different schemes and code with each one separately. We would, for example, ask our coders to first decide whether the animal was a chick or a goat and only later ask whether it was yellow or brown.

Moving to Nested Coding

Another option in dealing with what look like distinct dimensions of a phenomenon is to move to a nested coding scheme. Suppose, for example, that we do not care much about goats in the previous example, but only want to look at the chicks. In this case, rather than code all the data for color, we might code in two stages. In the first stage, we would ask our coders to decide if it was a chick or not. Only if the answer were yes, would we go on to ask whether the chick were yellow or brown.

Acknowledging the Limits of Interpretation

Finally, in inspecting disagreements, you may realize that your judgments are relying on knowledge so contextualized that you could not expect a second coder to duplicate your judgments. In this case, you have two alternatives.

One choice is to move to an enumerative coding scheme where you list all the cases that you, with your deep knowledge of the context, judge to be in a given category. Such an enumerative scheme can go a long way in communicating to your readers the substance of a analytic construct.

A second option is to admit the limits of interpretation on the analytic construct, attempt to describe and illustrate it as best you can in your report, but abandon the attempt to get a high level of agreement with a second coder. This step should be viewed as a last resort, of course; because what we often start out thinking cannot be made explicit can be done with more thought. Nevertheless, it is important not to narrow one's vision of verbal data in a way that unduly favors the relatively transparent (and perhaps less important) over that which is relatively opaque (and perhaps more important).

Occasionally, you will find that you have not reached anywhere near satisfactory levels of reliability even after several rounds of second coding. In such cases, you will want to step back from the analysis and think through the analytic constructs with which you are working. They may be unclear. Or the data may simply not be describable in their terms. Quite frankly, you may be looking for the rabbit in the wrong hole. While no one likes to abandon an analysis, sometimes that is the best recourse. Often, you can return to it at a later time when a fresh perspective and further insight may give you better guidance.

Finalizing Reliability

Once you have revised your analytic procedures, you should repeat the process of working with a second coder until an adequate level of reliability is reached. Generally, you would like to see simple agreements of .85 or better. This can usually be reached after one or two rounds of second coding.

Once you have reached this level of agreement, you need to stabilize your coding scheme. Take a new and as-yet uncoded section of data, and give it to a new second coder, someone who has not yet worked with you. The level of agreement you achieve with this fresh data and fresh coder, along with the stabilized coding scheme that produced it, is what you include in your report of the analysis.

Generally speaking, you need not have this final second coder code your entire data set, unless the set is small enough that the task can be completed in a reasonable time. Since verbal data sets tend to be quite large, a more selective approach to final second coding is required. Generally, at least 10% of the data ought to receive a second coding. Furthermore, each kind of data ought to be represented in this 10%: All the built-in contrasts, for example, ought to be included. Your overall goal is to verify the reliability of your coding scheme on the full breadth and depth of the data even when it cannot all be coded twice.

After data has received a final second coding, you will still find disagreements between coders. To prepare the data for the kind of analyses we describe in the next few chapters, you will need to reconcile those disagreements. Inspect each one carefully and decided which coding decision to adopt.

Make sure to retain records of each round of your coding, which version of the scheme was used, what level of agreement was received, how each segment of data was coded by each coder. For this reason, it is probably best to create a separate coding workbook for each round of coding and to label it with the date of the second coding. Then, if ever necessary, you can go back and recover your steps.

PROJECT: ACHIEVING RELIABILITY

Revise your coding scheme to achieve an appropriate level of reliability. A sample reliability workbook is available at the course website.

Give the sample of data you coded in the last project, along with your coding scheme, to a second coder to code.

Then calculate the simple inter-rater agreement as well as corrected agreement using Cohen's kappa.

Finally, review the results of the second coding to categorize disagreements. Revise your coding scheme to address these categories of disagreements.

Write up a short description that includes:

1. The interrater agreement, both simple and corrected.
2. The table of agreements and disagreements.
3. An analysis of categories of disagreements along with revisions made to the coding scheme to address these discrepancies.

Include the coding workbook with both sets of codings, the calculations for simple and corrected agreement, the table of agreements and disagreements, and the original and revised coding scheme.

For Further Reading

Cohen, J. (1960). "A Coefficient of Agreement for Nominal Scales." *Educational and Psychological Measurement, 20,* 37–46.

Gaskell, G., and M. W. Bauer, "Towards Public Accountability: Beyond Sampling Reliability, and Validity" in M. W. Bauer and G. Gaskell, *Qualitative Researching with Text, Image, and Sound* (pp. 336–350). Thousand Oaks, CA: Sage.

Goetz, J. P., and M. D. LeCompte (1984). "Reliability" in *Ethnography and Qualitative Design in Educational Research* (pp. 211–220). Orlando: Academic Press.

Miles, M. B., and A. M. Huberman (1994). "Standards for the Quality of Conclusions" in *Qualitative Data Analysis: An Expanded Sourcebook* (pp. 277–280). Thousand Oaks, CA: Sage.

Silverman, D. (2001). "Credible Qualitative Research" in *Interpreting Qualitative Data: Methods for Analyzing Talk, Text and Interaction* (Chapter 8). Thousand Oaks, CA: Sage.

)

Calculating Frequency

In this chapter, you will calculate the frequency and relative frequency with which you placed data in your coding categories. This process involves building a frequency table: naming its data ranges, defining its criteria, calculating its frequencies, and calculating its marginals. Formulas for calculating relative frequency are also included. Simple techniques for writing and copying formulas, designating data ranges, and working with databases are introduced.

Frequency

In this chapter we take the first step in detecting patterns in the data you have just coded. In particular, we ask, "How often did I assign data to this coding category?" The answer to this question is called its *frequency*. We also ask, "How often was this category used compared to my other coding categories?" The answer to this question is its *relative frequency*.

Answering these two questions involves relatively easy sets of calculations. Nevertheless, many researchers overlook their use. Sometimes we get so caught up in the details of specific parts of the data or so eager to go on to some of the more complex analyses that we overlook these basics: How often? In what proportion? Make it a habit of your analytic life to always have these answers ready, the first things you are dying to know as soon as your data is coded. The global perspective gained from answers to such questions allows you to begin to discern the underlying patterns in your data filtered through the lens of your coding scheme.

When you are working with data that has built-in contrasts, you will want to see measures of frequency for the contrasting data side-by-side. For example, if we had designed the analysis to contrast speaker participation data from Meeting 1 with Meeting 2, we would want some way to compare the frequency of each

Frequency # of t-units		Speaker	Speaker	Speaker	
		Ed	Cheryl	John	Total
	Meeting 1	314	314	115	743
	Meeting 2	314	314	314	942
	Total	628	628	429	1685

Figure 6.1 A frequency table.

speaker from two data worksheets. This can be most easily accomplished by building a frequency table.

A frequency table contains an array of frequency data, with the names of the coding categories across the top and the names of the data samples for your built-in contrasts along the side. In Figure 6.1, for example, we have set up a frequency table for the speaker data for Meeting 1 and Meeting 2. Across the side, we have labeled the source of the data (Meeting 1 or Meeting 2) as well as a total across the samples. Across the top, we have listed the categories (Ed, Cheryl, and John) as well as a total across the categories. The best place to put this frequency table is in a new worksheet called Frequency. In this way, you can pull out the patterns across multiple data sheets and look at them in their own sheet.

Coded data is usually organized so that a single column holds multiple data codes. In Figure 6.2, for example, the speaker categories of Ed, Cheryl, and John are mixed together in Column B. Building a frequency table from this kind of coded data involves working with your data as a database in Excel and includes four steps: creating a frequency table, naming the data range that holds the data, specifying the criteria by which you pick out the relevant data, and counting that data. In the following sections we review techniques for accomplishing these tasks.

Naming Data

A frequency table provides summary data across your built-in contrasts and, therefore, has relationships to ranges of data on several different data worksheets. The process of calculating the frequencies for coding categories in these data worksheets involves treating their data as databases and therefore begins by naming them.

To name the data on a data worksheet, use the Define Name command under the Insert menu as shown in Figure 6.3. In the dialogue box that pops up, give the database a descriptive name as we have done with our name "Meeting 1" shown in Figure 6.4.

Next, to specify the data range this name applies to, click on the spreadsheet icon next to the Refers to box, shown in the bottom right of Figure 6.4. Excel will close up the Define Name box to give you room to drag through the data range on the worksheet. To do this, click in the upper left-hand corner in the row of head-

	A	B	C
1	t-Unit #	Speaker	Text
2	1	John	Very
3	2	Cheryl	I don't know how anybody else would find it.
4	3	Ed	Well we're using specialized knowledge(?)
5	4	John	But that's just our directory :
6	5	John	that's just our directory structure.

Figure 6.2   Data for which frequency is to be determined.

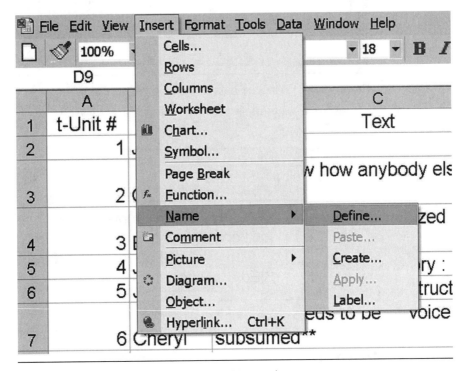

Figure 6.3   Using the Define Name command.

ings and drag to the bottom left hand corner of the last row of data. Make sure to include the header row! Excel will write the data range in the Define Name box as shown in Figure 6.5.

After you have entered the correct data range, click on the spreadsheet icon to the right of the Define Name box. Excel will reopen the full Define Name dialogue. Click OK to complete the naming process. Use this same procedure to give the data on each of your data worksheets a name.

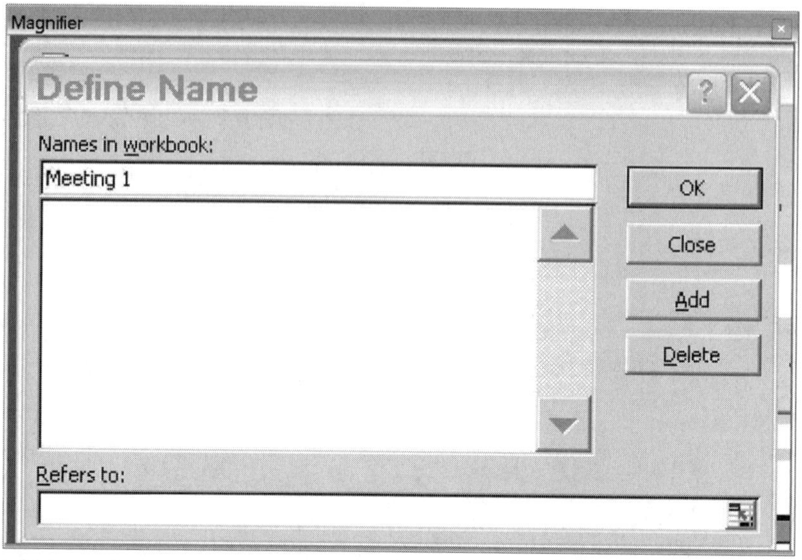

Figure 6.4   Giving the data range a name.

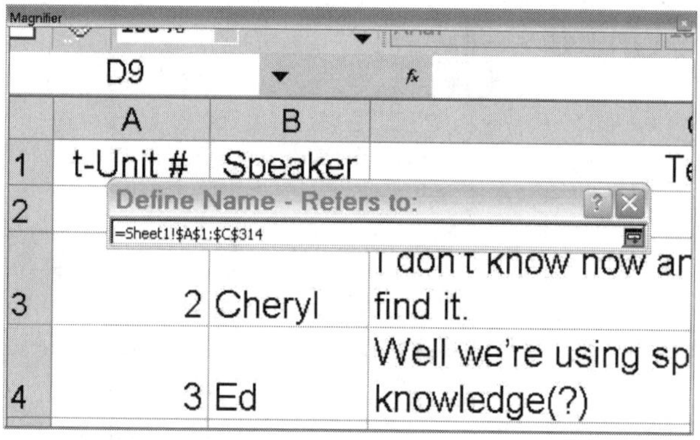

Figure 6.5   Specifying the range of the data.

Defining Criteria

The second step to building a frequency table is to tell Excel what criteria to use to pick out the data to count in the newly named databases. Because you are interested in the number of times each of your coding categories occurs, your criteria will naturally involve the names of these coding categories.

To facilitate our later calculations of frequency, we set up the criteria for each coding category in each of the databases using the same format we will use for the frequency table itself. In Figure 6.6, for instance, we see a table labeled "Criteria" that has the same structure as the frequency table underneath it: The names of the coding categories are arrayed across the top; the names of the data ranges are arrayed across the side.

	A	B	C	D	E
1					
2					
3	**Criteria**				
4		Ed	Cheryl	John	
5	Meeting 1	Speaker	Speaker	Speaker	
6		Ed	Cheryl	John	
7	Meeting 2	Speaker	Speaker	Speaker	
8		Ed	Cheryl	John	
9					
10	**Frequency**				
11		Ed	Cheryl	John	Total
12	Meeting 1	70	128	115	313
13	Meeting 2	0	106	104	210
14		70	234	219	627
15					
16	**Relative Frequency**				
17		Ed	Cheryl	John	Total
18	Meeting 1	0.22	0.41	0.37	1
19	Meeting 2	0.00	0.50	0.50	1
20		0.55	0.75	0.70	2

Figure 6.6   Tables for criteria, frequency, and relative frequency.

Within the criteria table itself, we need to specify two pieces of information for each cell of the table. On the first line, we write the label for the column on the data worksheets that holds the data codes. On the line underneath, we write the name of the specific data code we want to count for.

In Figure 6.6, for example, the criteria to be used to count the instances of the code "John" in Meeting 1 are placed on D5 and D6. In D5, we write "Speaker" because that is how we have labeled the coding column in the data worksheet (see Figure 6.5). In D6, we write "John" because that is the particular code we want to count for in this cell of the table.

Copying Fixed Values

Notice how the name of the coding column is the same for each cell in the criteria table. Because we have been consistent about naming the columns on our data worksheets, the coding columns in each data worksheet have the same fixed value. Of course, if you have not been consistent, these labels might have to be different.

If you have been consistent, however, you can take advantage of Excel's drag and copy function to write the name of the column once ("Speaker" in B5, for example), drag it across category columns in the first row of cells (to C5 for Cheryl and to D5 for John), and then copy this first row of cells (B5 to D5) for Meeting 1 to the second row of cells (B8 to D8) for Meeting 2. In this way, we can accomplish what would otherwise be a tedious task in three easy steps (type, drag, and copy).

Copying Formulas

Notice also how the names of the coding categories for Meeting 1 and Meeting 2 are the same: Ed, Cheryl, and John. These names, furthermore, echo the headings for the criteria table itself: Ed, Cheryl, and John. In fact, in any criteria table, the category names will be written n + 1 times, where n = the number of data ranges you include. For our criteria table in Figure 6.6, n is 2 (Meeting 1 + Meeting 2), so we will need to write Ed, Cheryl, and John three times.

We could, of course, manually type in these category names, but there's a lot of repetition here. Luckily Excel provides a more efficient alternative. Once we write the category names in the headings of the table (from B4 through C4), we write a formula that tells Excel to get the values for the criteria table cells from that heading. The formula to accomplish this task, written in B6 to start, is:

$$=B4$$

Once written in B6, we can then drag this formula across to fill in the rest of the row (C6 to D6). As we copy the formula to the right (B6 to C6, for example), Excel adjusts the references in the formula accordingly. So, for example, in C6, Excel will write:

$$=C4$$

and in D6, it will write

$$=D4$$

This is just what we want, of course, and now, with one formula, the entire set of category criteria have been specified for Meeting 1.

Continuing in this efficient mode, we now copy this first row of criteria for Meeting 1 (from B6 through D6) to the second row of criteria for Meeting 2 (from B8 to D8). Notice, however, that the formulas in the second row of criteria do not contain the same formulas as the first row. In B8 in the second row, we have

$$=B6$$

rather than

$$=B4$$

as we had in B6 in the first row. Because Excel uses relative references for both row and column values unless you tell it otherwise, when you copied the formula

$$=B4$$

down two rows, Excel adjusted the values in the formula down two rows to produce

$$=B6$$

In the case of a criteria table, it just so happens that B6 contains the same values as B4, so all is well. If, however, we need to make sure that Excel looks in B4 rather than B6 for the value of the criteria, we could fix that value by inserting a $ right before the row in the formula

=B$4

This is called a fixed rather than relative reference. Now, no matter where we copy this formula, it will always take its value from Row 4. we could also use the following version to make sure that Excel always looked in Column B:

=$B4

And we can even pin a value down by row and column combined:

=$B$4

Although the difference between relative and fixed reference is not important in the particular case of criteria table, it will be important many times. Thus, if you want to fix a reference to a particular row or column, insert that $!

6.1 Try It Out

The data shown in Figure 6.7 is from a database: Janet. A database with a built-in contrast to Janet also exists: Jane. Create a criteria table for Subject Coding for codes "I" and "other" across these two databases. Make sure to include two rows per cell, one for the coding column and one for the code.

	A	B	C	D
1	Item#	Session	t-unit	Subject Coding
2				
3	1	c-d2	I stopped	I
4	2	c-d2	the section was defining paternalism	other
5	3	c-d2	it was called Bernard Gert and Charles Culver paternalistic behavior	other
6	4	c-d2	it was just like defining it	other
7	5	c-d2	and giving examples	other
8	6	c-d2	I stopped at the end of the section...	I
9	7	c-d2	cause I didn't feel like starting a new section ...	I
10	8	c-d2	I was just reading it	I
11	9	c-d2	and taking .. some notes	I
12	10	c-d2	and jotting notes down next to the paragraphs ... in the margins in the booklet	I

Figure 6.7 Data in the database Janet.

For discussion: How would you have to adjust your criteria table if you added another code to this coding scheme?

Calculating Frequencies

Once you have named your databases and specified your criteria, you are ready to calculate the frequencies for your coding categories.

The Frequency Formula

The function used to accomplish this task is a database function, DCOUNTA. DCOUNTA is a function that counts every instance in a given coding column in a database that matches a given criteria. The general form for the formulas used in a frequency table is:

=DCOUNTA(database, "dataColumn",criteria)

Let's walk through the use of this formula to calculate the frequency of Ed in Meeting 1, a value that goes in B12 in Figure 6.6. We begin by typing an = followed by the function and an open parenthesis:

=dcounta(

There is no need to write the function in upper case; Excel will change it for you once you complete the formula.

Now let's enter the arguments for the function. For database, you insert the name you have defined for the data range:

=dcounta(Meeting 1,

For "dataColumn" insert the name of the column in which the data segments are stored—in double quotes:

=dcounta(Meeting1,"Text",

And for criteria, drag the two-row range from the previous criteria table:

=dcounta (Meeting1,"Text",B5:B6

Now close the parentheses and hit the return:

=dcounta (Meeting1,"Text",B5:B6)

Excel will show the formula:

=DCOUNTA(Meeting1,"Text",B5:B6)

and use it to calculate the number of instances in the column labeled Text that have "Ed" as its speaker in the database Meeting 1. In this case, that value is 70 as the frequency table in Figure 6.6 shows.

SUM   ▼ ✕ ✓ ƒ×   =DCOUNTA(Meeting1,"Text",B6:B7)

Figure 6.8   Editing a formula to insert the correct range for the criteria.

Filling the Frequency Table

Because you have set up your frequency table to echo your criteria table, you can begin to fill the rest of your frequency table by dragging this formula across Row 12 (to C12 and D12). Next, drag these formulas down to Row 13 (from B13 through D13). The resulting formulas in Row 13 must then be edited to insert the correct ranges for the criteria. For example, the formula in B13 will be:

=DCOUNTA(Meeting1,"Text",B6:B7)

The correct range for the criteria for this cell in the frequency table, however, is B7:B8 rather than B6:B7. To correct this formula, click in the cell with the formula and then move your cursor to the formula bar as shown in Figure 6.8. Select the incorrect data range (B6:B7) and then click and drag in the spread sheet to insert the correct data range (B7:B8), and hit Return. The formula should then read:

=DCOUNTA(Meeting1,"Text",B7:B8)

You can then drag this corrected formula to fill the rest of Row 13.

Producing a frequency table in this fashion is a powerful tool for the analysis of verbal data. The link between this frequency table and the named databases is fixed. Should you return to a data worksheet to refine a coding scheme or correct data entries, your frequency data will automatically update to reflect the revised values. Since the coding of verbal data is an iterative process, these automatic updates are priceless.

6.2   Test Your Understanding

The following formulas incorrectly designate the data range to be used as a database for the data shown in Figure 6.5. Describe what each will refer to and what will go wrong with the calculation of relative frequencies when the database is defined in these ways.

a. ='Meeting1'!$A$2:$C$314

b. =$A$2:$C$314

c. ='Meeting1'!A1:C314

d. ='Meeting1'!$A$2:$B$314

Calculating Marginals

In Figure 6.6, we show a completed frequency table with totals for each row and each column, as well as the grand total for the table itself. Taken together, these totals are known as the marginals—they are on the margins of the table.

Creating a Marginal Sum

The formulae for these marginals all involve the SUM function. In E12, the formula for the total for Row 12 is:

=SUM(B12:D12)

In B14, the formula for the total for Column B is:

=SUM(B12:B13)

Designating a Data Range

To designate a data range in an Excel formula like these, you can manually type in the names of its endpoints (for example, B12 and D12) separated by a colon. Excel, however, provides an easier way that does not require you to type in cell names. Begin writing the formula

=sum(

and when you get to the place where the data range should go, click and drag in the spreadsheet to select the data range. Excel will then automatically enter the selected data range in the formula:

=sum(B12:D12

Now all you have to do to complete the formula is close the parentheses:

=sum(B12:D12)

Using this technique to designate cell ranges within an Excel formula will save you the aggravation of finding and typing in cell names. You can even click in a single cell to insert its name into a formula.

6.3 Try It Out

Using data from Frequency Workshop (downloadable at the course website), create a frequency table for publication type. Make sure to name the data ranges, specify the criteria, calculate the frequencies, and calculate the marginals.

Calculating Relative Frequency

The final component of calculating frequencies is calculating relative frequency. Relative frequency tells you what proportion of coded segments were assigned to a given category. It is calculated relative to the total number of segments is in the data. Thus, the relative frequency of a category equals

$$\frac{\text{\# of segments assigned to the category}}{\text{\# of segments in all categories}}$$

For the data in Figure 6.6, then, we have divided the row totals for both meetings (313 and 210 respectively) into the frequencies in individual cells in each category. The proportion for Ed in Meeting 1, for example, equals 70 divided by 313; and for Cheryl equals 128 divided by the same 313.

The easiest way to calculate relative frequencies in Excel is with a formula containing an absolute reference to the total number of segments (the 315 that gets repeated in the previous example). The formula we have used in B18 in Figure 6.9 to accomplish this purpose is:

$$=B12/\$E12$$

With this formula, we tell Excel to divide the value in the cell (in B12) by the sum of the row (in E12). Once we have placed the following formula in B20 we can drag and fill Row 9 (from C20 across to E20) to finish calculating the relative frequencies for Meeting 1, and copy it (to B22 through E22) to finish calculating the relative frequencies for Meeting 2. Thus, with the right use of absolute references in our formulas, we can write one formula that will calculate the entire table of relative frequencies.

PROJECT: CALCULATING FREQUENCY

Calculate the frequencies and relative frequencies for your coded data. Sample data with its associated frequency tables can be found at the course website.

Make sure to name your databases and set up your tables (criteria, frequency, and relative frequencies) in a separate Frequency worksheet. Enter each data sample as a separate row in the tables.

Seeing Patterns of Distribution

In this chapter, you will look for patterns in how your verbal data is distributed across the categories of your coding scheme. Using the frequency table from the last chapter, you will create and interpret distribution graphs of their patterns. Graphing techniques are introduced.

Distribution

In this chapter we take the first step in detecting patterns in the data you have just coded. In particular, we ask, "How did the way I assigned data to my coding categories vary with my built-in contrasts?" The answer to this question is called its distribution, and graphs of these patterns are called distribution graphs.

Distribution refers to the way your data is distributed across the categories in your coding scheme. It is the topology of the data. The patterns shown in Figure 7.1, for example, are distribution graphs of speaker data across the categories of Ed, John, and Cheryl for Meetings 1 and 2.

The most obvious use for distribution graphs comes when you want to know whether the distribution of the data varies according to the built-in contrasts that you created in your original analytic design. With that design, you articulated a plan for selecting data that you expected to show contrasting patterns in the phenomenon of interest. With these distribution graphs, you can begin to see whether your expectations were met: Does the distribution of your data over the categories in your coding scheme vary by the source of the data?

If, for example, we had chosen to look at data from Meeting 1 and Meeting 2 because we expected a built-in contrast, we could use the distribution shown in Figure 7.1 to see how these two meetings differed along the dimension of speaker participation. When the frequencies are looked at graphically, we see two things im-

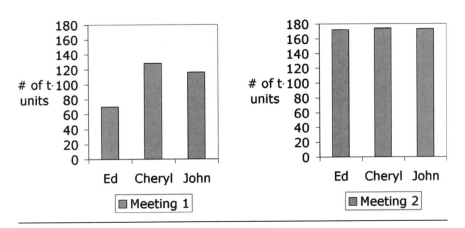

Figure 7.1 Actual distribution of speaker frequency in two meetings.

mediately: that Meeting 2 was a lot more talkative and that Meeting 2 was a lot more equitable.

While the graphs in Figure 7.1 showed us distribution in terms of actual frequency, those in Figure 7.2 show it in terms of relative frequency. That is, we have graphed the percentages of time that each category occurred. This data does not show us how talkative one meeting was compared to the other. For that we would have to go back to the graphs in Figure 7.1. But these graphs tell us what the relative contribution of each speaker was and how that relative contribution varied between the two meetings.

If the total number of segments in one set of data is quite different from the total number in a comparison set, then the actual frequencies can be quite deceptive. In Figure 7.1, for example, we see that the frequencies for John are 115 in Meeting 1 and

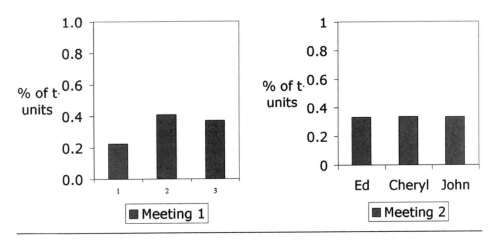

Figure 7.2 Relative frequencies of speaker distributions in two meetings.

173 in Meeting 2, two figures that seem quite different. But when we look at them as relative frequencies, as in Figure 7.2, we see that in Meeting 1, John spoke 37% of the time while in Meeting 2, he spoke 33% of the time, two figures that seem more similar. The difference here lies in the differences in the total number of segments in the two meetings. In Meeting 1 there were a total of 314 segments; in Meeting 2, there were 519 segments, two-thirds again as much. So while John spoke more often in absolute terms in Meeting 2, in relative terms, he spoke about as often.

Which of these two ways of looking at distribution is better, using the actual frequency as we have done in Figure 7.1, or using relative frequency as we have done in Figure 7.2? The answer is both. Both sets of graphs tell us important information about the way our data is distributed over the categories making up our coding scheme. As a consequence, you should always examine both. Techniques for doing so are introduced in the next section.

7.1   Test Your Understanding

The two graphs shown in Figure 7.3 show the actual and relative frequency of men and women 13 or more years past dissertation who have been promoted to the rank of full professor in the five colleges at a university. What do the actual frequencies tell you? What do the relative frequencies tell you? What are the differences between them?

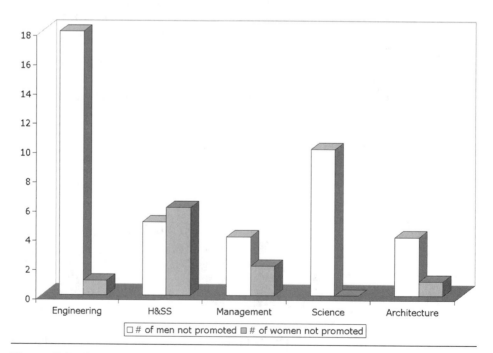

Figure 7.3   The actual and relative frequency of promotion to the rank of full professor.

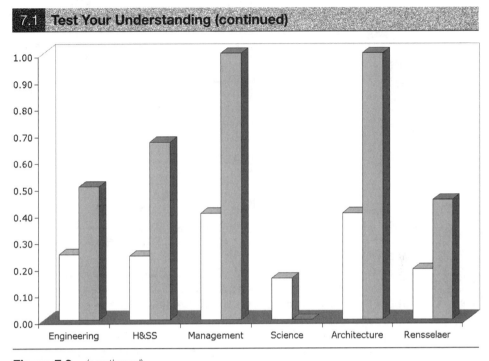

Figure 7.3 (continued)

For discussion: Which graph would you use to call attention to the problem of promotion among women faculty? Why?

Graphing Distribution

One of the best ways to see patterns in verbal data is through graphs—the spatial array of data points on a two- and sometimes three-dimensional coordinate system. Almost all of us are better able to see and interpret patterns through the spatial arrays shown in Figure 7.1 than the numeric frequency tables in Figure 7.4. Thank goodness, Excel makes it relatively easy to move from frequency table to distribution graph.

To create a distribution graph in Excel, select the data to be graphed and then use the Chart Wizard to walk you through a variety of choices in format. At the end, Excel places the graph in your workbook. You can later go back and modify the graph, and once you have a graph for a particular analysis, you can create a new Chart Style and then apply it to other graphs you make. In the rest of this section, we introduce the process of making distribution graphs, and then deal with modifying graphs and creating new chart styles.

Creating Distribution Graphs

To create your distribution graphs, begin by inserting a new worksheet in which to place them. It is generally a good idea to name this sheet in a way that

	A	B	C	D	E	F
1	**Actual Frequency**		Speaker	Speaker	Speaker	
2	# of t-units		Ed	Cheryl	John	Total
3		Meeting 1	71	129	115	315
4		Meeting 2	172	174	173	519
5		Total	243	303	288	834
6						

Figure 7.4   Selecting data to be graphed.

makes clear its relationship to the sheet containing the frequency tables from which the frequencies are drawn. If your frequency table is in the worksheet Frequency, for example, you might place your graphs on a sheet called Frequency Graphs.

To make a frequency graph, select the data to be graphed. Make sure to include the label for the kind of segment as well as the headers for the categories—but not the row and column totals—as we have done in Figure 7.4. Then click on the Chart Wizard on the toolbar.

In the first step in the Chart Wizard, shown in Figure 7.5, you choose the kind of chart you want to use. Charts for the distribution of coded data are usually column charts. The first and default choice (as shown in Figure 7.5) is an ordinary 2-D chart. This will work for the purposes of showing the distribution of simple frequency data.

In the next step in the Chart Wizard, choose the data to be graphed. As shown in Figure 7.6, the data you initially selected is shown in the field for the data range and a thumbnail of the graph of that data is shown above. You usually do not have to change anything here for a distribution graph.

In the third step of the Chart Wizard, select chart options as shown in Figure 7.7. For the graphs used in this chapter the following options were chosen:

- Under the Titles tab, the y-axis was labeled. For the graphs of actual distribution in Figure 7.1, we used the label "# of t-units"; for the graphs of relative frequency in Figure 7.2, we used the label "% of t-units."
- Under Axes, we used the defaults.
- Under Gridlines, we chose to remove major gridlines for the y-axis.
- Under Legend, we chose not to position the legend at the bottom.
- Under Data Labels, we used the default of none.
- Under Data Table, we chose the default of not showing the data table.

In the final step in using the Chart Wizard, select the chart location. As mentioned earlier, graphs are easier to work with when placed in their own sheet. In Figure 7.8, we place the chart as an object in the Frequency Charts worksheet.

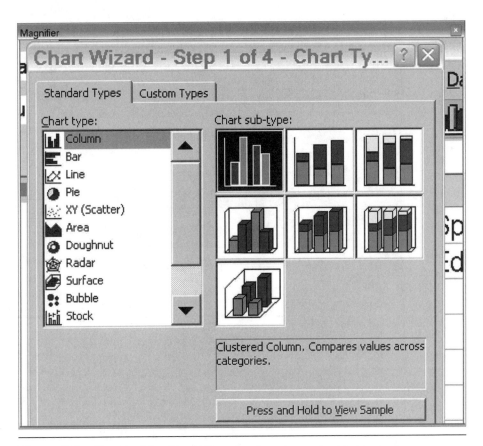

Figure 7.5   Step 1 of the Chart Wizard—choosing a chart type.

Modifying the Graph

The graph created by the Chart Wizard, as shown in Figure 7.9, will need some modifications in order to show distributions.

To begin with, we need to change the scale. Normally, the Chart Wizard uses a scale that represents the range of data it is given. But, as we see in Figure 7.1, our graph for Meeting 2 will have frequencies that range up to nearly 180. To insure that both distribution graphs are on the same scale, double click on the y-axis to bring up Format Axis as shown in Figure 7.10. There, change the maximum from 140 to 180 and click Okay.

In general, any feature of a graph can be changed to double clicking on it and changing the options. One feature I often change is the color of the plot area and the graph itself. Excel defaults to a dark plot area and uses color in its graphs, both of which look good in color presentations, but don't reproduce well in black and white in print. To change the color of the plot area, double click on the gray background and, in Format Plot Area, set the color of the background to None. To

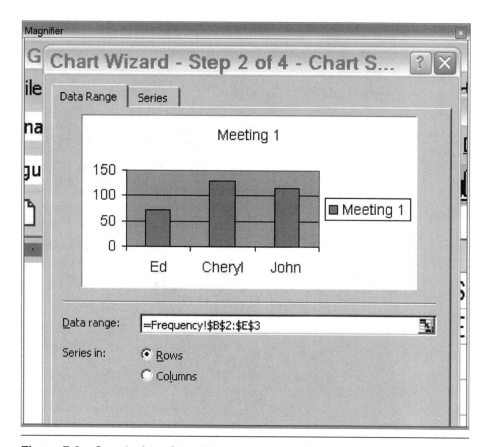

Figure 7.6   Step 2 of the Chart Wizard—choosing the data source.

change the color of the series, double click on one of the colored bars in the graph and select gray or black for the area color.

Using a Chart Style

Once you have created a distribution graph with the features you want for one of your data samples, you can easily transfer these features to the distribution graphs for other data samples using a Chart Style. To create a new Chart Style, with your cursor in the graph, select Chart Type from the Chart menu. Then, as shown in Figure 7.11, on the tab labeled Custom Types, click the User-Defined radio button and then the Add button. Finally, give a memorable name to the style.

To apply this new style to other distribution graphs using the Chart Wizard, in step 1 (see Figure 7.5), click on the tab for Custom charts, and then the radio button for User-Defined, and then select your newly defined chart as the chart type. All the features of your original graph will then be transferred to the new graph.

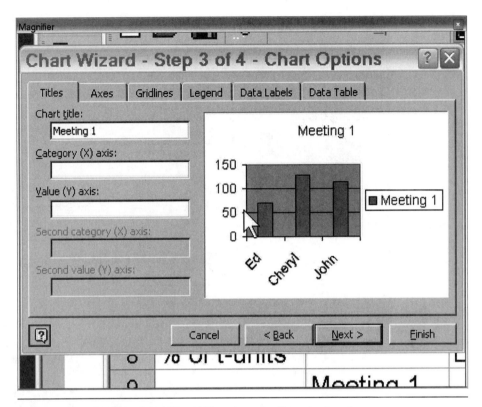

Figure 7.7   Step 3 of the Chart Wizard—selecting chart options.

7.2 Try It Out

In the file downloadable from the course website, create a graph of the distribution of speakers for Meeting 2 in the same style as the graph for Meeting 1. Do this by creating a new style for the Meeting 1 graph and then applying it to the Meeting 2 graph.

Interpreting Distribution Patterns

Once you have constructed distribution graphs for the actual and relative frequencies of your coding categories for each sample of your data, you are in a position to begin the process of interpreting the patterns they show. In other words, with the distribution graphs you have just created, you can begin to explore the nature of your built-in contrasts. To aid you in this endeavor, in the following sections we review the more common distribution patterns as well as ways you can look for patterns across cases and categories.

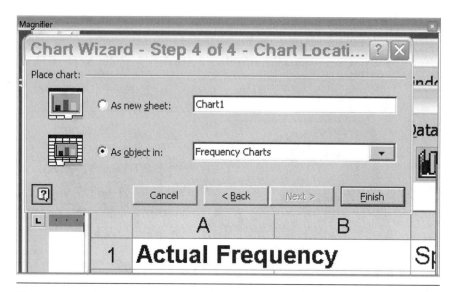

Figure 7.8   Step 4 of the Chart Wizard—choosing chart location.

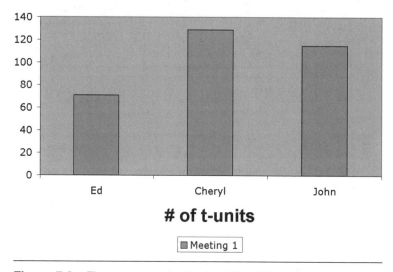

Figure 7.9   The graph created by the Chart Wizard.

Direct and Inverse Proportions

When is the distribution of coding categories across one sample of your data similar to the distribution in another sample? In the simple case, distributions are similar when the frequencies of each coding category are identical. In the case of Meeting 1 and Meeting 2, for example, we would certainly say that the distributions are similar if Cheryl, Ed, and John talked for exactly the same amount of time in each of the two meetings.

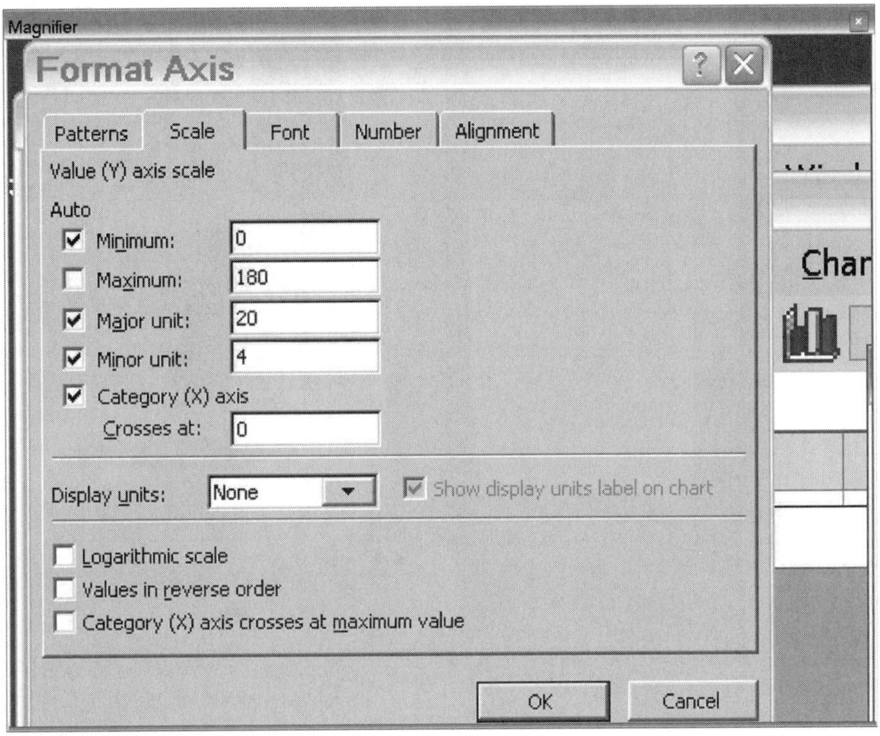

Figure 7.10 Changing the scale of the y-axis using Format Axis.

Our understanding of similarity goes beyond identical frequencies, however. Suppose that Meeting 2 was twice as long as Meeting 1, but that the relative frequencies with which Cheryl, Ed, and John talked were the same. In this case, we usually say that the distributions are similar— that Cheryl, Ed, and John talked about the same amount across the two meetings—despite the overall difference in the length of the meetings.

The underlying pattern for this larger sense of similarity is called direct proportionality: With direct proportionality, as the absolute frequency of one category changes, the absolute frequency of other categories change proportionately and in the same direction; if one goes up, the others go up. If one goes down, the others go down.

The two graphs in the top half of Figure 7.12 show distributions that are directly proportional to one another. Despite the fact that Meeting 1 is a lot longer than Meeting 2 (275 t-units versus 134 t-units), the relative frequencies of the coding categories are nearly identical between them: 64% for Ed, 24% for Cheryl, and 12% for John in Meeting 1; and 64% for Ed, 23% for Cheryl, and 13% for John in Meeting 2.

Sometimes frequency distributions are inversely rather than directly proportional. In inverse proportion, as the absolute frequency of one category changes, the absolute frequencies of other categories change proportionately but

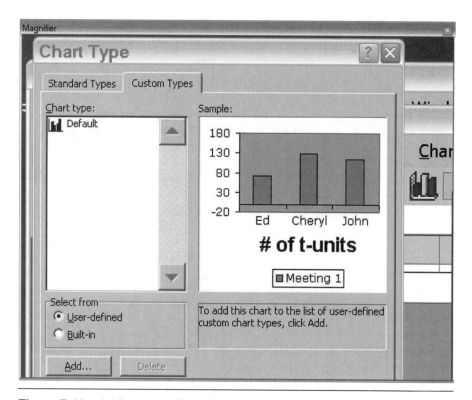

Figure 7.11   Adding a new Chart Style.

in the opposite direction. If one goes up; the others go down. If one goes down, the others go up. This is the case for the pair of distribution graphs shown in the bottom half of Figure 7.12. In Meeting 1, Cheryl talked for 34% of the time and John for 66%; in Meeting 2, the relative frequencies are reversed with Cheryl talking for 66% of the time and John for 34%. This is a clear case of inverse proportion.

Direct and inverse proportions are relatively common in verbal data. For example, suppose you have two conversations with the same person. In the first conversation, she is rather quiet; in the second conversation, she is more loquacious. If we were to look at the distribution of talk between speakers in these two conversations, we would probably find they were directly proportional. That is, as your interlocutor spoke more (or less), you probably also spoke more (or less) in reply. As a result, the speaker distributions in the two conversations, which vary in overall length, are nevertheless similar.

Suppose, however, that your conversations with your interlocutor occur within a formal 1-hour meeting. Now, when she speaks more, she leaves less time for you to speak. As a result, the speaker distributions become inversely proportional. On days she speaks more, you speak less; on days she speaks less,

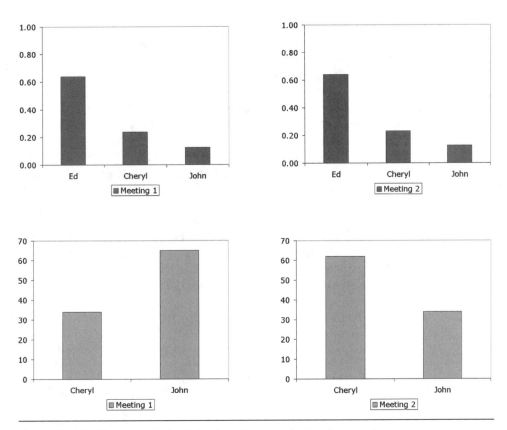

Figure 7.12   Patterns of direct (top) and inverse (bottom) proportion.

you speak more. As this example suggests, inverse proportion is fairly common in cases of fixed resources—such as the total time available for a meeting.

Constants, Absolute and Proportional

Direct and inverse proportionality are patterns that reflect systematic differences between distributions. By contrast, some relationships between distributions can be characterized more by what they have in common than by how they differ. In the top of Figure 7.13, for example, the two distributions show a common value for Cheryl's contribution: Cheryl spoke 94 t-units in both Meeting 1 and Meeting 2 even though Ed and John's contributions differed across the two meetings.

When one category has the same actual frequency in two or more samples, we see a pattern involving an absolute constant. In our example, the actual frequency of Cheryl's contributions—94 t-units—is an absolute constant across the two meetings.

A related pattern, shown in the bottom of Figure 7.13, involves a proportional constant. Here, the relative rather than actual frequency remains constant across samples. In both meetings graphed in the bottom graphs in Figure 7.13, for example, Cheryl speaks about 33% of the time in both meetings.

Absolute and proportional constants are not unusual in verbal data. Suppose, for example, a weekly meeting is always opened with a 5-minute recap of last week's meeting. All verbal phenomenon associated with that recap will tend to be fixed in quantity regardless of how long the rest of the meeting takes. In this case, meetings from two different weeks will tend to exhibit a pattern of absolute constant.

Proportional constants are even more common. Suppose, for example, that the number of questions asked by the prosecution and defense in a trial was a fixed percentage of the trial proceedings. Then the contribution of attorneys' questions will be a proportional constant, increasing as the length of the trial increases, but remaining more or less at a constant proportion of the proceedings. Witness contributions, on the other hand, may be quite variable, with some witnesses responding extensively while others have relatively little to say. In this case, in contrast to attorneys' contributions, the length of witness contributions might have no relationship to the length of the trial.

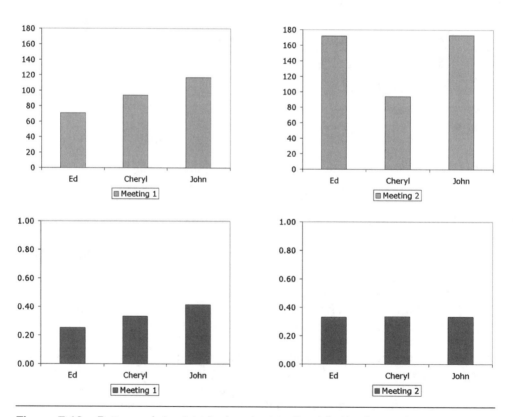

Figure 7.13   Patterns of absolute (top) and proportional (bottom) constants.

Equity and Dominance

The distribution patterns shown in Figure 7.14 are last but not least in the analysis of verbal data. Here, in Meeting 1, we see a situation in which one category, speaker John, dominates. In Meeting 2, by contrast, speaker contribution is equitably distributed across speaker categories.

Patterns of equity and dominance are significant in the analysis of verbal data. In most classroom conversations, for example, the teacher's contributions tend to dominate regardless of other participation. Equitable distributions like those shown to the right in Figure 7.14 are relatively rare.

Lack of Pattern

Finally, the last important pattern to be on the lookout for in the analysis of distributions is the pattern of no pattern. All verbal data is characterized by natural variations due to innumerable factors. Sometimes these variations add up to variation across distributions that cannot be described as falling into any particular pattern. In Figure 7.15, for example, no discernable pattern exists linking Meeting 1 and Meeting 2. Cheryl's contributions go way down; John's stay about the same; Ed's go up. While, as described in Chapter 11, we can develop narrative descriptions of these relationships, there does not appear to be an overall pattern as was in the cases described in the previous sections.

If you expected differences between data samples, the lack of pattern can be quite interesting. If, on the other hand, you are looking for ways to characterize the relationship between two data samples, the lack of pattern for the dimension analyzed should be a message to send you looking at other dimensions or to other phenomena altogether.

The patterns just reviewed are only some of those that you may encounter as you compare the distributions across the built-in contrasts of your design. They

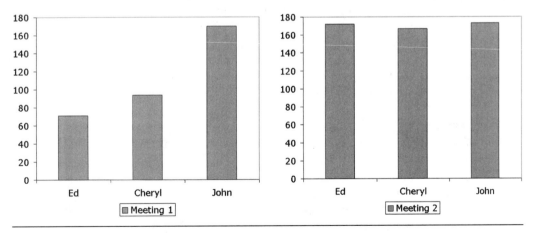

Figure 7.14   Patterns of equity and dominance.

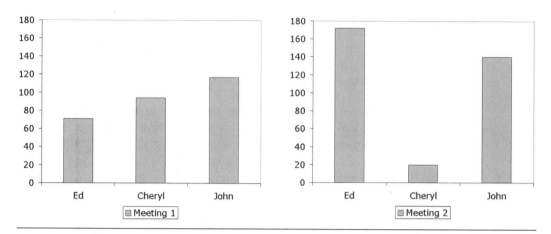

Figure 7.15 Distributions without pattern.

are tools to help you notice and characterize the contours of your data samples. If they indicate that something is "going on" in your data, you may want to refine your analysis to produce a better characterization of the phenomenon. In the remainder of this chapter, we deal with two such refinements—collapsing cases and combining categories—as well as some of the interactions that can make such refinements overly simple and thus problematic.

Refining Patterns Across Cases

Thus far, we have described the distributions you may want to analyze as if they consist of just one case on each side of your built-in contrasts. Yet many good analytic designs include multiple cases rather than just one case. Suppose, for example, we had designed our analysis to contrast two kinds of meetings—design meetings and managerial meetings—and we had data samples from two meetings of each kind—four meetings in total.

Our analysis would begin, of course, with the distributions of each of the four cases as shown in Figure 7.17. In this case, we find that there is a proportional similarity between the two design meetings, in which Ed and John talk with about the

7.3 Try It Out

The graphs in Figure 7.16 show the frequency and relative frequency with which texts that were private (intended for oneself as reader) and texts that were public (intended for other readers) were used during a working session that involved five different applications: desktop software for a personal digital assist (PDA), e-mail, web browser, word processing, and spreadsheet. How would you describe the differences between the applications in terms of these distributions?

7.3 **Try It Out (continued)**

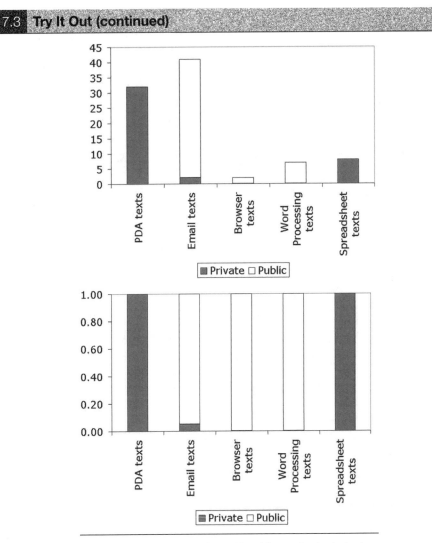

Figure 7.16 Distributions of public and private texts.

For discussion: Compare your descriptions with those of your classmates.

same relative frequency and Cheryl talks less frequently. The two managerial meetings are likewise similar to each other, though different from the design meetings. Here, Ed talks most frequently, followed by Cheryl, with John left far behind.

When cases have more in common with each other than they do with the cases across a built-in contrast, we may want to collapse cases in order to refine the pattern. In Figure 7.18, for example, we have collapsed the data from the two design meetings and from the two managerial meetings to give a portrait of how, overall, the design meetings and managerial meetings differ.

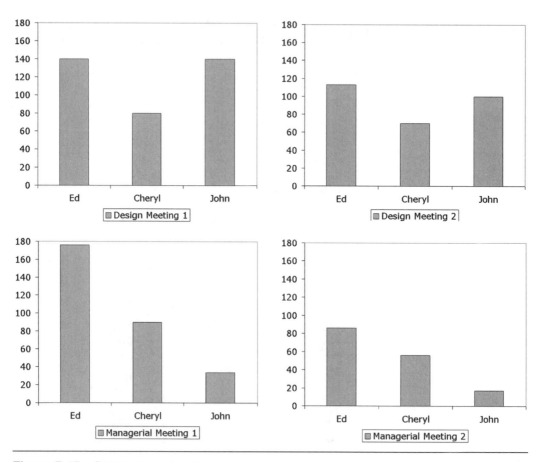

Figure 7.17   Distributions of multiple cases.

Collapsing Cases

To collapse cases, simply add together the frequencies across cases within a contrast. In Figure 7.19, for example, we show the frequency table used to construct the charts in Figure 7.18. The frequencies for the two design meetings appear in one table followed by the frequencies for the managerial meetings in a second table. A third table shows the frequencies for design meetings and managerial meetings overall and has been created by bringing down the column totals from the two tables above it. Thus the formula in C16 is

$$=C8$$

and the formula in C17 is

$$=C13$$

The rest of the table is filled in by dragging these two formulas across Columns D, E, and F.

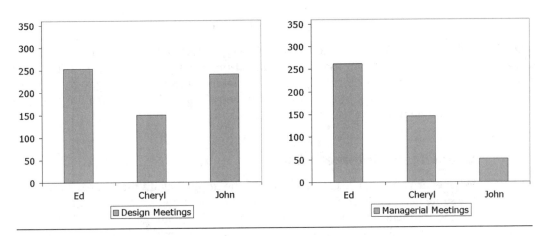

Figure 7.18 Collapsing cases.

Calculating Averages

The data graphed in Figure 7.18 represent the total frequency of speaker categories in two design meetings and two managerial meetings. Another, perhaps more meaningful statistic for this data is the average frequency of speaker contribution per meeting. These figures can be calculated using a formula with a similar structure to the formula for sums:

	A	B	C	D	E	F
1	**Collapsing cases**					
2						
3	**Actual Frequency**					
4	# of t-units					
5			Ed	Cheryl	John	Total
6		Design Meeting 1	140	80	140	360
7		Design Meeting 2	113	70	100	283
8		Total	253	150	240	643
9						
10			Ed	Cheryl	John	Total
11		Managerial Meeting 1	176	90	34	300
12		Managerial Meeting 2	86	56	17	159
13		Total	262	146	51	459
14						
15			Ed	Cheryl	John	Total
16		Design Meetings	253	150	240	643
17		Managerial Meetings	262	146	51	459
18		Total	515	296	291	1102

Figure 7.19 Adding frequencies to collapse cases.

$$=AVERAGE(C6:C7)$$

Values from this formula tell you the average frequency per meeting. Ed, for example, contributed an average of 126.5 t-units per meeting in design meetings and 131.0 t-units per meeting in managerial meeting. Such averages give a better sense of the average magnitude of a phenomenon (like Ed's speaking) and are thus sometimes more useful in communicating with your readers.

Checking for Interactions

Whenever you collapse cases, you make the implicit claim that those cases follow the same basic pattern. Such need not be the case. Look at the data in Figure 7.20. As the frequency table at the bottom of the figure suggests, the collapsed frequency for design and managerial meetings is the same here as it was in the data presented in Figure 7.18. In this case, however, this collapse presents a very misleading portrait of the individual cases.

To see how, compare the kinds of descriptions we might generate with the collapsed data with descriptions based on the individual cases. If we were to say, for instance, that Cheryl contributed, on average, 75 t-units per meeting in the design meetings, this characterization would hardly be a good description of her contribution in Meeting 1 (where she spoke for 140 t-units) or her contribution in Meeting 2 (where she spoke for 10 t-units).

Nor are comparisons between her total contribution and the total contributions of Ed and John valid. In the collapsed data, Cheryl looks as if she speaks less than either Ed or John. But the data for the individual cases makes clear that in Meeting 1 she spoke with about the same frequency as Ed and John, but in Meeting 2, she spoke far less.

The situation we have just been describing—one in which collapsing cases provides a misleading portrait of the individual cases—is called an interaction. In an interaction, pooling data across cases obscures major variations within the cases that makes the pooled statistics—either the collapsed frequencies or the averages—poor descriptions of the cases themselves. These are called interactions because the choice of samples interacts with the pattern of distribution.

So, for example, if we want to answer the question, "How did the distribution of speaker contribution differ between the design meetings and the managerial meetings?" for the data presented in Figure 7.20, we would have to answer, "It depends. . . ." The first design meeting (graphed to the left in Figure 7.20) looks a lot more equitable than the managerial meetings (graphed to the right in Figure 7.18). But the second design meeting (graphed to the right in Figure 7.20) does not look at all equitable. In this data set, as in all interactions, there simply is no way to generate a general characterization that fits the individual cases.

The overall lesson to be learned here is that while collapsing cases can be a very useful technique for refining patterns, it can also be misleading if it obscures real variation within cases. It is important to always look at the distribution of

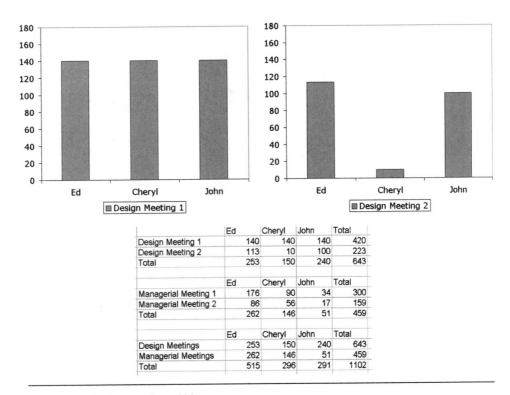

Figure 7.20   Interaction within cases.

each case individually before taking the step of collapsing them together across your built-in contrasts.

Refining Patterns Across Categories

A second technique for refining distribution patterns involves combining categories within your coding scheme. In Figure 7.21, for example, we show a meeting with four speakers combined into two categories, managers and subordinates. This 100% stacked column graph neatly suggests that in both meetings managers spoke about twice as often as subordinates, a very suggestive finding.

Two limitations need to be placed on the use of combining categories as a way of refining distribution patterns. To begin with, categories can only be combined in ways that make sense with respect to the phenomena. Combine apples with apples, not with oranges (unless you are interested in fruit!).

Second, you must always check the distributions of the individual categories in advance of combining them to make sure that no interactions exist. Look at the distributions in Figure 7.22, for example. These represent the individual cases

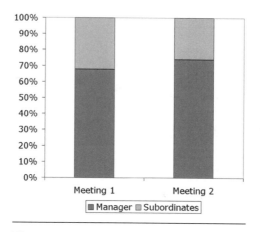

Figure 7.21   Combining categories.

combined to produce the patterns shown in Figure 7.21. Ed and Roger are the managers; Cheryl and John are the subordinates. Combining the categories as we have done makes the implicit claim that Ed and Roger have more in common with each other than they do with Cheryl and John. The individual cases in Figure 7.22 confirm this, but what if they told a different story? What if Roger, although a manager, looked more like Cheryl and John in his participation than he did like Ed. Combining his data with Ed's data to produce an overall picture of managers' contribution would, in this case, be misleading. There would be an interaction: How managers act would depend upon which manager—Ed or Roger. In such cases as this, you should avoid combining categories.

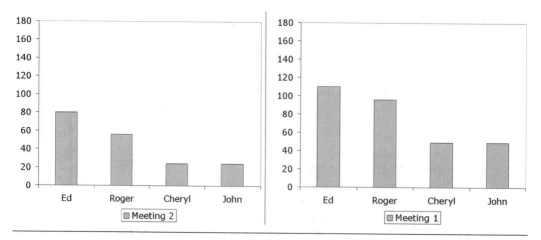

Figure 7.22   Interactions within categories.

PROJECT: SEEING PATTERNS OF DISTRIBUTION

Create graphs to represent the distribution of your data in the coding categories, across your built-in contrasts. A sample set of distribution graphs is available at the course website.

Make sure to look at both frequency and relative frequency for individual cases before refining the distributions by collapsing cases or combining categories.

Describe in one to two pages:

a. how your data was distributed across your coding categories, and
b. what these patterns may suggest about the phenomenon.

Attach the data workbook with all data worksheets and Frequency worksheet.

CHAPTER 8

Exploring Patterns
Across Dimensions

 In this chapter, you will look at patterns that indicate how one dimension of your data is associated with another dimension. You will build contingency tables showing the relationship across the categories of two dimensions and block charts to examine their patterns. A process for the stepwise comparison of dimensional patterns with patterns across your built-in contrast and across cases is introduced.

Dimensions

In the last chapter, we looked at the distribution of your data—the ups and downs created by the categories of your coding scheme. In this chapter, we take analysis into another dimension by looking at how these contours are related to the distribution patterns of a second coding scheme. This kind of analysis will help you to understand how the distribution of your data in one dimension is associated with its distribution in a second dimension.

Thus far in your analytic efforts, you have been concerned about describing the relationship between your built-in contrast and a phenomenon of interest. Taking the categories that made up a coding scheme, you looked for differences in the distribution of data across your built-in contrasts. In this chapter, we take that analysis one step further to look at the associations between these patterns and patterns across a second dimension.

Adding a second dimension to an analysis involves coding your already coded set of data with a second coding scheme. The goal is often to develop a greater understanding of the differences across your built-in contrasts. If, for example, you have discovered that design and management meetings are different along the dimension of speaker contribution, you might then begin to wonder

	A	B	C	D
1	**T-Unit #**	**Speaker**	**Text**	**Indexicality**
2				
3	1	Cheryl	I mean...	Not Indexed
4	2	Ed	Jesus.	Not Indexed
5	3	Cheryl	See I :	Not Indexed
6	4	Cheryl	see where	Not Indexed
7	5	Cheryl	this little thing is?	Indexed
8	6	Cheryl	It looks to me	Not Indexed
9	7	Cheryl	like it got wiped out.	Not Indexed

Figure 8.1   Data coded along two dimensions, speaker and indexicality.

how these types of meetings varied along a second dimension—indexicality, for instance. Figure 8.1 shows a sample of data that has been coded in this way both for the dimension of speaker contribution (in Column B) and the dimension of indexicality (in Column D).

Adding a Second Dimension

To add a second dimension to your analysis, return to the original data sheets and construct a second coding scheme whereby each segment of data is assigned to one of the categories associated with a second dimension. The procedures detailed in Chapters 4 and 5 for developing a coding scheme and confirming its reliability apply. The result will be data that has been coded along two dimensions.

Questions of Distribution

Once a second dimension is added to your data analysis, two kinds of questions can be asked. To begin with, you can ask how the distribution of data over the categories of the second coding scheme varies across your built-in contrast. This question is a question of distribution and parallels the question you asked concerning your first dimension. For example, with the two dimensions shown in Figure 8.1, we can ask not only a question about distribution of speaker contribution:

> Do design meetings differ from management meetings in the relative contributions made by speaker?

but also a question about the distribution of indexicality:

> Are design meetings more or less indexical than management meetings?

Answering these two questions will give us a picture of the distributions of the data in both dimensions, but it will not tell us how these two distributions are related to one another. To understand this, we must ask questions of association.

Questions of Association

If we stop our analysis with answers to questions of distribution, our understanding of the data will be less than complete. We would fail to explore the associations between the two dimensions—how they are interrelated. For this we have to ask questions of association.

Most generally, questions of association ask how variations along one dimension are associated with variations along the second dimension. In the case of the data in Figure 8.1, for example, we can ask a question about the association between speaker contribution and indexicality:

> Do some speakers employ more indexical language than other speakers?

Furthermore, we can also ask how that association plays out across our built-in contrasts:

> Does the rate of indexicality of a speaker vary by the kind of meeting they are attending?

The procedures outlined in the rest of this chapter are designed to help you answer questions of association.

8.1 Test Your Understanding

Decide whether each of the following questions is a question of distribution or a question of association. Then label the dimension being used in each question.

a. During what decade did Elvis record his best songs?
b. How is the productivity of rock stars related to age and gender?
c. Are men more likely than women to act aggressively in on-line interactions?
d. Are certain topics associated with greater aggression among men than among women?

For discussion: Discuss with your classmates the kind of data sheets that would allow you to answer each question.

Building Contingency Tables

The process of seeing associations across dimensions involves the use of contingency tables like the one shown in Figure 8.2. The categories of one coding scheme are arrayed across the top of the table (Indexed and Not Indexed). Down the side are arrayed the categories of the second coding scheme (Cheryl, Ed, John). In the cells are listed the frequencies with which the two dimensions intersect. For example, the upper left-hand cell represents the intersection of Cheryl with Indexed, and the cell itself tells us that 69 of Cheryl's t-units were coded as Indexed.

The process of building a contingency table is an extension of the database manipulations we used for building frequency tables. You (a) name the data, (b) build a criteria table, and then (c) use this criteria to fill the contingency table. You can review the procedures for these steps in Chapter 6.

	Indexed	Not Indexed	Total
Cheryl	69	73	142
Ed	40	32	72
John	1	2	3
Total	110	107	217

Figure 8.2 A contingency table for data coded in two dimensions: speaker and indexicality.

Two-dimensional Criteria

The criteria for a contingency table are more complex than those used for simple frequency tables. Because each cell in a contingency table like that shown in Figure 8.1 uses criteria for two dimensions, each criteria in the related criteria table occupies twice as many cells—that is, four rather than two.

A sample criteria table for a contingency table is shown in Figure 8.3. The two cells on the first line give the name of the two dimensions (Speaker and Indexicality). The two cells on the second line give the names of the relevant categories from each dimension (Cheryl and Indexed).

5		Indexed		Not Indexed	
6	Cheryl	Speaker	Indexicality	Speaker	Indexicality
7		Cheryl	Indexed	Cheryl	Not Indexed
8	Ed	Speaker	Indexicality	Speaker	Indexicality
9		Ed	Indexed	Ed	Not Indexed
10	John	Speaker	Indexicality	Speaker	Indexicality
11		John	Indexed	John	Not Indexed

Figure 8.3 Criteria for filling a contingency table.

Core Contingency Tables

A set of core contingency tables must be constructed for each of the cases sampled in your data. If, for example, we have data from four meetings—two design meetings and two management meetings—we must build core contingency tables for all four of these meetings. Figure 8.4 shows one way of setting up the criteria for multiple contingency tables.

Calculating Contingencies

In the core contingency tables themselves, the formulas for calculating the frequencies at the intersections for the two dimensions have the same structure as the formulas used to construct the more simple frequency tables:

=DCOUNTA(database,"dataColumn",criteria)

Management 1
Criteria

	Indexed		Not Indexed	
Cheryl	Speaker Cheryl	Indexicality Indexed	Speaker Cheryl	Indexicality Not Indexed
Ed	Speaker Ed	Indexicality Indexed	Speaker Ed	Indexicality Not Indexed
John	Speaker John	Indexicality Indexed	Speaker John	Indexicality Not Indexed

Management 2
Criteria

	Indexed		Not Indexed	
Cheryl	Speaker Cheryl	Indexicality Indexed	Speaker Cheryl	Indexicality Not Indexed
Ed	Speaker Ed	Indexicality Indexed	Speaker Ed	Indexicality Not Indexed
John	Speaker John	Indexicality Indexed	Speaker John	Indexicality Not Indexed

Design 1
Criteria

	Indexed		Not Indexed	
Cheryl	Speaker Cheryl	Indexicality Indexed	Speaker Cheryl	Indexicality Not Indexed
Lee	Speaker Lee	Indexicality Indexed	Speaker Lee	Indexicality Not Indexed
Ed	Speaker Ed	Indexicality Indexed	Speaker Ed	Indexicality Not Indexed
John	Speaker John	Indexicality Indexed	Speaker John	Indexicality Not Indexed

Design 2
Criteria

	Indexed		Not Indexed	
Cheryl	Speaker Cheryl	Indexicality Indexed	Speaker Cheryl	Indexicality Not Indexed
Lee	Speaker Lee	Indexicality Indexed	Speaker Lee	Indexicality Not Indexed
Ed	Speaker Ed	Indexicality Indexed	Speaker Ed	Indexicality Not Indexed
John	Speaker John	Indexicality Indexed	Speaker John	Indexicality Not Indexed

Figure 8.4   Criteria tables for the core contingency tables, one for each case.

8.2 Try It Out

A data set has been collected of written comments on three papers from professors across the disciplines, using the following design:

	Paper A	Paper B	Paper C
English professor			
History professor			
Biology professor			
Physics professor			

These comments have been coded using the two coding schemes shown here.

Force	Topic
Directive	Grammar
Facilitative	Style
	Content
	Argument
	Organization

Set up the criteria tables that will fill core contingency tables appropriately.

When selecting the data range for two dimensions, be careful to select all four cells of the criteria table. For example, to fill the cell at the interaction of Cheryl and Indexed, we must drag from B6 across to C6 and then down B6 and B7. The resulting formula then contains the criteria for both dimensions:

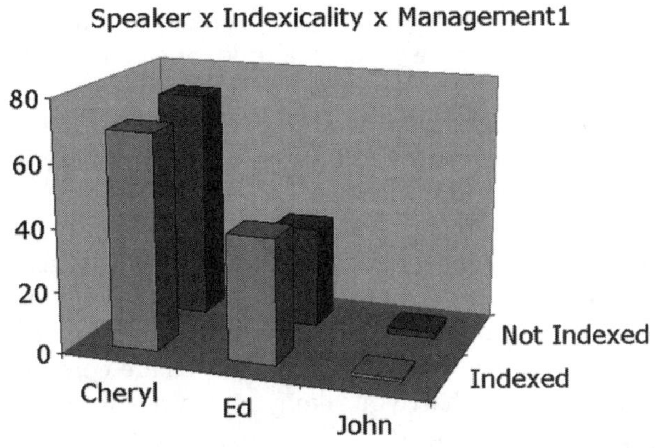

Speaker x Indexicality x Management1

Figure 8.5   A block chart showing two-dimensional data for the Management1 case.

=DCOUNTA(Management1data"Text",B6:C7)

Graphing Dimensions

The rest of this chapter outlines a stepwise process for analyzing graphs constructed from the core contingency tables described in the last section. Before you go on to this analysis, however, we introduce the general procedure for constructing these graphs.

Just as your analysis moves into two dimensions with the addition of a second coding scheme, so too do your graphing techniques. The basic graph used to explore two-dimensional data is called a block chart. As you can see from the example in Figure 8.5, a block chart is a two-dimensional graph. The coding categories of the first coding scheme are arrayed along the x-axis. The coding categories of the second coding scheme are arrayed along the z-axis. The graph itself shows the distribution of the data across these two dimensions.

In Figure 8.5, for example, we see that in the Management 1 meeting, Cheryl was the most frequent speaker, Ed the second most frequent, and John hardly spoke at all. We also see that this patterns holds true both for contributions that were indexed (shown in light grey) and those that were not indexed (shown in dark grey).

Creating a Block Chart

Creating a block chart for two-dimensional data involves the same basic process as creating a frequency chart. Select the data in the contingency table, including both column and row headers, but excluding the marginals, as shown at the top of Figure 8.6. Invoking the Chart Wizard, select the 3-D column graph in step 1 as shown at the bottom of Figure 8.6.

Block charts offer the same set of options that are available for frequency graphs. The block chart shown in Figure 8.5, for example, has the following options:

- For the chart Title, we used the names of the two dimensions as well as the name of the case (for example, Speaker × Indexicality × Management1) this helps us to keep track of what we have graphed.
- For Gridlines, we have removed the default gridlines.
- For the Legend, we have deselected the Show legend box since it provided redundant information.

The process of analyzing across dimensions, described next, involves creating and comparing a great many block charts. Consequently, creating a chart style for your preferred options in a block graph will save you considerable time. It will also help to insure that your block graphs are comparable. Thus, once you have produced a block chart you like, you can use it to create a Block style following the procedures described in Chapter 7.

Rotating the Chart

Although block charts have the value of showing distribution data in two dimensions, they have the flaw of being difficult to read and interpret. The forward plane of the graph often obscures the data on the planes behind it. Furthermore, the dimensionality of the graph often makes it difficult to compare magnitudes across planes.

	Indexed	Not Indexed	Total
Cheryl	69	73	142
Ed	40	32	72
John	1	2	3
Total	110	107	217

3-D Column. Compares values across categories and across series.

Figure 8.6   Selecting the data and the 3-D Column Graph to create a block chart.

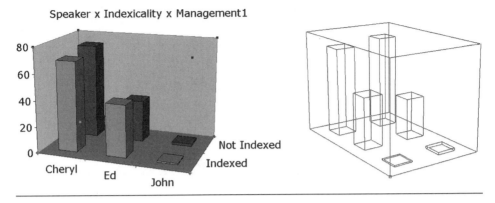

Figure 8.7 Rotating a block chart.

To deal with difficulties in viewing patterns in a block chart, you will find it useful to rotate the chart. To rotate a block chart, select the corners of the graph shown on the left in Figure 8.7. Then begin dragging in the direction that will provide you with a better view for what you want to inspect. As shown to the right in Figure 8.7, a skeleton view of the block chart will appear and help to guide your rotation. Continue rotating until you can see the data that has been obscured or have moved the data you want to compare into the same plane.

Rotating charts can help to refine your understanding of the patterns in three-dimensional block charts. In Figure 8.5, for example, while it was easy to see the contours across the dimension of speaker contribution, it was harder to compare across the dimension of indexicality. Are there more, less, or about the same numbers of indexed units as nonindexed? The view in Figure 8.5 made it hard to tell. Once the graph is rotated to the view shown in Figure 8.8, however, the answer is more easy to come by: The levels are more or less the same.

When you want to compare block charts, it is important that they have the same degree of rotation. Since it is nearly impossible to rotate two charts exactly the same amount by hand, a better system involves applying the values for the rotation of one chart to other charts. You can do this using the 3-D View . . . command under Chart on the menu bar. As shown in Figure 8.9, the 3-D view shows adjustments in elevation, rotation, perspective and height. You can also return a rotated graph to its default rotation—very useful if you mess things up and want to start over. To transfer the rotation of one block chart to another, simply note the values for an already rotated chart and then apply them to a second chart using the 3-D View . . . command.

Refining Patterns

As you create your block charts, you may find that the distribution patterns of certain categories are similar to one another and quite different from patterns for

Speaker x Indexicality x Management1

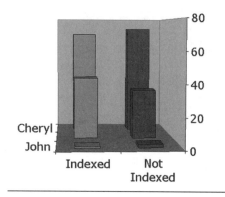

Figure 8.8 A rotated view of the same data shown in Figure 8.5.

other categories. In Figure 8.10, for example, there appear to be three different patterns. First, we can see business, technology, and special interest publications as sharing the same pattern of dominance through the years. Another group of publications, by contrast, seems to have started from relatively modest numbers in 1996 and to have been increasing. And finally, a third group of publications

Figure 8.9 Setting chart rotation.

wasn't even on the horizon in 1996, but seems to have become a regular if still small publication venue by 2000.

When you see possible clusters in the distribution patterns of your data, you can reorder the categories in your data sheet to create block charts that better represent these clusters. An example of a clustered block chart is shown in Figure 8.11. Here, we have placed the categories with the strongest incidence toward the left of the chart, the medium categories in the middle, and the relatively late-occurring categories toward the right. This kind of clustered display has greater ability to convey the publication patterns for the articles.

To create a clustered display, return to your contingency table and insert cluster values for each of the categories in your coding scheme. Assign the same cluster value to categories with similar patterns that you want to appear close together on the block chart. Assign low cluster values to those categories with relatively large values that you want to cluster to the left of your block chart and high cluster values for those with relatively low incidence that you want to cluster to the right of your block chart. As shown in Figure 8.12, for example, we have as-

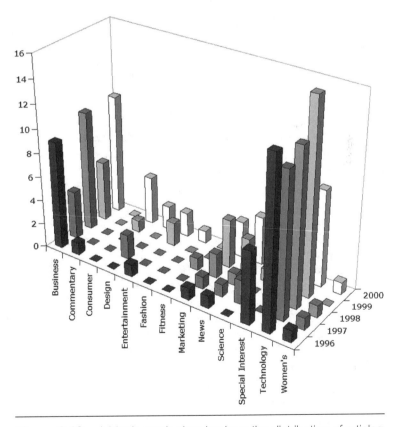

Figure 8.10 A block graph showing how the distribution of articles across publication type varies by year.

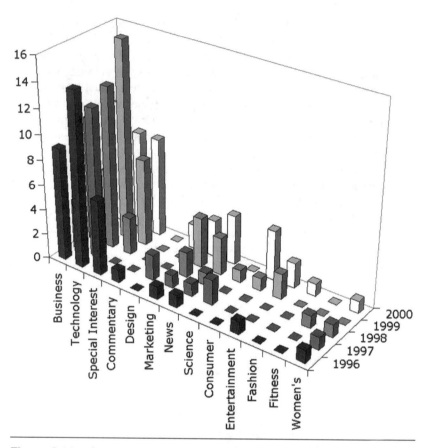

Figure 8.11   Clustering categories to reveal common patterns of distribution.

signed a cluster value of 1 to the dominant publication types, a 2 to the medium publications, and a 3 to the relatively late publications.

Now, as shown in Figure 8.12, sort the columns of the contingency graph by the row in which you assigned the cluster value, using the option to sort from left to right rather than from top to bottom. To get to this option, click on the Options button in the Sort dialogue box to bring up the Sort Option dialogue box. The result will be a clustered set of categories in your contingency table that will automatically update your associated block graphs to look like the one in Figure 8.11.

A second technique could be used to enhance the view of clustered categories in Figure 8.11. Each column within a cluster could be assigned the same color, with high-incidence columns colored black, medium-incidence columns colored gray, and low-incidence clusters colored white. To create this kind of color pattern, select each column individually and assign it a color.

To color an individual column, click once on the column to select the series and then click a second time to select just the column. Next, double click this column to bring up the dialogue box that will allow you to change its color to a cus-

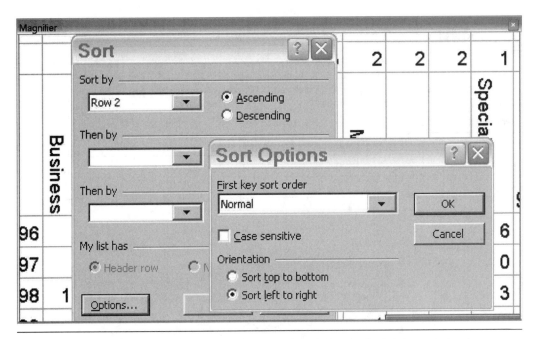

Figure 8.12   Assigning a cluster value to categories of data in the totals worksheet.

tom color. Individually select and assign this color for each of the remaining columns in this cluster, and color the other clusters in the same way.

Characterizing Dimensions

The analysis of verbal data across dimensions is a complex comparative process. One way to understand it is through the schematic given in Figure 8.14. You begin by characterizing the overall patterns in each dimension and comparing them to the patterns across contrast. You then go on to establishing the basic associations across dimensions and checking the patterns across contrast. Finally, you take

8.3 Try It Out

For a study of PDA (Personal Digital Assistants) users, we classified participants into three groups based upon the balance between work and life items in their PDAs: Strong Life, Strong Work, and Integrated. We want to understand the relationship between this Work-Life Balance classification and their home situation. The data are shown in the table in Figure 8.13 and the block chart following, downloadable from the course website.

   Use the techniques in this chapter to cluster together those participants with children, with partner but no children, and without family responsibilities.

(continued)

	Single, living alone	Single, living with partner	Single, living with friends	Single, with children	Married, no children	Married, with children at home	Married, children grown	Divorced, with children	Other	Total
STRONG LIFE	4	0	0	0	3	2	0	1	0	10
INTEGRATED	3	1	0	0	3	9	3	2	0	21
STRONG WORK	1	0	0	0	2	6	2	0	0	11
Total	8	1	0	0	8	17	5	3	0	42

Work-Life

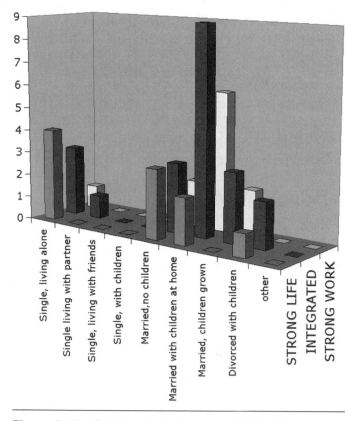

Figure 8.13 Relationship between work-life balance and home situation.

For discussion: What relationship, if any, do you see between work-life balance in the PDA and home situation?

whatever patterns you find across dimensions and contrasts and see whether they hold true across cases.

As this schematic indicates, then, the baseline pattern for any analysis of data across dimensions is the overall pattern for each dimension. While many factors arise that can complicate if not compromise the adequacy of these baseline characterizations, you will only be able to understand these complications if you begin with overall characterizations.

A characterization of the overall pattern for a dimension is a description of the general contours of the data as it is distributed in the categories of your coding scheme—without regard to specific cases and without regard to the built-in contrasts. If you have a coding scheme with three categories, for example, you ask yourself how, overall, the data has been placed in those categories: in the first category? in the second? in the third?

To answer these kinds of questions—to understand the overall pattern for a dimension—involves calculating the frequency of each category of a coding scheme and then calculating its relative frequency. Figure 8.15, for instance, shows the frequency and relative frequency of the coding categories for the categories of speaker (Cheryl, Ed, and John) and for the categories of indexicality (Indexed and Not Indexed). Notice that the totals for each table are identical because exactly the same set of segments has been classified according to each scheme.

Calculating Overall Frequencies

To calculate overall frequencies for each dimension and fill tables like those shown in Figure 8.15, sum the relevant frequencies from the core contingency tables for each case. If, for example, we have the same four meetings (two management, two design) described earlier, the overall frequency for Cheryl would be equal to the totals for Cheryl in Management 1, in Management 2, in Design 1, and in Design 2. The values we need to sum are, therefore, in all four core contingency tables, and we need to bring them together in one formula.

Dimension		
Dimension x Contrast	Dimension x Contrast	
	Dimension x Dimension x Contrast	Dimension x Dimension x Contrast
		Dimension x Contrast x Case

Figure 8.14 Schematic of the complex comparative process of analyzing data across dimensions.

Speaker	Frequency	Relative Frequency
Cheryl	512	0.43
Ed	269	0.23
John	407	0.34
Total	1188	1.00

Indexicality	Frequency	
Indexed	483	0.41
Not Indexed	705	0.59
Total	1188	1.00

Figure 8.15 Overall patterns for the dimension of speaker contribution and indexicality.

To construct the formula for the overall frequency for Cheryl, for example, we type the = and then click on the row totals for Cheryl in each of our four core contingency tables, inserting a + between each. The result pulls and sums values from the four contingency tables:

$$=D28+J28+D36+J36$$

Once the overall frequencies are calculated, the relative frequencies, like those shown to the right in Figure 8.15, are calculated using the procedures presented in Chapter 6.

Establishing Overall Patterns

Because you will be comparing the overall patterns for each dimension to the patterns across built-in contrasts, the relative frequencies give you the best understanding of the overall patterns for each dimension. We can see from Figure 8.15, for example, that overall, 41% of the segments were Indexed and 59% Not Indexed, a pattern in which, in general, the language is slightly less indexed than not indexed. Once we know this, we can then go on to see whether this overall pattern of indexicality holds across our built-in contrasts.

Graphing Overall Patterns

Sometimes you will want to create a graphic representation of the overall patterns for a dimension to compare with patterns across contrast. With a two-category coding scheme like indexicality, this is not particularly necessary, since the overall pattern of 41% versus 59% is not hard to understand. But with dimensions with more numerous categories, graphing can be helpful.

Although you are working with one-dimensional data, you will find it easier to use three-dimensional block charts to facilitate comparison with later block charts. Figure 8.17 shows block charts for the overall relative frequencies for both dimensions of the data seen earlier in Figure 8.15. You may notice that they are slightly different from one another. The dimension of speaker contribution is distributed along

8.4 Try It Out

Write the formula that will calculate the overall frequency with which the English professor made facilitative comments about content for the core contingency tables shown in Figure 8.16.

	A	B	C	D	E	F	G	H	I	J	K	L
1	**English Paper A**				**English Paper B**				**English Paper C**			
2		Directive	Facilitative	Total		Directive	Facilitative	Total		Directive	Facilitative	Total
3	Grammar	0	0	0	Grammar	1	0	1	Grammar	2	3	5
4	Style	2	1	3	Style	12	1	13	Style	3	0	3
5	Content	0	2	2	Content	1	3	4	Content	0	2	2
6	Argument	0	0	0	Argument	1	1	2	Argument	2	4	6
7	Organization	0	1	1	Organization	0	5	5	Organization	0	1	1
8	Total	2	4	6	Total	15	10	25	Total	7	10	17
9	**History Paper A**				**History Paper B**				**History Paper C**			
10		Directive	Facilitative	Total		Directive	Facilitative	Total		Directive	Facilitative	Total
11	Grammar	0	0	0	Grammar	0	0	0	Grammar	0	0	0
12	Style	0	0	0	Style	0	0	0	Style	0	0	0
13	Content	3	1	4	Content	2	1	3	Content	5	0	5
14	Argument	0	0	0	Argument	0	0	0	Argument	0	0	0
15	Organization	0	0	0	Organization	0	1	1	Organization	1	0	1
16	Total	3	1	4	Total	2	2	4	Total	6	0	6
17	**Biology Paper A**				**Biology Paper B**				**Biology Paper C**			
18		Directive	Facilitative	Total		Directive	Facilitative	Total		Directive	Facilitative	Total
19	Grammar	2	0	2	Grammar	1	0	1	Grammar	5	0	5
20	Style	0	0	0	Style	0	0	0	Style	0	0	0
21	Content	6	0	6	Content	3	0		Content	2	1	3
22	Argument	0	0	0	Argument	0	0	0	Argument	0	0	0
23	Organization	0	0	0	Organization	0	0	0	Organization	0	0	0
24	Total	8	0	8	Total	4	0	4	Total	7	1	8
25	**Physics Paper A**				**Physics Paper B**				**Physics Paper C**			
26		Directive	Facilitative	Total		Directive	Facilitative	Total		Directive	Facilitative	Total
27	Grammar	0	0	0	Grammar	0	0	0	Grammar	0	0	0
28	Style	0	0	0	Style	0	0	0	Style	0	0	0
29	Content	0	3	3	Content	0	5		Content	0	4	4
30	Argument	1	0	1	Argument	3	0	3	Argument	1	0	1
31	Organization	0	0	0	Organization	0	0	0	Organization	0	0	0
32	Total	1	3	4	Total	3	5	8	Total	1	4	5

Figure 8.16   Core contingency tables for data on written comments.

the x-axis; that for indexicality along the z-axis. This facilitates comparison with the block charts we will create in general, like that shown in Figure 8.5.

When you use the Chart Wizard to create a three-dimensional graph using two-dimensional data, it will by default array that data along the x-axis. This will work well for your first dimension, but is not as easy to work with for your second dimension. To move a second dimension from the x-axis to the z-axis, make the selection shown in Figure 8.18. That is, in step 2 of the Chart Wizard, select Rows rather than Columns as the series. If you have already constructed a chart with the default option, you can change it by choosing Source Data under Chart on the menu bar, and making the same selection shown in Figure 8.18.

One final note about producing these block charts. With data laid out as shown in Figure 8.15, you cannot simply drag to select the data to produce block

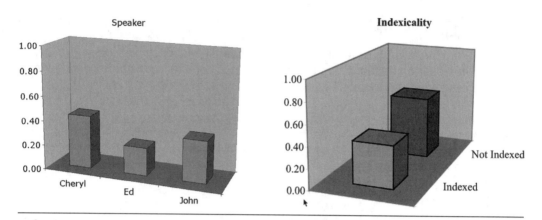

Figure 8.17   Block charts of the overall patterns for speaker contribution and indexicality.

Figure 8.18   Moving a dimension to the z-axis in Step 2 of the Chart Wizard.

charts like those shown in Figure 8.17. As you can see, the data for relative frequency are not adjacent to the category names on the spreadsheet. While you could copy and rearrange the data in a more appropriate manner, a way does exist to select nonadjacent data.

To select nonadjacent data for graphing, begin by selecting the first block of data (perhaps the category names). Next, while holding down the command key (on Macintosh computers) or the control key (on Windows computers), drag to select the second block.

Checking Patterns Across Contrast

Once you understand the overall patterns for each dimension of the data, you can begin to explore the way these patterns change across your built-in contrast. These patterns need to be examined separately for each dimension.

Establishing the Contrast

Begin by constructing a set of contingency tables for each dimension that show the data on either side of your contrast. In Figure 8.19, for example, you can see two sets of contingency tables, one for the dimension of speaker contribution and one for the dimension of indexicality. These have been created by summing the relevant data from our core contingency tables.

Making the Comparison

Using these contingency tables, we then construct a set of block graphs for each dimension and make comparisons with the basic pattern for that dimension. Two outcomes are possible for these comparisons. On the one hand, the patterns on either side of the contrast may mirror the overall pattern for that dimension. In this case, we have evidence that the contrast may be irrelevant to the dimension. If, on the other hand, the patterns on either side of the built-in contrast shift as we move from one side of the contrast to another, we have evidence that the dimension may be relevant to the contrast.

For example, Figure 8.20 shows a comparison between the overall pattern for the dimension of speaker contribution and the patterns across the built-in contrast of management versus design. In the top right-hand of the figure, we see that the contour of the distribution for talk by Cheryl, Ed, and John in the management meetings pretty much mirrors the overall contour on the left-hand side. The same is the case for the design meetings on the bottom right-hand side.

To confirm your comparisons, compare the relative frequencies for the dimension overall with the frequencies across contrast. If the patterns are parallel, the general order as well as the general magnitude of the relative frequencies of the categories should be more or less equivalent.

Thus, to confirm the similarity of patterns suggested by the block graphs in Figure 8.20, we compare the relative frequencies for the design and management data with the overall relative frequencies:

	Overall	Management	Design
Cheryl	0.43	0.49	0.40
Ed	0.23	0.24	0.22
John	0.34	0.28	0.38

Speaker x Management	
Cheryl	208
Ed	101
John	118
Total	427

Speaker x Design	
Cheryl	304
Ed	168
John	289
Total	761

Indexicality x Management		
Indexed	Not Indexed	Total
227	200	427

Indexicality x Design		
Indexed	Not Indexed	Total
256	505	761

Figure 8.19 Contingency tables across a built-in contrast.

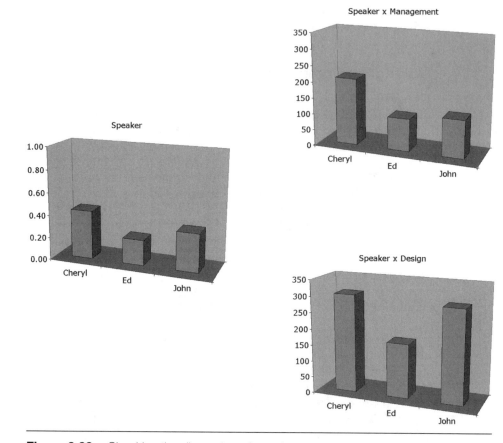

Figure 8.20   Checking the dimension of speaker across contrast of management versus design meetings.

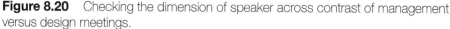

   This comparison confirms our interpretation of the graphs. The general order of speakers—Cheryl, John, Ed—and the general magnitude of the difference between them—Cheryl in the 40% range, John in the 20% range, and Ed in the 30% range—provide preliminary evidence that the dimension of speaker contribution is not strongly associated with the contrast between design and management meetings in this data set. As we shall see later on, this evidence is complicated by patterns revealed by later stages of our analysis, but at this stage, it is important to understand the preliminary evidence.

   The sample comparisons across contrast suggest a different story when we look at the second dimension of indexicality. Figure 8.21 shows this comparison. Here, unlike for speaker contribution, we do see substantial difference between the patterns on either side of the contrast and the overall patterns. As you can see, indexicality appears to be lower, across the board, in design meetings than in management meetings. A look at the relative frequencies confirms this association:

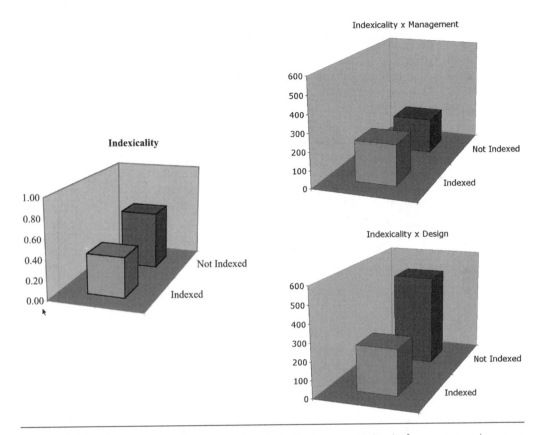

Figure 8.21 Checking the dimension of indexicality across contrast of management versus design meetings.

	Overall	Management	Design
Indexed	0.41	0.53	0.34
Not Indexed	0.59	0.47	0.66

In the management meetings, the majority of the units are indexed; the opposite is the case in the design meetings, where the majority of units are not indexed.

In a situation where the overall patterns are not born out by the patterns across the built-in contrast, you find evidence that the contrast is associated with the dimension. What this means is that the overall pattern for a dimension—41% indexed, for example—is not an adequate characterization of the data on either side of your built-on contrast—in this case, of neither the management data (where the ratio was 53% versus 47%) nor of the design data (where the ratio was 34% versus 66%). Such a pattern suggests, then, that your built-in contrast makes a difference—is associated with—this dimension.

Speaker x Indexicality

	Indexed	Not Indexed	Total
Cheryl	213	299	512
Ed	108	161	269
John	162	245	407
Total	483	705	1188

Speaker x Indexicality x Management

	Indexed	Not Indexed	Total
Cheryl	105	103	208
Ed	50	51	101
John	72	46	118
Total	227	200	427

Speaker x Indexicality x Design

	Indexed	Not Indexed	Total
Cheryl	108	196	304
Ed	58	110	168
John	90	199	289
Total	256	505	761

Figure 8.22   Basic associations across dimensions.

Checking Patterns Across Dimensions

Once you have compared the overall pattern within each dimension with the patterns by contrast, the next step is to compare the patterns across dimensions. Looked at in isolation from one another, dimensions of data may appear to be unassociated when a deeper look shows an association.

˙Establishing the Associations

The foundation for checking patterns across dimensions is an understanding of the basic associations across dimensions. How are variations in the first dimension associated with variations in the second dimension? A contingency table that shows variations in the two dimensions of your analysis, such as that shown at the top of Figure 8.22, will help you to answer this question.

Developing a contingency table of the basic associations requires summing data from the core contingency tables both across cases and across contrasts. For example, if we began with four core contingency tables, one for each of the two design meetings and one for each of the two management meetings, the contingency table of basic associations will sum across those four contingency tables to produce one contingency table, the one shown in the top of Figure 8.22. A block chart of these basic associations is shown to the left in Figure 8.23.

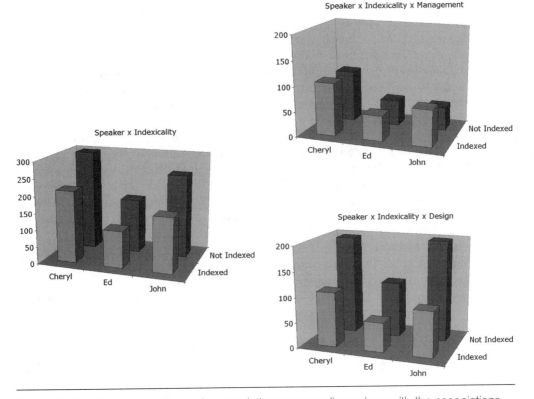

Figure 8.23   Comparing the basic associations across dimensions with the associations across contrasts.

Checking the Patterns

After establishing this basic association across dimensions, your next step is to look at the two-dimensional patterns formed on either side of your built-in contrast. At the bottom of Figure 8.22, we see an example of contingency tables that represent the intersections of the first and second dimensions (Speaker and Indexicality) with the built-in contrast (Management versus Design).

To construct these contingency tables, return to your core contingency tables and sum across cases, but not across contrast. In the case of our sample data, then, the original four contingency tables are collapsed to produce two: one for design and one for management.

Block charts are then constructed from these contingencies like those shown to the left in Figure 8.23. Make sure to adjust their scale to be equivalent if necessary.

Interpreting Comparisons

To make comparisons between the basic two-dimensional contours and the contours found in the data across contrast, trace the basic contour and then see whether that same contour is found in the data by contrast.

For example, as shown to the left in Figure 8.23, we see that the basic contour for speaker contribution in the indexed data (in the front plane of the chart) goes from a high with Cheryl, to a low for Ed, and then rises to an intermediate value for John. Next, we look to see whether this same contour is repeated in the management data graphed in the top right-hand corner. Here we find the same contour, albeit at a lower rate: starting from a high with Cheryl, moving to a low for Ed, rising to an intermediate value for John. In terms of the indexed data, then, the management data looks a lot like the data overall.

Next, we compare the contours for the Not Indexed data. In the basic associations, we see, as noted earlier, that across all speakers, contributions are less likely to be indexed than not indexed. In the management data, however, this is not the case: There, the data appear to be about equally indexed and not indexed. That is, the dark columns in the back plane are not that much higher than the light columns in the front plane. Thus this contour looks quite unlike the basic patterns of falling and rising that held true for the overall pattern.

Furthermore, John's contributions do not appear to mirror the general pattern. Indeed, in the nonindexed data, they appear to be no higher than Ed's. That is, the contour here is relatively flat as we move from Ed's column to John's column. Again, this is quite different than either the overall pattern or the pattern for indexed data where John's contributions were higher than Ed's.

Having seen two ways in which the management data does not parallel the two-dimensional contours of the data overall, we next look to see what is going on in the design data. Here we see what looks like a more expected picture. That is, we see a contour that goes from a high with Cheryl, moves to a low for Ed, and then rises to an intermediate value for John in both data that is indexed and data that is not indexed.

Clearly then, something appears to be going on in the management meetings along both dimensions. In the management meetings, talk is relatively more indexed than usual and John's talk stands out as particularly highly indexed. These unusual patterns suggest that the two dimensions, speaker contribution and indexicality, have some association in this data set.

8.5 Try It Out

Using the data on written comments in Figure 8.16 and downloadable from the course website, create the contingency tables showing Force × Topic across the contrast of Humanities (English and History) and Sciences (Biology and Physics).

Checking Patterns Across Cases

The last stage in an analysis across dimensions is to look at the patterns on a case by case basis. That is, for any pattern that has emerged in the earlier stages of analysis, we need to know whether that pattern holds true for all cases in our data.

Two outcomes are possible here. In the first situation, we may find that the patterns suggested in earlier stages of analysis hold true in specific cases. In this situation, we can report the more general patterns as good characterization of our data set. In the second situation, we may find that the patterns suggested in earlier stages do not hold true of specific cases. In this situation, we must acknowledge that the more general patterns do not provide an adequate characterization of our data set, that there are case-by-case differences.

Block graphs of individual cases can be constructed from the core contingency tables with which we started this chapter. For our sample data, this yields four block graphs, two for design meetings and two for management meetings. We can then compare these to the contours for the graphs established in the last section. That is, we can ask, do the patterns of association that seem to hold overall —between the dimensions of speaker contribution and indexicality and across the contrast of management and design—hold for the individual cases?

In the design data, the pattern we want to confirm is that the general contours shown to the left in Figure 8.24 parallel the contours in the two cases-specific graphs to the right. This means that

a. the contributions should, in general, be less indexed than indexed, and
b. that Cheryl should make the greatest number of contributions, followed by John, followed by Ed.

A preliminary comparison suggests that these two patterns do hold in the specific design meetings. That is, the contours of the block chart for Design 1 and

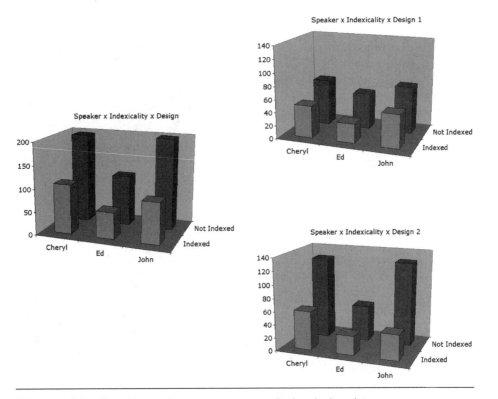

Figure 8.24   Checking patterns across cases in the design data.

Design 2 suggest both that the language is less indexed than indexed and that the speaker contributions are ordered and of the same magnitude as in the general pattern.

As we noted earlier, the patterns in the management meetings were more complex than those in the design meetings. In particular, we found preliminary evidence that

a. talk is relatively more indexed than usual and
b. that John's talk was particularly highly indexed.

At this final stage in our analysis, we need to understand how these complex patterns play out in the two management cases. Block graphs for the management data are shown in Figure 8.25.

Here, unlike in the design data, we find that the general patterns for the management data do not hold for the individual cases. That is, as we see in Figure 8.25, neither Management1 nor Management2 look like each other nor like the general pattern already discussed. The patterns for Cheryl and Ed look relatively as expected, but John's talk is very different across the two management meetings. He talks more than anyone else in Management 2 and almost not at all in Management 1. In Management 2, furthermore, his talk is relatively more indexed than not indexed.

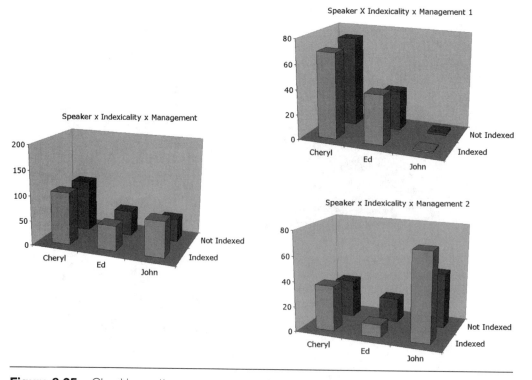

Figure 8.25 Checking patterns across cases in the management data.

Putting It All Together

The process presented in this chapter, the process of analyzing across dimensions, involves so many comparisons and distinctions that it is not unusual, when you are finished, not to be able to see the big picture. Keeping track of what you find at each stage of analysis can be complex, and figuring out the relationships among the stages can be a real challenge.

You will find that the best technique for putting it all together is to write it out. That is, for each level of the analysis, write out any characterizations true at that level. Then, move to the next level of analysis and see whether those characterizations remain true or must be qualified or withdrawn entirely.

With our sample data, then, we begin with the dimensional analysis. Is there anything we can say about the dimension of speaker contribution that seems to hold overall? Originally it looked liked speakers were ordered in terms of relative contribution: Cheryl, John, Ed. This pattern held true, more or less, for the design meetings, but not for management meetings. In Management 2, John dominated, whereas in Management 1, he hardly talked.

What, then, might we say about the dimension of speaker contribution in this data set? The answer is that while speaker contribution was relatively stable in design meetings, and relatively stable for Cheryl and Ed in management meetings, John's contribution in management meetings was highly variable.

Next we ask about the second dimension. Is there anything we can say about the dimension of indexicality that seems to hold overall? Originally, it looked like the language was generally less indexed than indexed. This pattern held true for the design data in both cases. It was, however, reversed in the management data except in Ed's talk in Management 2. In terms of indexicality, then, we see some consistency across our built-in contrast, with talk in the management meetings being more indexed than in the design meetings, with the exception of Ed in Management 2 whose language was not as highly indexed.

Characterizations like these, characterizations built on systematic analysis across dimensions, reflect both possible general statements about a given data set—

Talk in the management meetings was more indexed than in the design meetings.

—and qualifications specific to particular cases:

Ed's language in Management 2 meeting was not as highly indexed.

Such characterizations help you to know what is going on in a given data set. They form a rock-solid foundation for the analyses described in the remaining chapters of this book:

- They become the source of questions you pursue through the temporal analysis described in Chapter 9.
- They form the patterns whose significance you can test in Chapter 10.
- They become the substratum of the detailed analysis you carry out in Chapter 11.

And they represent the results you present in Chapter 12.

Take a moment to appreciate what you now know!

Look at the block charts in Figure 8.26 below showing the association between the dimensions of force and topic as they are played out across the contrast of Humanities versus Sciences. Use the data given in Figure 8.16 to decide whether the following characterizations provide an adequate description of this data.

a. Whereas the faculty in the humanities focused primarily on style, those in the sciences focused primarily on content.
b. The professors in the sciences were more directive than the professors in the humanities.
c. The professors in the humanities made more comments than the professors in the sciences.

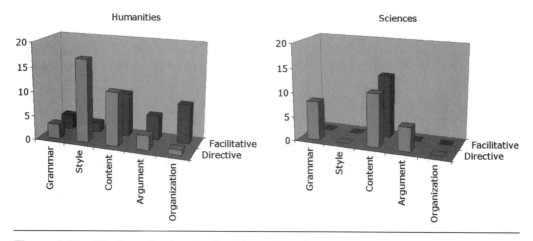

Figure 8.26   Block charts showing the Dimension x Dimension x Contrast contours for the data in Figure 8.16.

For discussion: How can these claims can be modified to be more adequate characterizations?

PROJECT: EXPLORING PATTERNS ACROSS DIMENSIONS

Explore the patterns in your data across a second dimension. A dimensional exploration is available at the course website.

Add a second dimension to your analysis and use the stepwise schematic in Figure 8.14 to guide your analysis of its association with the contours of your first dimension.

Begin by constructing your core contingency tables and then use them to construct block charts for each stage of analysis.

When you are finished, use writing to put the results of your analysis together, making sure to include an appropriate mixture of general statements and qualifications specific to cases.

CHAPTER

9

Following Patterns over Time

  In this chapter, you will look at patterns in your verbal data that indicate how aspects of your data vary over time. Looking for patterns in time helps to define the temporal shape of your coding categories. We will consider simple temporal indexes and then go on to look at aggregate patterns.

Time

Verbal data is inherently temporal. That is, we expect language to be ever changing—minute by minute in oral interactions, line by line in written interactions, and minute by minute as well as line by line in electronic interactions. We all recognize that topics shift in conversation, that texts change as they structure the reader's experience, that what we say in an interview this week will be different from what we say a week from now. Surprisingly, however, relatively few researchers try to describe the patterns in language that occur over time—what I have elsewhere called *temporal shape* (Geisler, 2001).

The neglect of time as an analytic construct in the analysis of verbal data may arise from the belief that the temporal shape of verbal data is unpredictable. The exact temporal shape of language might be thought too indirect and messy to be worth examining. Verbal interactions are, however, often more regular than might first appear. Conversations don't bounce from topic to topic without rhyme or reason, but often progress with some kind of rationale. Texts likewise don't shape the reader's experience without pattern. Indeed, genre conventions exist to provide a kind of routinized shape that can structure the reading experience and help us make sense of what we're reading. The same is true in both oral and electronic interactions. The techniques described in this chapter will help you to discover underlying temporal patterns in your verbal data and thereby better understand how the stream of language shapes human experience over time.

Indexing in Time

The simplest temporal patterns involve indexing the distribution of your coding categories across any unit by which you have segmented the data. These can range from the obvious units of time itself (minutes, seconds, etc.) to segments of continuous discourse (words, lines, t-units, paragraphs, etc.). We might, for example, index how speakers change by t-unit.

As you saw in Chapter 7, the overall distribution of speaker contribution can be examined by using distribution graphs like those in Figure 7.1 that show us, relatively speaking, how often speakers speak. When we index this data in time, we take this question one step further and ask how the speakers' contributions shift segment by segment during the course of the meeting: Did all speakers speak consistently throughout the meeting or were there clusters of interaction between one or more of the participants at some times and not at others?

A temporal index can help us to answer questions about temporal distribution. In Figure 9.1, for example, we see movement across the four speakers, Cheryl, John, Ed, and Lee, as we move across the first 180 t-units of a meeting. This temporal index suggests that although interaction between John and Cheryl was fairly even throughout this time, contributions by Lee and Ed were more sporadic. Lee came in just twice and said very little; Ed came in five times, three for relatively short contributions, but once for an extended interaction with Cheryl and a second time for a conversation primarily with John. Simple scatterplots like this can tell us a great deal more about how a phenomenon of interest, like speaker contribution, plays itself out over time.

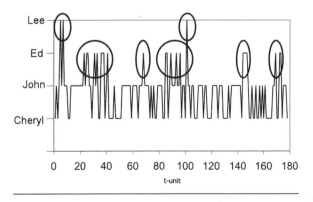

Figure 9.1   A temporal index showing speaker change by t-unit.

In Figure 9.2 and downloadable from the course website, you will find a temporal index of the agents a student talked about during an interview about a writing project on paternalism. Use this temporal index to match the phenomenon listed on the left with the portions of the index listed on the right.

1. The first time during the interview when the student talked a lot about the paternalist as agent.
2. The second time during the interview when the student talked a lot about the paternalist as agent.
3. The last time during the interview when the student talked a lot about the paternalist as agent.
4. A time when the student talked almost exclusively about herself as agent.
5. A time when the student talked not at all about herself as agent.
6. A period in which the student talked a great deal about agents other than herself or a paternalist.

a. 12–24
b. 27–48
c. 52–55
d. 52–67
e. 64–67
f. 70–109
g. 79–89
h. 106–128
i. 111–125
j. 129–141
k. 153–155
l. 164–181

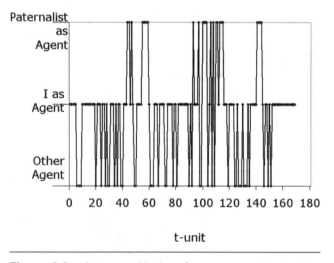

Figure 9.2   A temporal index of agency over the t-units of an interview.

For discussion: Which of the following seems to happen more often: Mixing "I as agent" with "others as agent" or mixing "I as agent" with "paternalist as agent"?

The Temporal Index

In Excel, a temporal index can be created with a scatterplot like that in Figure 9.1. Scatterplots map two variables against each other. One variable is temporal, the unit of segmentation such as the t-unit we have used in Figure 9.1. The second variable is the categorical dimension of the data you wish to index over time. In Figure 9.1, this dimension is speaker contribution.

Conventionally, time goes on the x-axis; the categorical dimensional data on the y-axis. To read a temporal index, then, you move from left to right through time and up and down across the categories of your data.

Assigning Numeric Values to Categories

Unlike the distribution graphs you have worked with in earlier chapters, the scatterplots you use for temporal indexing only work with numeric data. To create a temporal index, you must assign a numeric value to each category in your coding scheme. In Figure 9.3, for example, we have placed numeric values for the speaker categories in a new column inserted to the left of the categories themselves—in Column B.

The numeric values you assign to categories will determine where, on the y-axis, each category is plotted. In Figure 9.3, for example, we have assigned a numeric value of 1 to Cheryl; 2 to John; 3 to Ed and 4 to Lee. The assignment of these values is purely arbitrary, but it does determine the order in which categories are plotted.

It is often best to assign the most frequently occurring categories lower numeric values so that they will be plotted in the lower region of the scatterplot. For

	A	B	"),3,(IF((C5="Lee:"),4)))))))	
1	T-Unit#	Speaker #	Speaker	Text
4	1	1	Cheryl:	We need a little hole in the middle of this table.
5	2	2	John:	Oh, Jesus! We could just go get a drill right now.
6	3	1	Cheryl:	We need one of these don't we?
7	4	2	John:	Or a big hammer.
8	5	4	Lee:	It wouldn't actually have to be in the middle
9	6	2	John:	I mean
			Lee:	You could put it like right here off to

Figure 9.3   Assigning numeric values (in a new Column C) to categories of speaker (in Column D).

example, by assigning the two most frequent speakers, Cheryl and John, to the numeric values 1 and 2, we have created a temporal index where their interaction becomes a base against which we can more easily see the more intermittent participation of Ed and Lee.

Although numeric values can be assigned by hand you will find it easier to use a formula that will assign them automatically. For the data shown in Figure 9.3, we used the following formula:

=IF((D4="Cheryl:"),1,(IF((D4="John:"),2,(IF((D4="Ed:"),3,(IF((D4="Lee:"),4)))))))

Though quite complex, this formula is really a variation on the conditional formulas we have used earlier. Its underlying structure is shown in Figure 9.4.

Each step in the formula tests the values in the original dimensional column to see whether a category is present; if so, it records the numeric value to be assigned to that category. If this category is not present, the formula goes on to test for the presence of the next category. Again, if present, it records a numeric value; if not, it goes on to test for the next category. This continues until all categories have been tested for, at which time, you close all the open parentheses.

The tests for each category have the now-familiar syntax:

IF(D4="Cheryl:")

This formula tests for a match between the contents of the column (D4) and the alphanumeric string used as the category code (Cheryl:). Make sure that you have been consistent in using the same alphanumeric string each time you code. If not, Excel will not find a match and will return False. If, for example, the code "John" had been used without the colon used elsewhere ("John:"), the formula would return FALSE.

If you find you have a problem with inconsistent alphanumeric strings for a code, you may want to create a new column and recode the data more consistently using something like the following formula:

=IF(D5="John","John:",D5)

=IF(First Category, 1,	¤	¤	¤	
¤	(IF(Second Category, 2,	¤	¤	
¤	¤	(IF(Third Category, 3,	¤	
¤	¤	¤	(IF(FourthC ategory,4)))))))¤	

Figure 9.4 The underlying structure of a formula for assigning numeric values to categories.

which will change miscoded data ("John") to properly coded data ("John:") while leaving the other data unchanged. You will then be ready to assign numeric values to categories.

9.2 Try It Out

Write a conditional formula that will assign numeric values to the topic codes listed here. Use the data distribution shown in Figure 8.26 to help you decide what numeric values to assign to each code. Assume the topic codes are in Column D and that the data begins on Row 3.

> Grammar   Style   Content   Argument   Organization

For discussion: What are the differences in your formulas, especially in the ways you assigned numeric values to categories? How will the resulting indices be different?

Making the Temporal Index

Once the data has been prepared, select the two columns to be graphed, including the headers. Then invoke the chart wizard. In step 1, choose the XY chart type. In step 3, make sure to label the graph and the temporal dimension as shown in Figure 9.5. The resulting graph will look like that shown in Figure 9.6.

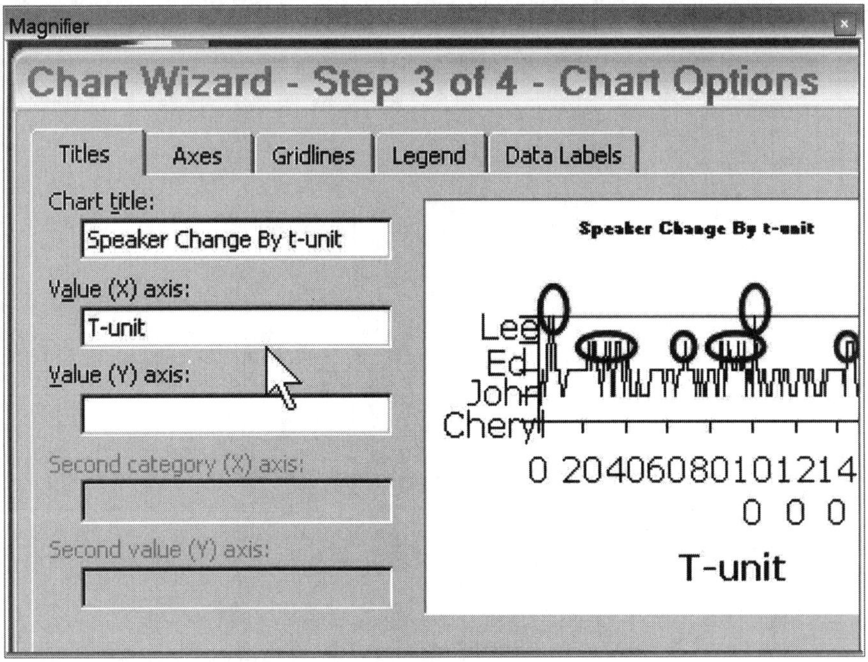

Figure 9.5 Labeling the chart and temporal axis.

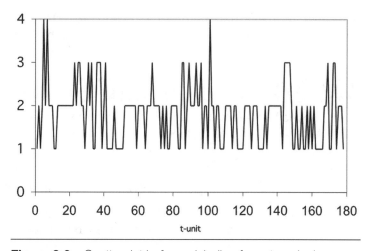

Figure 9.6   Scatterplot before relabeling for categorical dimension.

Relabeling the Categorical Dimension

Scatterplots like those shown in Figure 9.6 do a nice job of showing temporal change, but need some adjustment in order to communicate more effectively about the categories being used. Because we have assigned numeric values to categories, they appear as numeric values on the y-axis of our scatterplot. To be more effective, we need to label them with the names of the categories themselves.

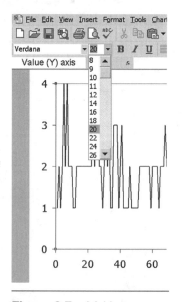

Figure 9.7   Making room for the categorical labels.

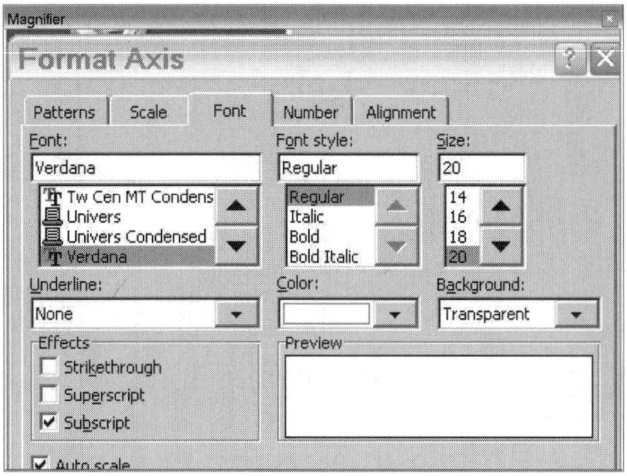

Figure 9.8   Making room for the categorical labels.

Begin by making room for the category label. The easiest way to do this is to increase the size of the existing numeric labels. As shown in Figure 9.7, select the y-axis and then increase the font size. Excel will automatically move the y-axis over, thereby providing you with room for your category labels.

Next, as shown in Figure 9.8, hide the numeric labels on the y-axis by

a. coloring them white and
b. making their background transparent.

Now you have room to add new categorical labels.

To add labels, click on the Text Box button on the Drawing Toolbar. Then, as shown in Figure 9.9, click the approximate place you want your first label and type it in. Repeat until you have all of your labels and get a result like that shown originally in Figure 9.1.

Aggregating in Time

Temporal indices track segment-by-segment change across coding categories and often provide too much detail to be useful—a real case of not being able to see the forest for the trees. If you find your temporal index obscures the differences that your distribution analysis suggests are there, you should consider aggregating your data into larger units of analysis. To see more of the forest, that is, you might make moves like the following:

- from the turn to the interchange,
- from the t-unit to the topic,
- from the second to the minute, and so on.

Aggregating data is a form of resegmenting the data, a task that, as we hinted in Chapter 3, is no easy matter. If, however, you simply move up a level in your

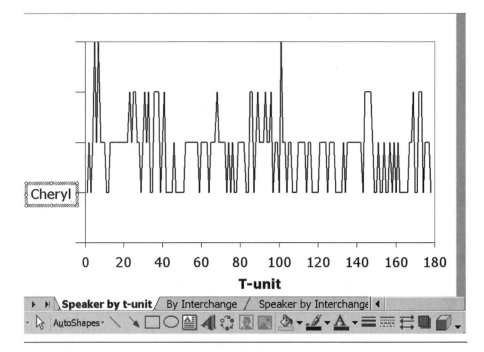

Figure 9.9   Adding categorical labels to the y-axis.

unit of analysis so that you are gathering a number of segments into a larger aggregate, the task is somewhat simpler. It involves three steps:

1. demarcating borders of the new aggregates,
2. doing a count of the frequency of each code within the aggregates, and
3. doing a cumulative count for each aggregate.

Once this process is repeated for each code of your coding scheme, you can create an aggregate temporal graph like the one shown in Figure 9.14.

Demarcating the Aggregates

Aggregation is best done on a copy of your original data sheets, so make a copy first and then go on to the following steps.

We begin by creating a new column to the left of the original units of segmentation as shown in Figure 9.10. Use it to demarcate the border of adjacent aggregates. Basically, your goal is to place a number in this column for each aggregate. Place this number next to the *last* segment in the aggregate. So, in Figure 9.10 for example, an aggregate number has been placed next to t-unit 2 because that is the last t-unit in the aggregate. The next aggregate starts with the following t-unit, t-unit 3, and runs to t-unit 5, so we place an aggregate number next to t-unit 5.

Continue this process of deciding where aggregates begin and end, marking their borders with an aggregate number next to the *last* segment in the aggregate. Put a 0 to demarcate the border of the first segment.

	A	B	C	D	E
	Interchange	T-Unit#	Speaker #	Speaker	Text
1					
2					
3	0	177			
4		1	1	Cheryl:	We need a little hole in the middle of this table.
5	0	2	2	John:	Oh, Jesus! We could just go get a drill right now.
6		3	1	Cheryl:	We need one of these don't we?
7		4	2	John:	Or a big hammer.
8	0	5	4	Lee:	It wouldn't actually have to be in the middle
9		6	2	John:	I mean
10	0	7	4	Lee:	You could put it like right here off to the side.
11	0	8	2	John:	Yeah

Figure 9.10   Demarcating the borders of adjacent interchanges.

	A	B	C	D	E
1	Interchang ▾	T-Unit#	Speaker #	Speaker	Text
3	0	177			
5	1	2	2	John:	Oh, Jesus! We could just go get a drill right now.
8	2	5	4	Lee:	It wouldn't actually have to be in the middle
10	3	7	4	Lee:	You could put it like right here off to the side.
11	4	8	2	John:	Yeah
14	5	11	1	Cheryl:	Yeah, right.

Figure 9.11   Assigning numbers to aggregates once aggregating is complete.

As shown in Figure 9.10, to simplify the task of demarcating aggregates, you may want to begin by marking the borders of your aggregates with 0's rather than numbers. This way, you can first concentrate on the task of deciding where the borders are without worrying about what number to assign. This method also eliminates the problems that arise when you insert new aggregate borders later on, thereby throwing off your numbering.

Later, once your aggregation is stable, you can replace those 0's with continuous numbering. As shown in Figure 9.11, the easiest way to make this replacement is by filtering your data for those 0 and then replace each 0 with a number.

Shading may also be a useful technique. In Figure 9.10, we have marked the interchanges with alternating bands of shading to make the boundaries between the aggregates more clear. This kind of alternate shading can be helpful, although it must be done by hand and thus takes considerable time if your data set is long.

9.3 Try It Out

The following data downloadable from the course website has been segmented by the second. For example, 002.36 equals 2 minutes and 36 seconds. Aggregate the data by the minute. That is, demarcate the boundaries for minutes 1–6.

Sequence	Time in Minutes	Time in Seconds	Text	Tool
1	000.00			PDA
2	000.10		Make second Palm Movie (Mar 21)	PDA
3	000.13		Send Teri Pilot proposal (Mar 21)	PDA
4	000.18			PDA
5	000.45		Take in leave request (Mar 26)	PDA
6	000.58			PDA
7	001.01			PDA
8	001.13		email programmer (Mar 26)	PDA
9	001.26			PDA
10	001.28			PDA
11	001.36			spreadsheet
12	001.39			spreadsheet
13	001.47			PDA
14	001.49		call about hotel bill [Mar23, Maint]	PDA
15	002.08			PDA
16	002.17			PDA
17	002.18			PDA
18	002.19		email programmer (Mar 26)	PDA
19	002.24			PDA
20	002.25		Take in leave request (Mar 26)	PDA

Sequence	Time in Minutes	Time in Seconds	Text	Tool
21	002.32			PDA
22	002.34		hotel bill	Off-line
23	005.27			PDA
24	005.27		call about hotel bill [Mar23, Maint]	PDA
25	005.34			spreadsheet
26	005.38			PDA
27	005.41			spreadsheet
28	006.33		Book Prospectus	spreadsheet
29	006.49		Discipline	spreadsheet
30	006.53		Book Prospectus	spreadsheet

Getting the Counts

The next step in creating an aggregate temporal graph is to get a count for each coding category for each aggregate. The easiest way to do this is to separate the data by coding category and then develop counts for each one.

If you have already created a temporal index for your data, you will have created a single column like that shown in Column B in Figure 9.10. This column records the numeric codes you have assigned to each of your categories. Now, you will need to separate each code into its own column so it can be counted.

To separate the data by code, enter a new column for each coding category. Then create a conditional formula to record a 1 if the code is present and 0 if absent. In Column F of Figure 9.12, for example, we used the following formula to place a 1 in the column if the code "Cheryl" is present in Column C and a 0 if it is absent:

=IF(($C4="Cheryl"),1,0)

We use an absolute value for column C ($C) because the data codes are always found in the same column. We use a relative value for the row (4) because we want this value to change as we drag the formula down the new column.

Doing the Cumulative Counts

The final step involves counting off the code within each aggregate. We start counting with a 1 at the beginning of the aggregate and count until the cumulative count for the aggregate is complete. For the next aggregate, we start over again with 1.

	A	B	C	D	E	F	G
1	**Interchange**	**T-Unit#**	**Speaker #**	**Speaker**	**Text**	**Cheryl Count**	**Cheryl**
2							
3	0	177					
4		1		1 Cheryl:	We need a little hole in the middle of this table.	1	1
5	1	2		2 John:	Oh, Jesus! We could just go get a drill right now.	0	1
6		3		1 Cheryl:	We need one of these don't we?	1	1
7		4		2 John:	Or a big hammer.	0	1
8	2	5		4 Lee:	It wouldn't actually have to be in the middle	0	1
9		6		2 John:	I mean	0	0
10	3	7		4 Lee:	You could put it like right here off to the side.	0	0
11	4	8		2 John:	Yeah	0	0

Figure 9.12   Creating the count (Column F), and cumulative count (Column G) for the code "Cheryl:".

As usual, such tedious work can be considerably reduced with an Excel formula. For the data in Figure 9.12, we used the following formula in G4 to get the cumulative counts shown in Column G:

=IF(ISNUMBER($A3),F4, G3+F4)

This formula tests the previous row in Column A (where we find the aggregate borders) to see whether the previous segment was the last one in an aggregate (designated by the presence of a number):

ISNUMBER($A3)

If an interchange has just ended and a new one is starting, A3 will cointain a number and this formula will therefore record the count value from Column F, Row 4:

IF(ISNUMBER($A3),F4

If Row 4 is not the beginning of a new aggregate, the formula adds the count value to the cumulative count so far:

IF(ISNUMBER($A3),F4, G3+F4

This formula for cumulative counts is quite versatile. It will work on counts that are simply 1 or 0 like that shown in Figure 9.12, but it will also work on data with higher count values like those shown for indexicals in Figure 9.13, Column G, where the count values in Column F can be greater than 1.

	B	C	D	E	F	G
1	T-Unit#	Speaker #	Speaker	Text	Indexicals Count	Indexicals
2						
21	18	2	John:	But what do you think about the general configuration there?	2	2
22	19	2	John:	Is it achievable?	0	2
23	20	2	John:	Does it achieve what	0	2
24	21	2	John:	we want	0	2
25	22	2	John:	and is it achievable?	0	2
26	23	3	Ed:	I think	0	2

Figure 9.13   A cumulative count of data with counts greater than 1 per segment.

You will need to create a count and cumulative count for each category in your coding scheme—inserting two columns for each coding category.

Once the cumulative counts have been calculated for each coding category, use an autofilter on Column A to filter for NonBlanks. Also hide the columns for the counts so that you see only one column for each category in your scheme.

Exploring Aggregate Patterns

One of the most informative graphs for displaying aggregate patterns in time is the aggregate temporal graph like the one shown in Figure 9.14. In this graph, the aggregate counts for each speaker are stacked one on top of the other for each interchange. The total height of the stack shows you how much activity any individual aggregate exhibited. We can tell from Figure 9.14, for example, that interactions around Interchange 19 were quite lively compared to the interactions around Interchange 32.

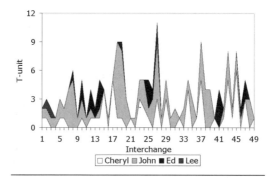

Figure 9.14   A stacked area graph showing aggregate speakers change over time.

Making an Aggregate Temporal Graph

To make an aggregate temporal graph, select the data to be graphed (for example the data in Columns H, K, N, and Q, including the headings) and invoke the chart wizard. In step 1, select area graph and choose the stacked version. Continue through the rest of the steps, as for a scatterplot. The result should look like the one shown in Figure 9.14.

Interpreting Aggregate Patterns

Aggregate temporal graphs like that in Figure 9.14 help you to understand the relative contribution of each of the coding categories to the total activity in an interchange. In Figure 9.14, for example, we can see that activity starting roughly at Interchange 16 and continuing through Interchange 28 was lively and involved all three major participants. Interaction between Interchange 33 and 40, by contrast, though somewhat lively, took place between just Cheryl and John. Such patterns can send us back into the data itself to explore what was going on.

To see how aggregate temporal graphs differ from temporal indices, compare the graph in Figure 9.14 with the one in Figure 9.1. Figure 9.1 does a better job of pinpointing the exact locations of contribution from each speaker and the relative infrequency of participation by Lee and Ed. For this reason we call it an index—there is a one-to-one relationship between each point on the graph and each segment of the data.

The aggregate temporal graph in Figure 9.14 does a better job, however, of helping us to see who is interacting with whom over more extended periods and gives us a much better sense of the level of activity in any given period. All this in-

9.4 Try It Out

In Figure 9.15, you will find an aggregate temporal graph of the agents talked about by a student during an interview about a writing project on paternalism, aggregated by turn. Each turn represents the student's response to a question by the interviewer. These were the questions asked:

1. At what point did you stop today?
2. Why did you stop?
3. Can you sort of describe to me generally what you put in the introduction?
4. Can you summarize what you put in that paragraph too?
5. Can you summarize what you put in that paragraph too?
6. Do you feel better now that you've gotten those first two paragraphs written?

Given the pattern of activity and attention to agency shown in Figure 9.15, what kinds of questions would you ask to elicit attention by a writer to agents others than the writer herself? What kinds of questions would you ask to elicit a lot of discussion? What kinds seem to elicit attention only to the writer herself?

For discussion: What aspects of the verbal data are clearer in Figure 9.14 than in 9.1? What aspects of Figure 9.1 are less clear in Figure 9.14?

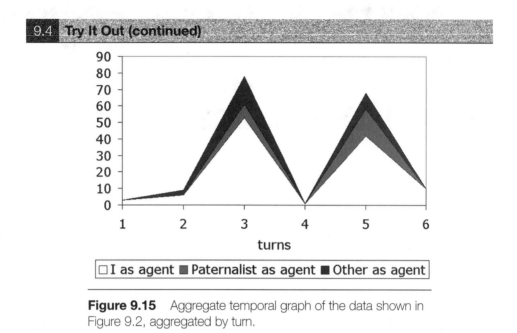

9.4 Try It Out (continued)

turns

☐ I as agent ■ Paternalist as agent ■ Other as agent

Figure 9.15   Aggregate temporal graph of the data shown in Figure 9.2, aggregated by turn.

formation is, of course, very useful in pulling together a complete description of the way that the stream of verbal data plays itself out over time across the categories in your coding scheme.

PROJECT: FOLLOWING PATTERNS OVER TIME

Analyze the way the distribution of your data over the categories of your coding scheme varies over time. A sample temporal analysis is available at the course website.

Begin by creating a temporal index for each case. Then try aggregating the data in a way that seems appropriate and constructing an aggregate temporal graph to display the results. Finally, write a discussion describing the temporal shape of your data.

Turn in both your Excel file with data and graphs and the Word file with the discussion of the patterns.

For Further Reading

Geisler, C., and R. Munger (2001). "Temporal Analysis: A Primer Exemplified by a Case from Prehospital Care" in E. Barton and G. Stygall, *Discourse Studies in Composition*. Cresskill, NJ: Hampton Press.

10

Evaluating Significance

Over the last four chapters you have been looking at ways of seeing patterns in verbal data. In particular, you have been asking how the distribution of data into coding categories varied across contrast, across dimension, and across time. In some cases, you may have found small variations; in some cases, large variations. In this chapter, we turn to considering the issue of evaluating the significance of those findings by using χ^2 tests.

Significance

The concept of evaluating the significance of results is often associated with experimental methodology, controlled conditions, and what many have thought is an inappropriate commitment to treating people like corn—that is, as lacking the reflexivity and contextuality that is fundamental to language use. Unknown to many, the allusion to fields of corn comes from R. A. Fisher's work (the Fisher of the F-test) who developed statistical methods to evaluate the comparative advantages of growing corn under experimental conditions. His classic work, *The Design of Experiments,* will still reward any reader interested in understanding the underlying theory behind experimental methods and statistical inference.

Fisher and statisticians following him made the assumption that sufficiently large samples of data sampled from any population would distribute itself in the shape of a normal curve like that shown in Figure 10.1. Most of the data would cluster around the center or mean, with 68% of the data lying within one standard deviation of this mean, within the further boundaries of two standard deviations from the mean we find 95%, and almost all data (99.7%) lying within the further boundaries of three standard deviations. The standard deviation is de-

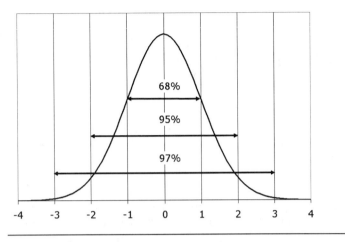

Figure 10.1 A normal distribution.

fined as the point along the normal distribution where the curve changes from down to curving up. A very nice animation of a normal distribution can be found at *http://members.aol.com/discanner/balldrop.html*.

Many people have come to think of the normal distribution as a normative statement about the world: that samples of data from a population *should* follow a normal distribution. Perhaps the most obvious normative use comes when a teacher uses a normal distribution to insure that the majority of students receive a C on a test, with a smaller but equal number of students receiving higher or lower than a C.

What most statisticians now understand, however, is that not all phenomenon have the shape of a normal distribution; that the normal curve is only one—though perhaps the best understood—of the underlying distributions possible in data. With respect to the kind of analysis of verbal data introduced in this book, in fact, the normal curve is usually not the best way to go.

Models of Underlying Expectations

The best perspective to take on the evaluation of significance is to understand it as the comparison of what we have *observed* against a model of what we would *expect* to observe if nothing much was going on. This kind of comparison of observations to expectations actually guides our evaluation of significance in all kinds of everyday activities. We judge, for example, the significance of Jenna not returning our morning greeting against our expectations for what Jenna would do if nothing much were going on. If our model of expectations is that she always returns our greeting, her failing to do so this morning can seem highly significant. If, however, she is often lost in thought on days when she has a lot of work to do, her failure to return our greeting will be seen as far less significant.

In the same way, evaluating the significance of the results from an analysis of verbal data involves specifying a model for what we would expect the results to look like if nothing much were going on. In classical methods of statistical inference, the model of what we would expect if nothing were going on is encapsulated in the normal curve we just discussed. Parametric methods ask how far from the expected distribution of a normal curve a set of observations fall. The further away from expectations, the more significance the results in this case, just as in the case of Jenna's lack of morning greeting.

The assumption that an appropriate underlying model of expected distribution follows a normal curve works very well for some phenomena. The number of times a coin turn up heads in a set of tosses, for example, follows a normal distribution, assuming the coin is not dinged up a way that favors one side or the other. Many phenomenon cannot be expected to be normally distributed, however. If we ask what the distribution of distances is of a group of high school students trying the long jump, for example, we would expect to find a distribution skewed to the left, with a fairly broad range of students able to jump some way, and with a very long tail to the right and an eventual ceiling as fewer and fewer students are able to pass the normal limits of human performance, not at all a normal curve.

Many researchers use parametric methods for evaluating significance without understanding that they are implicitly making a choice about how to model their underlying expectations for the data. If the assumption of normalcy is inappropriate, such parametric tests will tell you little about how you should evaluate the outcome of your analysis. It would be as if you had taken Jenna's behavior and inappropriately compared it to your model of expectations for Ralph: Ralph always returns my greeting, we might think, so Jenna's silence must be highly significant. As this example is meant to indicate, using the wrong model of underlying expectations can warp your evaluation of significance.

Modeling Expectations about Categorical Data

For the kind of analysis we have been using in this book, the normal curve is inappropriate as a model of underlying expectations in one obvious way. Verbal data coded into categories—categorical data—can never be expected to approach a normal distribution because a normal distribution is continuous while categorical data is, well, categorical.

To see the difference, imagine an analysis that yields values up to 4. If this data were continuous, the values might include .01, 3.3, 1.2, 1.27, and so on. But if the data were categorical (and if there were only four categories), the values would always be 1, 2, 3, and 4. As we saw in Chapter 5, if the probability that a segment was assigned to a given code was equal to the probability that it would be assigned to any other code, we would expect the distribution of data to look like the random distribution in Figure 10.2 rather than the normal curve in Figure 10.1. Statistics that use this kind of random model as their underlying model of distribution for evaluating the significance of results are called nonparametric statistics. At their simplest, they assume the kind of flat distribution shown in Figure 10.2 where the probability of each category is equal to every other category.

The assumptions in the underlying random distribution of nonparametric statistics are a lot more forgiving than those of parametric statistics based on the nor-

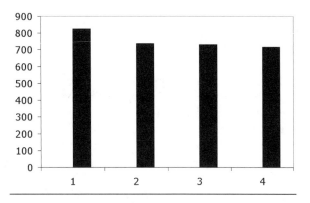

Figure 10.2   A random distribution of categorical data.

mal curve. To continue our comparison of evaluating the significance of Jenna's failure to return our greeting, we might say that a more forgiving underlying model of expectations might be that if Jenna responded at all to our greeting, she would respond with a greeting of her own. Using this as our underlying model of expectations, we would think it significant only when Jenna responded in a negative manner to our greeting, not when she didn't appear to hear us at all. Such a model is more forgiving, then, because it includes in its definition of expected normalcy a whole range of possible behavior associated with being distracted or lost in thought that the original model would have classified as significant.

In the same way, normal nonparametric statistics evaluate a lot more potential behavior as normal than do parametric statistics because they do not expect to see increasingly smaller distributions at the tails of their curves than at their centers. Under a parametric evaluation, then, a high value for category 1 as in Figure 10.2 would be judged significant because the normal curve distribution tells us to expect low numbers in the tails. Under a nonparametric evaluation, however, high numbers at the tails are as likely as in its middle.

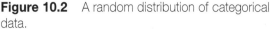

10.1   Test Your Understanding

Decide whether you would expect the following distributions to be parametric or nonparametric if nothing much were going on.

a. The number of times heads and tails arise in 150 coin tosses.
b. The length of essays written in a writing assessment.
c. The number of students who pass and who fail as the result of a writing assessment.
d. The number of times a computer user checks email in an average day.
e. The number of personal and work-related e-mails a computer user receives.

For discussion: What aspects of a distribution are important to consider?

The χ^2 Test of the Homogeneity of Distributional Variation

The most frequently used parametric test for categorical data is the χ^2 test. χ^2 is pronounced *chi-square*. For distribution patterns like those described in Chapter 7, the χ^2 test can help you evaluate the significance of differences across your built-in contrast. Such a test is often called a test of homogeneity because we are asking whether the distribution in one sample of data is similar to—or homogeneous with—the distribution in another sample.

Questions of Homogeneity

As you found in Chapter 7, graphic representations like the one shown in Figure 10.3 can suggest that the distribution of data across a built-in contrast looks quite different. The question remains, how different? A χ^2 test of homogeneity can help you decide.

For example, we might wonder whether the distribution of talk across speakers in design meetings was similar to the distribution in managerial meetings. A look at the data in Figure 10.3 suggests that there are some differences in the frequencies with which Cheryl, Ed, and John talked. To evaluate the significance of these differences, we perform the χ^2 test of homogeneity.

Models of Homogeneity

As we noted earlier, every test of significance involves a comparison between what was actually observed and what we would expect to observe if nothing much was going on. Earlier, we described a model for expectations where we had variation across four categories with an equal probability that data would be placed in each category. The model of expectations in our χ^2 test of homogeneity is a bit more complex. We have variation not only in categories arrayed from left to right, but also variation across contrast arrayed from back to front, as in Figure 10.4.

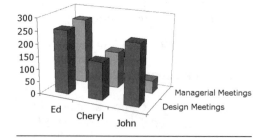

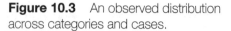

Figure 10.3   An observed distribution across categories and cases.

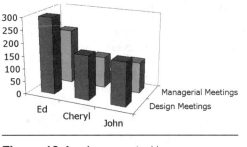

Figure 10.4   An expected homogenous distribution.

In such a situation, the expected homogeneous distribution is one in which the proportional distribution across contrast is the same. In the expected homogeneous distribution shown in Figure 10.4, for example, we see that the proportional differences between the speakers in the design meetings are equal to the proportional differences in the managerial meetings. Specifically, in both kinds of meetings, Ed is shown as speaking 47% of the time, Cheryl 27% of the time, and John 26% of the time. These two expected distributions, one in the design meetings and one in the managerial meetings, are thus no different from one another—they are homogeneous.

A more precise definition of the model of expected homogeneity can be given in terms of the marginals for observed distributions. As you may recall from Chapter 6, the marginals in a frequency table are the sums of the rows and columns of data. In Figure 10.5, for example, we see the marginals for the data graphed in Figure 10.3. From these marginals, we can see that, overall, there were 643 segments in the design meetings and 459 in the managerial meetings. We can also see that, overall, there were 515 segments with Ed as speaker, 296 with Cheryl as speaker, and 291 with John as speaker.

	Ed	Cheryl	John	Total
Meetings				643
Meetings				459
Total	515	296	291	1102

Figure 10.5   Marginal values for the distributions across speakers and meetings.

In developing a model of expected homogeneity, we take these observed marginals and ask the following question of homogeneity:

> Given these marginals, what would we expect the distribution in each of the cells to be if the distribution were homogeneous?

For example, given that there were 643 segments in design meetings and that there were 515 segments contributed by Ed, what is the expected frequency of Ed talking in design meetings, if the distribution were homogeneous?

The answer to this question can be given in terms of the joint probability of

1. a segment being in a design meeting and
2. a segment being from Ed,

or, more generally, the probability that a segment will fall in a given row (the design row or the managerial row) and in a given column (Ed's, Cheryl's or John's). Recall that a joint probability is simply the product of the simple probabilities that compose it. Thus, the joint probability of a given row and a given column equals the simple probability of a given row times the simple probability of a given column.

The following formula defines the simple probability of a given row:

Probability (Row) = # of segments in the row / # of segments overall

And this formula defines the simple probability of a column:

Probability (Column) = # of segments in column / # of segments overall

When we multiply the two together to get their joint probability of a segment being in a given column and given row, we get

$$\text{Probability (Row} \times \text{Column)} = \frac{(\text{\# of segments in the row} \times \text{\# of segments in column})}{\text{number of segments overall}}$$

Thus, the expected frequency for Ed speaking in design meetings if the distribution in homogeneous is

$$(643 \times 515) \, / \, 1102$$

or

$$300.49$$

Once we have this expected value for Ed talking in design meetings (300.49), we can compare it with the observed value, which was 253. Is the difference between these two values bigger than expected? Did Ed talk less in design meetings than we would have expected if the distributions were homogeneous? The only way to get at an answer to this question is to complete the full computation of the x^2 test, the task we turn to in the next section.

10.2 Try It Out

Create a model of the expected homogeneous distribution for the following data downloadable from the course website.

Frequency

	Ed	Cheryl	John	Total
Meeting 1	70	128	115	313
Meeting 2	104	106	104	104
	174	234	219	627

Computing a χ^2 Test of Homogeneity

The six steps shown in Figure 10.6 and discussed here will take you through the χ^2 test. They aim to compute χ^2 using the following formula:

$$\chi^2 = \text{Sum of } \left[\frac{(O - E)^2}{E} \right]$$

	A	B	C	D	E
1					
2	**Step 1. O**	Ed	Cheryl	John	Total
3	Design Meetings	253	150	240	643
4	Managerial Meetings	262	146	51	459
5	Total	515	296	291	1102
6					
7	**Step 2. E**	Ed	Cheryl	John	Total
8	Design Meetings	300	173	170	643
9	Managerial Meetings	215	123	121	459
10		515	296	291	1102
11					
12	**Step 3. O-E**	Ed	Cheryl	John	Total
13	Design Meetings	-47.49	-22.71	70.21	0.00
14	Managerial Meetings	47.49	22.71	-70.21	0.00
15		0.00	0.00	0.00	0.00
16					
17	**Step 4. (O-E)²/E**	Ed	Cheryl	John	Total
18	Design Meetings	7.51	2.99	29.03	39.52
19	Managerial Meetings	10.52	4.18	40.67	55.37
20		18.02	7.17	69.69	**94.89**
21					
22	**Step 5. DF**				
23	Number of samples	2			
24	Number of categories	3			
25	Number of samples -1	1			
26	Number of categories -	2			
27	df	2			
28					
29	**Step 6. Table Lookup**				
30	With df = 2, values greater than 9.21	p<.01			
31					

Figure 10.6 Steps to calculating the χ^2 test for homogeneity.

Translated into English, this formula means that χ^2 equals the sum of the squares of the differences between the observed and expected values for each cell in your frequency table, each difference having been divided by the expected value for that cell. Now, let's take this computation one step at a time.

In the first step, you record the observed frequencies (the "O" in the formula) in a table. The values for these frequencies should be found in your distribution worksheet and linked into a new sheet labeled "Chi-Square."

In the second step, you calculate the expected frequencies (the "E" in the formula). For each cell, we must multiply together the probability for a given row and the probability for a given column as explained in the last section. In effect, this means that the expected value in any cell in the second table in Figure 10.6 equals the total for the row times the total for the column, with this all divided by the grand total for the table. For B8 in Figure 10.6, then, we use the Excel formula

$$=(\$E3*B\$5)/\$E\$5$$

where

$$\$E3$$

is the row total,

$$B\$5$$

is the column total, and

$$\$E\$5$$

is the grand total. Because we have fixed the reference appropriately, we can drag this formula both down and across without having to adjust the values.

In the third step, you subtract the expected frequencies from the observed values (the "O − E" in the formula) for each cell in the table. In the Excel sheet shown in Figure 10.6, we have used the following formula for this calculation in cell B13:

$$=B3-B8$$

and then dragged it across the row to fill in the other values.

In the fourth step, for each cell you square the value from step 3 and divide the result by the expected value (the "$(O − E)^2/E$" in the formula). In the Excel sheet shown in Figure 10.6, we use the following formula:

$$=(B13*B13)/B8$$

The sum of the rows (94.89) is the χ^2 value.

Once you have the χ^2 value, in the fifth step you calculate the degrees of freedom for the χ^2 test. The degrees of freedom for the row is the number of categories minus 1 ($r − 1$). The degrees of freedom for the column is the number of cases minus 1 ($c − 1$). To get the total degrees of freedom, multiply the two together (r-1 times c-1).

In the sixth and final step, you use this degrees of freedom (df) to look up the value on the table of χ^2 distribution found in Appendix A at the end of this book. There we see that our value of 94.89 exceeds the value of 13.81 given for p = .001. This means that the chance that the distribution of our data across is homogeneous is less than 1 in 1000 or p < .001 for short.

Interpreting the Results

The final step in the computation of the χ^2 test—looking up the values on the table—tells you what the chances are that the distribution of your data over categories and across contrast is homogeneous. Generally speaking, we think of any probability of less than .01 as significant, less than .001 as highly significant, and less than .05 as in the direction of being significant.

Such numbers do not tell you, however, what in your observed data is departing from the model of expected homogeneity in such a fashion as to lead to a significant outcome for the χ^2 test. If we superimposed Figure 10.3, the observed distribution, on Figure 10.4, the expected distribution, we would see that some points lay close to each other and some more distant. The greater the difference between the points, the more they contribute to a large χ^2 value.

Thus, interpreting a significant χ^2 result involves pinpointing the greatest differences in the values making up the χ^2 value. To see these, you must return to examine the table in step 4 of Figure 10.6 where you computed $(O - E)^2/E$ for each cell. Since these are the numbers you added to get the final χ^2, extremely high values tell you what is so unexpected in the distribution of your data.

In step 4 of Figure 10.5, for example, we see that almost all the value for the significant χ^2 value comes from the values in both meetings for John (29.03 and 40.67 out of the 94.89 total). We also see that a lesser but still sizable contribution to the χ^2 value has come from Ed's talk in the managerial meetings (10.52). The other three values (7.51, 2.99, and 4.18) pale by comparison.

Having pinpointed the cells that make the greatest contribution to your significant χ^2 value, you next try to understand what makes the observed values in these cells so different from the expected values. You can do this by looking at the pinpointed differences between the observed and expected values, O − E, calculated in step 3 in Figure 10.6. For example, looking back to the table in step 3, we look for the three areas of largest effect—John in both kinds of meetings, and Ed in managerial meetings. For John, we see that he talked far less than expected in the managerial meetings (−70.21) and far more than expected in design meetings (+70.21). For Ed in the managerial meetings, we see that he talked more than expected (+47.49).

The final step in interpreting the results of the χ^2 test is looking at the observed data in light of the pinpointed effects. In our example, we see, for instance, that John does appear to follow an unusual pattern of making contributions in the two kinds of meetings. In the design meetings, he is one of the most talkative participants. In the managerial meetings, he trails way behind both Ed and Cheryl in his contributions. This clearly is far from a homogenous pattern of participation.

For the third pinpointed difference, for Ed in managerial meetings, we see that although Ed is the most talkative participant in both kinds of meetings, in the managerial meetings, he is proportionately more talkative—contributing 262 segments rather than the 215 predicted by the expected homogeneous model. Looking into the matter a little further, we notice there is very little change in Cheryl's rate of participation across meeting types. Thus, what appears to have happened in the managerial meetings is that as John spoke hardly at all; Ed who took up the slack.

Overall then, the χ^2 test of homogeneity can give you some sense of the magnitude of the differences across your built-in contrast as well as clues to the interpretation of those differences.

The χ^2 Test of the Independence of Dimensional Variation

The χ^2 test of distributional variation introduced in the last section is a test that asks whether the categories in your coding scheme were homogeneously distributed across contrast. This test is the most appropriate test for the distributional variations you may have discovered in Chapter 7. In this section, we go on to describe applications of the χ^2 test to the dimensional variations you explored in Chapter 8.

Questions of Independence

As you may recall from Chapter 8, dimensional variation involves adding another layer of analysis onto your data by coding your segments for a second phenomenon. Continuing with the example introduced in Chapter 8, we might add a second dimension of indexicality to data already coded for the dimension of speaker contribution. The χ^2 test of dimensional variation asks whether these two dimensions are independent of one another. That is, is the distribution of data across the coding categories in one coding scheme unrelated to the distribution across the coding categories in a second coding scheme? For this reason, the χ^2 test of dimensional variation is often called a χ^2 test of independence.

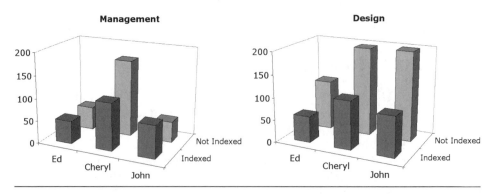

Figure 10.7 Observed distributions with dimensional variation.

Block graphs like those discussed in Chapter 8 and shown in Figure 10.7 can suggest that dimensions are not acting independently of one another. The proportion of indexical language used, for example, appears to depend both upon which speaker is talking and upon the kind of meeting the speaker is in. Although most of the speakers have a smaller proportion of indexed to nonindexed language, this ration changes for Ed and John in the management meetings. To what extent are there interdependencies between these two dimensions? This is the question that a χ^2 test of independence is designed to answer.

Models of Independence

The expected model for χ^2 test of independence is a model in which the distributions of data in the two dimensions are independent of one another. To understand what this means, recall that, like all χ^2 tests, expectations are defined in terms of the joint probability of a segment of data being placed into a given cell. Data like that graphed in Figure 10.7 has been analyzed as having three kinds of variation: variation across the first dimension, variation along the second dimension, and variation across contrast.

Figure 10.8 shows the expected model of independence for the data graphed in Figure 10.7. Unlike the observed data, this model of expected independence shows no unexpected contours. Both graphs show the same contours moving from left to right through the first dimension and the same contours back to front in the second dimension. The proportional difference left to right is the same regardless of the graph; the proportional difference front to back is also the same. Both dimensions appear to matter to the data—that is Not Indexed is always higher than indexed; Cheryl always speaks more, no matter which part of the data you look at. But in this model, they do not matter to each other—how much talk is indexed does not depend upon the speaker, for instance. For this reason, we speak of this expected model as a model of independence.

As in the χ^2 test of homogeneity, mapping the contours of the expected model begins with the observed marginals and asks the following question:

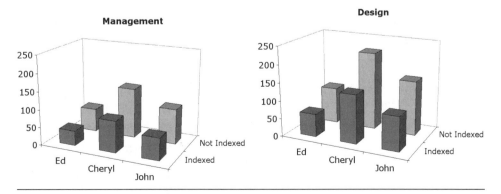

Figure 10.8 Expected independent distribution.

Given these marginals, what would we expect the distribution in each of the cells to be if the distribution were independent?

The answer to this question can be given in terms of the joint probability,

$$p(\text{dimension 1}) \times p(\text{dimension 2}) \times p(\text{contrast})$$

For a set of observations like those shown in Figure 10.8, then, we can calculate the probability of a given cell, like Ed's indexed talk in management meetings, as the product of these three simple probabilities:

the probability of talk being contributed by Ed,
the probability of talk being indexed, and
the probability of talk being in management meetings.

The formula for this joint probability is:

$$\frac{\text{\# of Ed segments} \times \text{\# of indexed segments} \times \text{\# of management segments}}{\text{total \# of segments} \times \text{total \# of segments}}$$

or

$$\frac{269 \times 483 \times 494}{1255 \times 1255}$$

which equals 40.75. This, then, is the expected value for Ed's indexed talk in management meetings. How does this compare with the observed value of 50? It does not look that different, but to get a measure of the significance or lack of significance of this difference, we need to look at them in the context of the computation of the full χ^2 test of independence—we turn to in the next section.

Computing a χ^2 Test of Independence

The steps for computing a χ^2 test of independence are similar to those for a χ^2 test of homogeneity. Because we have two rather than one contingency table for our observations, however, the calculation of the marginals is a bit more complex and is best pulled out as a separate step as in Figure 10.9. Here in step 2, we see three sets of marginals, one for the first dimension (Ed, Cheryl, John), one for the second dimension (Indexed, Not Indexed) and one for the contrast (Management, Design).

Notice how the total for each set of marginals is the same figure (1,255)—this makes sense because the sum of any set of marginals will be the total number of segments in the data set. Thus, to insure that your calculation of marginals is correct, check that each of these totals show the same grand total.

Given these marginals, the expected values for the data can be calculated using the formula discussed in the last section, stated generally as

$$P(D1 \times D2 \times C) = \text{marginal for D1} \times \text{marginal for D2} \times$$
$$\text{marginal for C} / \text{grand total}^2$$

The expected values for the sample data are given in Figure 10.10.

As this figure indicates, we also calculate the marginals for these expected values to make sure they equal the observed marginals—as they should if our

	A	B	C	D	E	F
1	**Step 1. Observed**		Ed	Cheryl	John	Total
2	Management	Indexed	50	105	72	227
3		Not Indexed	51	170	46	267
4		Total	101	275	118	494
5						
6			Ed	Cheryl	John	Total
7	Design	Indexed	58	108	90	256
8		Not Indexed	110	196	199	505
9		Total	168	304	289	761
10						
11	**Step 2. Marginals**					
12	Dimension 1	Ed	Cheryl	John	Total	
13		269	579	407	1255	
14						
15	Dimension 2	Indexed	483			
16		Not Indexed	772			
17		Total	1255			
18						
19	Contrast	Management	494			
20		Design	761			
21						
22	Totals	Total	1255			
23		Total squared	1575025			

Figure 10.9 Calculating observe frequencies and their marginals.

			Ed	Cheryl	John	Total
48	**Step 3. Expected**		Ed	Cheryl	John	Total
49	Management	Indexed	40.75	87.71	61.66	190.12
50		Not Indexed	65.13	140.20	98.55	303.88
51		Total	105.88	227.91	160.21	494.00
52						
53			Ed	Cheryl	John	Total
54	Design	Indexed	62.78	135.12	94.98	292.88
55		Not Indexed	100.34	215.97	151.81	468.12
56		Total	163.11	351.09	246.79	761.00
57						
58			Ed	Cheryl	John	Total
59	Marginals	Indexed	103.53	222.83	156.64	483
60		Not Indexed	165.47	356.17	250.36	772
61		Total	269	579	407	1255
62						

Figure 10.10 Calculating expected frequencies.

computations are correct. We see, for example, that the expected marginal for Ed's talk is 269, which equals the observed frequency with which he talked (see Figure 10.9). Although we won't use these expected marginals in our calculation of χ^2, it is still a good idea to calculate them and check that they match marginal figures for the observed data.

To calculate expected marginals, simply sum across the expected values in the two tables. For the expected marginal for Ed's indexed talk, in C36, for example, we simply add up the expected value for his indexed talk in management meetings and his indexed talk in design meetings with the formula

$$=C49 + C54$$

This formula can be dragged across and down through the table to calculate all the expected marginals. The row and column totals for this table, then, should match the marginals for the observed data. If they do not, check your computation of expected values.

Finally, complete the computation of the χ^2 test of independence the same way as you did the χ^2 test of homogeneity, calculating $O - E$, and then $(O - E)^2/E$ as shown in Figure 10.11. The sum of these values is your χ^2 value.

63	**Step 4. O-E**		Ed	Cheryl	John	Total
64	Management	Indexed	9.25	17.29	10.34	36.88
65		Not Indexed	-14.13	29.80	-52.55	-36.88
66		Total	-4.88	47.09	-42.21	0
67						
68			Ed	Cheryl	John	Total
69	Design	Indexed	-4.78	-27.12	-4.98	-36.88
70		Not Indexed	9.66	-19.97	47.19	36.88
71		Total	4.89	-47.09	42.21	0
74	**Step 5. (O-E)sq/E**		Ed	Cheryl	John	Total
75	Management	Indexed	2.10	3.41	1.73	7.24
76		Not Indexed	3.07	6.33	28.02	37.42
77		Total	5.17	9.74	29.76	44.66
78						
79			Ed	Cheryl	John	Total
80	Design	Indexed	0.36	5.44	0.26	6.07
81		Not Indexed	0.93	1.85	14.67	17.44
82		Total	1.29	7.29	14.93	23.51
85	**Step 6. Degrees of Freedom**					
86	# of rows	2				
87	# of columns	3				
88	# of tables	2				
89	df	2				
90						
91	**Step 7. Table Lookup**					
92	sum of chi squares	**68.18**				

Figure 10.11   Calculating χ^2 as differences between observed and expected.

For degrees of freedom, you have three variables to consider: the number of categories in dimension 1, the number in dimension 2, and the number in the contrast. Substract 1 from each of these and multiply them together to get your total degrees of freedom. You can then use them with the lookup table in Appendix A using the procedures described earlier.

Interpreting the Results

The process of interpreting the results of a χ^2 test of independence begins, as you might expect, with pinpointing the cells that make the largest contribution to the significant χ^2 value and understanding the direction of their difference from the expected model. For our sample calculations shown in Figure 10.11, for example, we have pinpointed four cells in step 5 that seem to contribute the most to the total sum of χ^2 as well as the direction of their difference:

1. John's nonindexed talk in management meetings was lower than expected.
2. John's nonindexed talk in design meetings was higher than expected.
3. Cheryl's nonindexed talk in management meetings was higher than expected.
4. Cheryl's indexed talk in design meetings was lower than expected.

These differences we seek to interpret are highlighted in Figure 10.12.

As we have already seen, our expectations for the value of any given cell of a distribution have been set as a combination of our expectations for the first dimension, our expectations for the second dimension, and our expectations for the contrast. To interpret the significant contribution of a given cell to a significant χ^2 value, then, we must compare it to our expectations in these three areas.

If, for example, we want to understand why John's nonindexed talk in management meetings was lower than expected, we need to compare this to our expectations for

a. John's talk in management (dimension 1).
b. Nonindexed talk in management (dimension 2).
c. Talk in management (contrast).

In essence, we need to go back and look at our marginals.

Beginning with our expectations for the contrast, we see that the ratio of talk in management meetings to the talk in design meetings was 494 to 761. Thus, management meetings were, in general, less talkative than design meetings. John's nonindexed talk in management meetings was lower than expected. This suggests that—even given that all talk was, on average, lower in management meetings—John's nonindexed talk was especially low.

Moving to our expectations in Dimension 1, speaker contribution, we see that overall, John contributed less talk than Cheryl, but more than Ed. For his nonindexed talk in management meetings, however, this expectation was not met: there he contributed far less nonindexed talk than Cheryl, about as much as Ed. Notice how the expected pattern is, however, maintained for indexed talk:

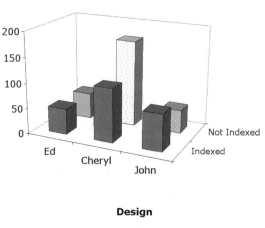

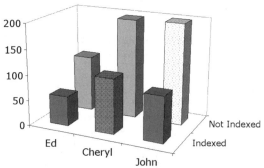

Figure 10.12   Pinpointing the cells that make the largest contribution to the significant χ^2 value.

Cheryl contributes the most indexed talk, John next, and Ed bringing up the rear. Here we begin to see that there was some interaction between the dimension of speaker contribution and the dimension of indexicality as our significant χ^2 value indicated.

Finally, moving on to our expectation for Dimension 2, indexicality, we expect there would be far more nonindexed talk than indexed talk. When John's nonindexed talk in management meetings was lower than expected, then, it goes against our general expectation that the speaker would have more rather than less talk that was not indexed.

Pulling together an overall interpretation of the result, we can now see that John's nonindexed talk in management meetings was lower than expected because, in general, he talked less in the management meetings than we expected him to and, furthermore, this reduction came almost entirely through a reduction in nonindexed talk. Put in concrete terms, John was relatively silent in management meetings and this relative silence arose out of him making fewer nonindexed contributions.

Differences in a significant χ^2 value tend to come in pairs. That is, if something is lower than expected in one area, there will be a balancing value that is higher in another area. Once we have interpreted the result that John's nonindexed talk in management meetings was lower than expected, we immediately move to building an interpretation of the balancing result that John's nonindexed talk in design meetings was higher than expected. Again we compare this result with our expectations for Dimension 1, Dimension 2, and the contrast.

As we have already noted, we generally expected design meetings to have been more talkative, so when John's nonindexed talk was high, we see no surprise. We have also seen that we generally expected John to have been in the middle in terms of speaker contribution. Here, this result produces some surprise for his contribution to nonindexed talk in design meetings was more than equal to Cheryl's contribution, even though his contribution to indexed talk was about where we would expect it. Finally, we have seen that we generally expected more nonindexed talk than indexed talk from speakers. Here our result that John's nonindexed talk was high in design meetings is in line with that expectation, but very different from what is going on in the management meetings, where his indexed talk was higher.

Pulling together an overall interpretation of this second result, we can now see John's nonindexed talk in design meetings was higher than expected because, in general, he talked more in the design meetings than we expected him to and, furthermore, this increase came almost entirely through an increase in nonindexed talk. Put in concrete terms, we can say John was relatively talkative in design meetings and this loquacity arose out of him making more nonindexed contributions.

For John, then, increases or decreases in his overall contribution to talk came almost entirely through changes in the level of his nonindexed talk: When he talked more in design meetings, it was through an increase in nonindexed talk; when he talked less, it was through its reduction. His contribution to indexed talk, by contrast, stayed relatively stable throughout.

Producing an interpretation of the two significant differences for Cheryl's talk follows the same process: comparing the difference to our expectations along Dimension 1, Dimension 2, and the contrast. While we will not take the time to carry out this interpretive process fully here, we will note that, for Cheryl, the impact of indexicality on level of contribution did not entirely follow the same pattern as John. It is true that, like John, when Cheryl talked more than expected (in management meetings), it was through a higher than expected increase in nonindexed talk. But when she talked less than expected (in design meetings) it was through a reduction in indexed talk. For most speakers, then, the proportion of nonindexed talk rises and falls with the speaker's overall level of contribution. For Cheryl's talk in design meetings, however, something else was going on, something that involved unexpected decreases in indexed talk.

Developing a deeper understanding of "what was going on"—of the actual patterns of language use that are pointed to by the interpretation of these significant differences—is a matter of detailing, the process we describe in Chapter 11. Before we turn to this topic, however, let us briefly discuss the use of the χ^2 test for evaluating the significance of temporal patterns, the task we turn to in the next section.

The χ^2 Test of Temporal Variation

Application of the χ^2 test to the kinds of temporal analyses discussed in Chapter 9 can help to focus on the way that the distribution of data across categories varies over time.

The key move is to aggregate the data across a relatively large temporal unit and then to use that unit as a set of categories constituting, in effect, a second dimension. For example, if we have classified a set of articles by the dimension of publication venue, we could use year of publication to create a set of temporal categories such as:

1950–1959
1960–1969
1970–1979
1980–1989
1990–1999

We could then look at the way the distribution of articles across publication type varied by decade with a contingency table structured like that shown in Figure 10.13. Such a table then becomes a set of observed values that can be compared against a model of the expected distribution across a decade if nothing much were going on. As you may have realized, such a χ^2 test is a test of homogeneity since you are asking whether the distribution of articles across decade is homogeneous or whether there are significant differences in their distribution. It will follow the procedure outlined in Figure 10.6.

A second approach to aggregating temporal data is to create categories that represent meaningful temporal units. If we were looking at talk in design meetings, for example, we might use temporal categories related to the design process:

- Requirements Phase
- Specification Phase
- Building Phase
- Testing Phase

	A	B	C	D	E
1					
2		news	business	fashion	general
3	1950-1959				
4	1960-1969				
5	1970-1979				
6	1980-1989				
7	1990-1999				

Figure 10.13   A contingency table with time as a second dimension.

Unlike the categories created by looking at decades in our earlier example, these design-process categories have adopted through their relevance to the stream of language under consideration. Unlike decades, they are not necessarily equal in size, though they do follow one another temporally. The appropriate χ^2 test is still one of homogeneity. It will also follow the procedure outlined in Figure 10.6.

If you want to use a χ^2 test to examine the significance of a set of data already structured by a built-in contrast, move the analysis into a third dimension as shown in Figure 10.14. Here we have added a contrast to the data shown in Figure 10.13, so our model of the expected values for this data is a combination of our expectations for the dimension, our expectation for time, and our expectation for the contrast:

$$D \times T \times C$$

Structurally, then, the analysis will follow the procedure outlined in Figures 10.9 through 10.11 for a χ^2 test of independence.

Restrictions on the χ^2 Test

In concluding this chapter, we call attention to some of the important restrictions on the use of the χ^2 test. They are:

1. The data used in the calculation must be raw data, not proportions;
2. along each dimension, each segment must have been assigned to one and only one coding category;
3. the assignment of a segment to a category must be independent of the assignment of other segments to a category; and
4. the expected frequencies in each cell (in step 2) must be at least 5.

	A	B	C	D	E
1					
2	With by lines	news	business	fashion	general
3	1950–1959				
4	1960–1969				
5	1970–1979				
6	1980–1989				
7	1990–1999				
8					
9	Without by lines	news	business	fashion	general
10	1950–1959				
11	1960–1969				
12	1970–1979				
13	1980–1989				
14	1990–1999				
15					

Figure 10.14   A contingency table with time as a third dimension.

If you have followed the methods outlined in this book, your data should meet these restrictions. Restrictions 3 and 4 bear brief comment however.

If you were to have a coder consider previous coding decisions in assigning a segment to a category, then coding decisions would not be independent as required by restriction 3. Such coding schemes would be hard to use in any case and are best avoided.

If you were to have a very small data set so the expected frequencies in any cell were very low, your analysis would not meet the criteria outlined in restriction 4. Such a situation might arise if you had categories in your scheme that were seldom used. One option in such a case is to combine infrequent categories into a single category. Such a move makes sense as long as this grouping makes intuitive sense and does not amount to classifying apples with oranges.

PROJECT: EVALUATING SIGNIFICANCE

Choose an appropriate χ^2 test to evaluate the significance of the distribution of your data across categories. A sample significance testing workbook is available at the course website.

Use Excel to calculate the χ^2 test.

Write up a discussion of your results in Word. Make sure to address:

a. The question you are asking;
b. The appropriate model of your expectations;
c. The χ^2 sum, its degrees of freedom, and its level of significance; and
d. If appropriate, an interpretation of the areas in which the observed data was significantly different from the expected model.

Detailing Results

In this chapter, you will develop the details necessary to support the analyses you developed in earlier chapters. Using the living language of streams of verbal data, you will learn to detail codes, patterns, and discrepancies in a way that will make your findings come alive for you and your readers. Techniques for locating detail and criteria for choosing detail are introduced.

Detailing

When you began the analysis of verbal data that has occupied you for awhile, you began with a living stream of language—text, talk, protocols, or electronic interactions made salient to you in their contexts of production. Now, through analysis, this living stream has been made meaningful to you in a context of interpretation. That is, you have used analytic techniques to articulate and test your intuitive understandings and explore its patterns.

Not surprisingly, the final stage in your analytic journey brings you back full circle to the details of language that drew you to your project in the first place. These details can illuminate your analysis both for your and your readers.

Defining Detail

For our purpose, detail can be defined as selections from a stream of verbal data chosen to provide specific examples of more general patterns. Detail can range in size from a single word or phrase to extended passages of interaction selected for their relevance to a point you want to make. Here, for example, is how a paragraph from a writer's text has been used to detail the concept of a "problem case in paternalism" (Geisler, 1994):

A prototypic problem case in the issue of paternalism, taken from Roger's final draft, is as follows:

> Mister N, a member of a religious sect which strictly forbids blood transfusions, is involved in a serious automobile accident and loses a large amount of blood. On arriving at the hospital, he is still conscious and informs the doctor that his religion forbids blood transfusions. Immediately thereafter he faints from loss of blood. The doctor believes that if Mister N is not given a blood transfusion he will die. Thereupon, while Mister N is still unconscious, the doctor arranges for and carries out the blood transfusion.

Details like this one can be presented in many contexts ranging from illustrating the way your coding scheme works to giving an in-depth description of the writing produced by a high school student for her English class.

What makes something a detail is its relationship to the larger patterns you have already established by earlier analyses:

- Some of those patterns may involve the varying distributions of contrasting data over a set of coding categories. You may have found, for example, that Cheryl talked more in design meetings than in management meetings. Detail can then help you understand what she was talking about in both meetings.
- Some of those patterns may involve associations across dimensions of analysis. You may have found, for example, that Cheryl tended to use more indexical language in design meetings. Detail can then help you understand what points Cheryl was making about the design and why those points were more highly indexed.
- And some of those patterns may involve changes over time. You may have found, for example, that Cheryl didn't begin making significant contributions in a design meeting until more than halfway through. Detail can then help you to understand what changed at that halfway point that led to her increased contributions.

Detail, then, does more than illustrate the general patterns found through analysis: It enriches your understanding of those patterns, allows you to explore potential explanations for these patterns, and can even become the source of schemes and codes that launch a second wave of analysis or the design of a further study.

The Meaning of Detail

To understand the meaning of detail, consider what an analysis shows without it. The general patterns revealed by distribution graphs, block charts, and temporal indices are significant abstractions from what are usually massive volumes of living language. As you now understand, such abstraction is one of the few ways to get a handle on the overall picture of what is going on. Nevertheless, such abstractions run the danger of becoming disconnected from the intuitive understanding that, as we saw in Chapter 4, is the unavoidable and invaluable foundation of verbal data analysis. By returning from the abstraction to detail, you reconnect with core intuitions.

When you return to the detail of language, you return as a different person, however. Analysis has given you both articulated concepts with which to understand phenomena and important understandings of the overall patterns. In other words, having gone through analysis, your intuition is now better prepared to interpret detail. Coming back to detail, then, can be understood as the "big payoff" for the entire analytic process. You now see the verbal data through the lens of intuitions tutored by the analytic process.

Detail thus forms a key component of the interpretive process in which you, the analyst, engage to make meaning of verbal phenomena. Detail also forms a key component of the interpretive processes in which your reader will engage with your analysis. As we shall see in the next chapter, some readers in some forums will be willing to engage fully with your study—following the intricacies of your coding and reaching for the abstractions of your analysis. Many, however, will not. Instead, they will rely on you to use details to make your results both concrete and meaningful.

Detail can help these readers in the meaning-making process in three ways. First, detail helps readers with understanding. Anchoring generalizations in concrete instances helps them to better understand what you are talking about—how you define the phenomenon, how you saw the associations. Second, detail helps readers to evaluate the credibility of your analysis—weighing it against their own intuitions and experience to see if it makes sense. And, finally, detail helps readers to see the significance of your results—to recognize its applications to the contexts in which they operate and to the policy issues in which they debate.

Areas for Detailing

Opportunities for detailing are associated with nearly every component of analysis. In this section, we provide examples of some of these opportunities.

Introducing the Phenomenon

Just as a picture is worth a thousand words, so too is one well-chosen detail worth a thousand vague descriptions of the phenomenon in which you are interested. Here, for example, is the opening of an article that distinguishes between the use of reading and writing by academic experts and academic novices in terms of authority (Penrose and Geisler, 1994):

> By early March, Janet is ready to set aside the notecards she's been laboring over since midwinter. She begins to write:
>
>> This paper will define paternalism and discuss its justification. Paternalism is the action of one person interfering with another person's actions or thoughts to help him. The person who interferes, called the paternalist, breaks moral rules of independency because he restricts the other person's freedom without that

person's consent. He does it, however, in a fatherly, benevolent way, and assumes that the person being restrained will appreciate the action later.

Across town a few days later, Roger makes a similar decision. Setting aside his scrawled pages of notes, he, too, begins his text:

> Consider the following situations:
>
> Situation One: Mister N, a member of a religious sect which strictly forbids blood transfusions, is involved in a serious automobile accident and loses a large amount of blood. On arriving at the hospital, he is still conscious and informs the doctor that his religion forbids blood transfusions. Immediately thereafter he faints from loss of blood. The doctor believes that if Mister N is not given a blood transfusion he will die. Thereupon, the doctor arranges for and carries out the blood transfusion. Is the doctor right in doing this? [Two more cases are presented.]
>
> Sometimes paternalistic actions seem justified, and sometimes not; but always, paternalism seems at least to be a bit disquieting . . . The authors whose efforts will be reviewed here have undertaken the task of trying to spell out conditions which must be satisfied for paternalistic actions to be justified . . . [S]o a preliminary task is that of giving an account of what are paternalistic actions; that of settling on a definition in order to gain a clearer notion of what we are talking about, and of what, if anything, has to be justified.

The contrast between these two introductions is striking. Though they share a common focus on the definition and justification of paternalism, Janet's text views the definition and justificatory conditions as established truths, while Roger introduces them as matters yet to be resolved.

Notice here how the extended and contrasting detail from different texts is used to help the reader understand what differences in authority amount to. Good detail often works this way to introduce a reader to a phenomenon.

Illustrating Segmentation

The next opportunity for using detail is describing the kinds of segments that you have used to break up the verbal stream. Often, such segments do not need to be explained because they represent well-known choices (sentences, t-units, etc.). At other times, however, you may anticipate that the segment will be unfamiliar to readers. In these cases, detail will go along way toward reader understanding as in the following case (Geisler, Rogers, and Haller, 1998):

> We expected that the lists these participants produced would be indicative of the kinds of issues to which they normally attend in a software engineering design task. They produced such issues as the following:
>
> ▪ "How should system respond if a credit card transaction is declined by the issuer? If credit card was reported stolen?" [Last of nine issues listed by a software engineering expert]
> ▪ "Can user query how much charges they've run up?" [Eighth of nine issues listed by an advanced technical communication student]
> ▪ "Can the user select a bus any time that it runs or must they take the next available bus?" [Fourth of nine issues generated by an advanced software engineering student]

■ "If the machine doesn't work, you can't get to where you want to go" [First of five issues generated by an advanced chemistry student]

The four details used in this example not only clarify the nature of the segment "issue" but also represents the range of issues produced by the four groups in the study. These details, then, not only serve their current purpose (illustrating segmentation), but also prepare the reader for later findings.

Understanding Codes

As noted in Chapter 4, a good coding scheme will provide not only definitions of coding categories, but also sample segments that would be coded in that category. These sample segments, you may now realize, can become details that help readers to understand what your coding scheme really amounts to, as in the following example (Geisler, 1994):

> To analyze participants' use of the construct of authorship, I examined the protocol data for the presence of *author mentions,* which were defined to include: (a) names of specific authors (e.g., "Childress"), (b) nominals standing for an aggregate of authors (e.g., "these guys"), (c) nominals standing for roles of authors (e.g., "a moral philosopher"), and (d) pronouns standing in for any of the aforementioned ("she"; "they").

Illuminating Patterns

The greatest opportunity for detail comes in the service of understanding the overall patterns revealed by your analysis. Good detail here will be linked to the overall patterns as in the following example where details are directly referenced to patterns in the graphs shown in Figure 11.1 (Geisler, in press):

> Actions "to say" are foundational verbs of articulation. Some of them were literal:
>   "Jamie and I talked about this at great length."
> But most were metaphorical, describing giving voice in text:
>   "that I . . . I *said* was impurely paternalistic."
> "Say" was the preferred action for Janet who used it in more than half (54%) of her public accounts. Figure 5 suggests that she used it both to describe her own actions and the actions of the authors that she read, and that "saying" occurred in accounts throughout her sessions.

As this example shows, details can help to provide a more intuitive understanding to the otherwise dense abstractions represented in graphs.

Locating Detail

In large data sets like those typically used by verbal data analysts, finding details can seem an easy task since details are, if anything, overly abundant. Yet finding the right detail to do the work can be more of a challenge. As we have seen, good details don't simple illustrate; they illuminate and persuade. Several approaches can be helpful in locating just that right detail.

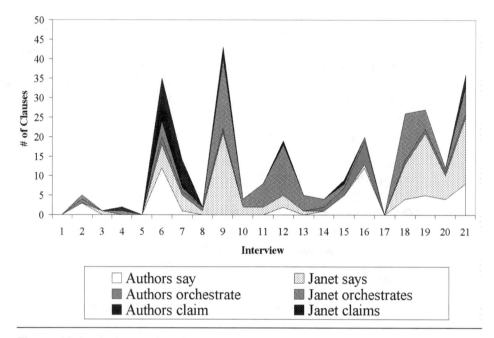

Figure 11.1   Actions in Janet's 22 sessions (Figure 5).

Stratified Sampling

Once analyzed, data can look like a variety of intersecting strata formed by distinctions in your data. Not only do the distinctions found in your analytic design—by case and by contrast—form strata, but also the new distinctions that have arisen in your patterns—by code, by association, by time. When using details to illuminate patterns, it is important to find details across these various strata, so you can understand the full range of phenomenon underlying a pattern.

In a study of five classrooms, for example, if you had found that teachers contributed more ideas about content than students did, you might look for details in the following strata:

■ Teachers' talk about content in each of the five classrooms—are they doing similar things when they all talk about content?
■ Students' talk about content in each of the five classrooms—what do students talk about when they actually do talk about content? Is there something in this talk that shows why it doesn't happen more often?
■ Teachers' talk about other things in each of the five classrooms—is teachers' talk about content somehow distinctive from other kinds of talk they engage in?
■ Students' talk about other things in each of the five classrooms—is students' talk about other things more compelling for students?

- Students' talk in response to teachers' talk about content—When teachers talk about content, why aren't students responding on the same topic? What topic do they respond to?
- Teachers' talk in response to students' talk about content—is there something about the way that teachers respond to students' talk about content that keeps them from pursuing it further?

As this partial list of strata and questions illustrates, a single overall result can lead to a whole host of follow-up inquiries that can be addressed and illuminated by detail.

11.1 Test Your Understanding

In the following excerpts Geisler, 2003 downloadable at the course website, underline the details that have been added. Rewrite the text to eliminate the details.

1. Before 1988, I used the still-common academic year calendar, Week-at-a-Glance, available from most university bookstores. A little bigger than the PalmPilot (4 × 6.5), it offered seven days in a 2-page spread as diagrammed in Figure 3. Monday through Friday provided 7 full blank lines; the weekend (on which I would presumably be loafing) provided 7 half-lines per day. A sample week, that of Dec 7, 1987, showed that I recorded four kinds of information in the Week-at-a-Glance. First, I listed daily appointments by writing a time followed by the name of the appointment: "9:30 Graduate Review Committee." Second, I noted deadlines such as "Final project due." Third, I created numbered task lists like the following:

   1. Annenberg
   2. Book revision plans

   And finally, I recorded untimed events that, nevertheless, were scheduled to occur on specific days: "David Phillips visits, New Zealand." As might be expected with all of these kinds of entries, the seven lines provided for each day often made space tight in my Week-at-a-Glance.

2. Activity theory requires us to understand how a tool builds upon the user's prior tools, responds to her desires and dissatisfactions, and, through its affordances, extends the capacity of the user in unexpected directions. We can see all of these factors at work with my use of the Day-Timer. The same kinds of information that we noted in the Week-at-a-Glance—daily appointments, deadlines, task lists, and untimed events found their place in the new Day-Timer technology. In addition, my desire for better control over project tasks and a mechanism through which to assure that I did not neglect my scholarship led me to develop new mediating means built on tool affordances: not only task lists created in a space whose label ("To Be Done Today") invited such use, but also time-keeping notes ("9:30–12:30") in spaces (Diary Record) designed for other purposes (billable hours).

(continued)

3. The largest of these activities could be characterized as "doing e-mail," though the work accomplished through this activity was broader than might be expected. In its simplest form, as shown in the activity graph in Figure 10, doing e-mail involved reading messages and taking one of a number of simple actions in response to messages received:

   - archiving many (action sequences 17, 19, 29, 22, 23, 25, 27, 30),
   - replying to one (action sequence 21),
   - trashing a couple (action sequences 18 and 26),
   - holding one for later reply (action sequence 37), and
   - responding to one by modifying an earlier reply (action sequence 24).
   - For most of these actions sequences, texts were processed serially in the order in which they were encountered. Only two new texts were created: Text 31, which served as a reply to Text 30; and Text 35, which became an addition to that same reply later on in action sequence 24.

4. While "doing e-mail," I invoked Palm Technologies when messages were linked to task management issues. As shown in Figure 11, for example, I responded to one e-mail message (Text 12) in three different ways, all involving the Palm:

   - First, I created the event (Text 19) mentioned in the message by going to my daily calendar for today (Text 1), moving forward 3 weeks (Texts

	A	B	C	D	E	F	G
15		15-Jan	16-Jan	17-Jan	18-Jan	19-Jan	20-Jan
16	Deadlines						
17	Work		NSF IT Proposal	NSF IT Proposal	NSF IT Proposal	NSF IT Proposal	
18	Events	No school					
19		M	T	W	Th	F	S
20		22-Jan	23-Jan	24-Jan	25-Jan	26-Jan	27-Jan
21	Deadlines			NSF ITR			
22	Work						
23	Events						
24		M	T	W	Th	F	S
25		29-Jan	30-Jan	31-Jan	1-Feb	2-Feb	3-Feb
26	Deadlines				JBTC		
27	Work	JBTC	JBTC	JBTC	Palm Tech	Palm Tech	
28	Events						
29		M	T	W	Th	F	S
30		5-Feb	6-Feb	7-Feb	8-Feb	9-Feb	10-Feb
31	Deadlines					NRC	
32	Work	Palm Tech	Palm Tech	Palm Tech	Palm Tech	Palm Tech	
33	Events						
34		M	T	W	Th	F	S
35		12-Feb	13-Feb	14-Feb	15-Feb	16-Feb	15-Feb
36	Deadlines						
37	Work	Palm Tech	Palm Tech	Palm Tech	Palm Tech	Palm Tech	
38	Events						
39		M	T	W	Th	F	S
40		19-Feb	20-Feb	21-Feb	22-Feb	23-Feb	24-Feb
41	Deadlines						
42	Work						
43	Events		Tucson	Tucson	Tucson	Tucson	Tucson

Figure 11.2   Figure 13 for Exercise 5.

13, 14, and 15) and 3 days (Texts 16, 17, and 18) to the date of the event.

■ Second, in the course of replying (Text 20) to the message, I sought to confirm the time for an upcoming meeting—going back to my Palm (Text 17), returning to the daily calendar for today (Text 1), changing to the weekly view (Text 21), and then checking the start time I had listed for the appointment (Text 22), which I then included in my reply (Text 23).

■ Third, while viewing my weekly schedule, I also decided to cancel another meeting (Text 24) earlier in the week, deleted it from the Palm, and then added a note about this (Text 25) to my e-mail reply (Text 40).

5. "Planning work" involved the use of a special purpose task management tool, the Project Inventory, created in a spreadsheet and shown in Figure 13 (shown in Figure 11.2). Calendar-like in structure, each week provided room to array three kinds of texts: deadlines such as that for the "NSF ITR" shown for Tuesday, January 16; events such as "Tucson" shown for the week of February 20; and work such as "Palm Tech" shown for Monday, February 5. To the right of the week's array and off screen in Figure 13, texts represented a variety of projects, unscheduled but waiting my attention. Weeks that represented time past were usually grayed out though this was not true at the start of this session.

For discussion: How does the rewrite change the meaning and impact of the text?

Filtering Data by Codes

Once you have decided what kinds of strata to illuminate through detail, you can use filtering techniques (see Chapter 4) to pick out segments that meet these criteria. If, for example, you wanted to look at teachers' comments about content, you could filter a data file first by speaker, choosing teacher as speaker code, and then by topic, choosing content as your topic code. The resulting selection would show you all the segments that might serve as details.

If you are simply picking out individual segments for details, a simple filter like the one just described will work. If, as is more often the case, you want to look at these segments in context, you will want to see more than a filtered list shows you. One way to achieve this is shown in Figure 11.3. On top you see data that has been filtered by the speaker code "Cheryl." The results have been selected and the font changed. On the bottom, the filter has been removed. The previously filtered segments clearly stand out, but the context for these segments can be seen. Such a display makes it easier for you to look at details in their full context.

Using a Temporal Index

A second technique for locating good detail involves the use of a temporal index. If you have constructed a temporal index, you can use it to locate specific

	A	B	C
1	**T-Unit #**	**Speak ▾**	**Text**
3	1	Cheryl	This is a little cumbersome
5	3	Cheryl	I don't know how anybody else would find it.
9	7	Cheryl	Yeah, it needs to be ***voice subsumed**
15	13	Cheryl	Should we talk about this stuff ...
17	15	Cheryl	A little bit ...
19	17	Cheryl	To remember this? I don't remember
20	18	Cheryl	what we said last week.
32	30	Cheryl	Ah, we need a time line
34	32	Cheryl	Okay, you take control
35	33	Cheryl	and let's write this out.
41	39	Cheryl	Now, take control and write it in here.
43	41	Cheryl	Don't you get a pen out – come on!

	A	B	C
1	**T-Unit #**	**Speak ▾**	**Text**
2			
3	1	Cheryl	This is a little cumbersome
4	2	John	Very
5	3	Cheryl	I don't know how anybody else would find it.
6	4	Ed	Well we're using specialized knowledge(?)
7	5	John	But that's just our directory :
8	6	John	that's just our directory structure.
9	7	Cheryl	Yeah, it needs to be ***voice subsumed**
10	8	Ed	I would suggest
11	9	ED	th-at we each sort of brainstorm individually :
12	10	ED	at least that's
13	11	ED	what I would like to do first : just get a few things on my private unit
14	12	ED	and then with this open one we can then write with it ...
15	13	Cheryl	Should we talk about this stuff ...

Figure 11.3   Marking filtered data with color and then looking at it in context.

interesting details. In the temporal index shown in Figure 11.4, for instance, we see that Lee did very little talking. To find those places where he did talk, we can simply hold our cursor over the point in the graph where he is talking and Excel will give us the information about that point. In this case, we see that one point of Lee's talk is associated with x coordinate of 101 and y coordinate of 4. Returning to the data sheet from which this graph was constructed, we can easily

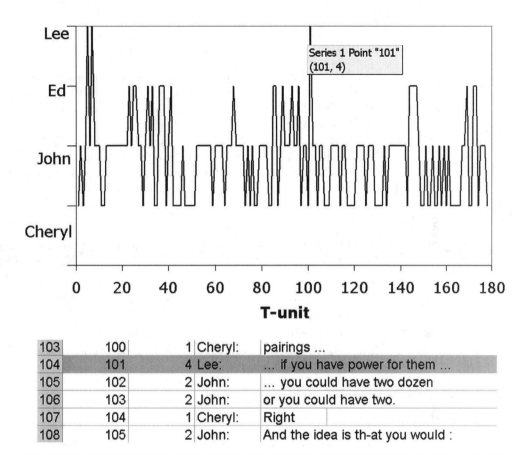

103	100	1	Cheryl:	pairings ...
104	101	4	Lee:	... if you have power for them ...
105	102	2	John:	... you could have two dozen
106	103	2	John:	or you could have two.
107	104	1	Cheryl:	Right
108	105	2	John:	And the idea is th-at you would :

Figure 11.4   Using a temporal index to locate detail.

11.2   Try It Out

Use filtering to locate five details on either side of your built-in contrast that illustrate what you take to be the major differences you have found in your analysis. Share them with a partner and ask him or her to describe the differences observed. Now write one to two sentences characterizing them for the rest of your classmates.

For discussion: To what extent do details speak for themselves? What needs to be added to details to make them interpretable?

find point 101, shown in grey at the bottom of Figure 11.4, and begin our interpretive process.

Using Memory

One final way to find details to illuminate overall patterns is through the use of memory. After coding and analysis, many analysts find that certain passages in the data stand out in their memories, are striking for what they show, and even haunt them as they develop the overall picture. Picking details for their salience can lead to serious mischaracterization of the data if done *without* the kind of systematic analysis described in this book. But picking such details after analysis insures that you can place them in the big picture of what was going on generally. Using memory to find your details can, under this kind of situation, be one of your most powerful techniques.

PROJECT: DETAILING RESULTS

Make a list of three to five main patterns of your analysis.

Now find details from each of the strata of your data that illuminate these patterns.

Finally, write up a description of your results that makes use of both the general patterns (illustrated graphically or in tables) and the details.

For Further Reading

Geisler, C. (1994). *Academic Literacy and the Nature of Expertise: Reading, Writing, and Knowing in Academic Philosophy*. Lawrence Erlbaum Associates, 1994.

Geisler, C. (2003). When Management Become Personal: An Activity-Theoretic Analysis of Palm Technologies. In C. Bazerman and D. R. Russell (Eds.), *Writing Selves and Societies: Research from Activity Perspectives*. San Diego, CA: Mind, Culture, and Activity and Fort Collins, CO: academic.writing. Available at http://wac.colostate.edu/books/selves_societies.

Geisler, C. (in press). Upon the Public Stage: How Professionalization Shapes Accounts of Composing in the Academy. In B. Couture and T. Kent (Eds.), *The Private, the Public, and the Published: Reconciling Private Lives and Public Rhetoric*. SIU Press.

Geisler, C., E. H. Rogers, and C. R. Haller (1998). Disciplining Discourse: Discourse Practice in the Affiliated Professions of Software Engineering Design. *Written Communication, 15*, 2-24.

Penrose, A. M., and C. Geisler.(1994). *Reading and Writing Without Authority. College Composition and Communication*, 71-86.

CHAPTER 12

Presenting Results

In this chapter, you will work out your options for presenting your results. The basics of a full accounting are reviewed as well as maxims to keep you on track in your presentation. Techniques for inserting graphs and details are also included.

Full Accounting

When you began the analytic process, you began by anchoring your endeavor in a literature. Now, by presenting your results, you come back to that same literature—to make a contribution of your own. In this chapter, the basics of a full account of results are first reviewed. We then go on to discuss some of the options you face in making an account as well as a few maxims to help guide your presentation.

What do readers expect to see when they encounter a presentation of your results? As we shall discuss later, the answer to this question depends upon the publication venue. Nevertheless, conventions do exist concerning what is expected of a full accounting. The following material is organized in the canonical order for a full account. We begin with the literature review, move to define the phenomenon, describe the data, survey the analysis, present the patterns, elaborate with detail, provide a discussion, and conclude with significance. Whether you use this particular ordering will depend upon the genre conventions of a specific journal. In any case, however, when a full accounting of your analysis is called for, these topics will be covered.

The Literature

What is the state of the art in the literature to which your analysis aims to contribute? What have been the relevant issues? The previous findings? The controversies? The missing links?

Your work began with the survey of the literature you did in Chapter 1 to anchor your project in the literature. As you have carried out your analysis, you probably added to your reading and developed a more focused interpretation of the state of the art. In presenting your results, then, you provide readers with a revised picture of this literature and its current state so that they may better understand the contribution your study makes.

The Phenomenon

What is the phenomenon examined in your analysis? In what context does it arise? Of what importance is it? Does it create problems for us? Does it present us with opportunities?

Your definition of the phenomenon of interest is critical to your readers' being able to understand and take an interest in your work. Sometimes the phenomenon is a well-established topic in the literature. At other times, you must work to get your readers to see something they may not have thought much about before.

Occasionally, striking details (see Chapter 10) can be used to call attention to a phenomenon and provide the basis for analyzing its characteristics. Because different audiences have different interests and levels of familiarity, the way you define a phenomenon can vary from one publication venue to another. But you must always make sure your readers know what phenomenon you are examining and why it's important.

The Design

By what design did you structure your analysis? What contrasts were built in to it? How does this contrast relate to the phenomenon in general? What categories of phenomenon did your sample? What questions were you seeking answers to?

A full accounting of a research project includes a description of the entire design that structured data gathering and analysis. You present some version of your descriptive framework as well as your research questions (see Chapter 2). Through these, you set up readers' expectations for a discussion of the results of both the analyses that were illuminating and those that were less interesting.

Sometimes, aspects of your descriptive framework turn out to be uninteresting. Some research questions may not have answers; some analyses lead nowhere. In these situations, many accounts of research do not review the full set of analyses conducted. Rather, they review only those that make a contribution to the literature. The conventions of your discipline, the expectations of your readers, and your own intentions will guide your decision on how fully to describe your initial design and questions.

The Data

What data did you collect? Where did it come from? How did you select it? How is it related to the phenomenon in general? Did you analyze all of it? If not, how did you make your selection?

A full accounting of your data makes clear what data you collected and/or analyzed and your reasons for selecting it. A data table (see Chapter 2) can provide an economical way of giving a full accounting. It can be included in a table in the body of the presentation for a full accounting or moved to an appendix for a more abbreviated account.

Always make sure to describe how you selected your data samples. Many studies using verbal data do not make selection clear enough. This can leave readers without an understanding of the criteria by which you selected the data and, therefore, without a way to assess how well your results represent the phenomenon. If, on the other hand, you show you had a process for selecting data and reasons for using that process, you enhance your credibility.

Data collection and selection is always described in a full accounting. For a more abbreviated account, some details can be moved to endnotes. It is also not uncommon to see authors referring readers to other published papers for more complete descriptions of data collection and selection.

The Analysis

How was the data segmented? How was it coded? What reliability was achieved between coders? What is the relationship of your analytic procedures to the phenomenon under investigation? To the research questions you have asked?

The bulk of the technical detail in a full accounting rests in the description of the analytic methods. These details represent a significant investment of a researcher's time and the merit of the study rests on the quality of these procedures.

Nevertheless, most readers are less interested in these analytic details than in other aspects of your research. Even those with the competence to evaluate your methods will often not have the interest—at least initially. Readers often focus first on results and only later may begin to pick apart your analytic process. Peer reviewers in research journals do, of course, look carefully at the analysis. Other readers, in fact, count on them to do so. In fact, many readers assume that if a study has made it into print, the analytic methodology must be sound. For this reason, even technical readers feel free to skim your analytic methods.

In a more abbreviated accounting, the analytic methodology is often the first thing to go from the body of the text. Segmentation may not be described. Coding schemes may not reproduced in full. Reliability figures may not be mentioned. Nevertheless, as a responsible researcher, you should make sure information about these topics is available in some peripheral way. Otherwise it will be impossible for others to assess and build on your work.

The Patterns

What patterns has the analysis revealed? How has the contrast built into the design actually played out? How does what you actually observed compare to what we might have expected had nothing really been going on?

The patterns you find through an analysis of verbal data are the heart of a presentation of results. It is here that the "news" of your presentation should be found. As you have already learned, such patterns can be complex. In presenting them, you need to decide how to orchestrate their presentation. Some of your options include:

BY QUESTION—If your research questions have addressed several different aspects of the phenomenon, you may want to adopt an organization that takes up and reviews the answer to each research question in turn.

BY CONTRAST—If your analysis has confirmed significant differences across your built-in contrast, you may want to begin with the overall evidence of this difference and then move to characterize each side of the contrast in turn.

BY DIMENSION—If your analysis has involved multiple dimensions, you may want to review the basic results in each dimension first and then turn to their interrelationship.

BY CASE—If your analysis has suggested a basic pattern with lots of variation by case, you may want to begin with the basic pattern and then present the individual variations.

Other organizational patterns do exist and can be imagined. The important point is this: Your results are complex and you need to find the best way to present them simply for a full accounting.

If you want to give a more abbreviated account of results, focus on the main results, the ones with the greatest significance in terms of theory or practice. Abbreviated accounts may also reduce the presentation of graphs and tables in favor of more discursive descriptions of patterns.

The Discussion

How do you interpret the patterns found? What is the nature of the phenomena under investigation? What meaning do they have in terms of the issues raised in the literature? What answer can be given to your research questions?

The results section presents the nitty gritty of the patterns you found and their significance compared to expectations. It is filled with tables and graphs. When you move into discussion, you are still focused on the patterns you found, but rise to a higher level of seeing the patterns in the context of the prior literature. In an abbreviated accounting, most of the presentation of results may be focused on discussing those results for readers.

The Significance

Of what significance are the findings? Why should readers care? Of what import are they theoretically? Of what important practically? If the results found here were to hold true more generally, what would be the implications? What further work needs to be done to confirm these patterns?

The final section of a canonical presentation of results concerns itself with assessing the significance of the contribution made by the study. This significance may lie in the realm of theory, of practice, of methodology, or in all three. Contribution may be in a single field or across several fields. The study may answer questions or raise them. It may confirm existing claims about a phenomenon or raise doubts about them. The study may put to rest an issue or set the stage for a continuing line of work. All of this should be made clear in a discussion of significance.

12.1   Test Your Understanding

In the following table, downloadable from the course website, match the claims (Geisler and Lewis, in press) on the left with the functions on the right. What functions appear to be missing?

1. Figure 5 shows graphically how the students' production of design ideas about the movement mechanism of their design was directly related, in every case, to the requirement to produce text:	a. The literature b. The phenomenon c. The data d. The patterns e. The interpretation f. The significance

2. We illustrate the purposes to which language is put in engineering design by drawing on a detailed case study of a team of four undergraduate engineering students—Sam, Paul, Tim, and Jack—who worked together over 15 weeks to develop a design for a motorized device that would provide mobility for children with cerebral palsy. The team was given this assignment by their professor, George, as part of their "capstone" experience in mechanical engineering design at our university, an experience required of students graduating with engineering degrees by the Accreditation Board of Engineering and Technology (ABET). The assignment George gave the students told them that children with cerebral palsy needed to experience independent movement through their environment and observe its effects, an experience that was currently expensive and hard to provide.

3. As this example from household technology illustrates, engineering design is "the strategy for causing the best change in a poorly understood or uncertain situation within the available resources." (Koen, 1987)

4. In the language arts classroom, shaped by the culture of literary interpretation, we often think of talk and text as distinct realms of activity, talk as something we do together; text as something—ideally at least—we do alone. We need to recognize, however, that in engineering design, as in many other workplace settings, texts and talk do not exist in isolation, but are almost always linked to one another. In their work on the mobility device, for example, Sam, Paul, Tim, and Jack used talk to make nearly 1,300 separate proposals about the frame, but over 70% of those proposals were made using some kind of text.

5. Despite the plethora of technological artifacts that surround us, many of us find the technical detail of engineering design to be a barrier to understanding what turns out to be a very human process. As a consequence, we may be missing opportunities to help students learn important language practices.

6. Engineering design is only one of the most obvious processes of cultural production by which citizens attempt to remake the world. As many have noted before us, the traditional language arts classroom has tended to present talk and text as the handmaidens of the society's justified concern with the transmission of a world already made. From design engineers, however, we can begin to understand talk and text as also useful for remaking that world.

For discussion: Can you imagine kinds of presentations in which these topics might not appear?

12.2   Try It Out

Return to the anchoring work with which you began this process in Chapter 1. Look at its presentation of results and identify the basic components found there. Are any of the components missing? How does this affect the power of the work to persuade you of its results?

For discussion: Compare your findings with those of your classmates. Are there differences by specialty?

Options in Placement

The analysis of verbal data can be used to make a contribution in any number of publication venues within a discipline. Each will have its own conventions about what kinds of reports are appropriate. Some specifically invite full accounts answering all the questions outlined in the last section. Others are more interested in what might come out of the analysis rather than the analysis itself—its general findings, their theoretical importance, or their practical implications. Such venues will expect a more abbreviated account.

As you make plans for publication, then, you need to decide on the appropriate mix of technical and nontechnical readers for your work. You may find that the number of readers interested in reviewing a full accounting of your results may be comparatively small—just that handful of peers working in your specialty perhaps. But the number of readers who may be interested in an abbreviated account of your work may be much greater.

To help you sort things out, make a point of discussing your publication options with advisers and colleagues as well as analyzing possible publication outlets. The descriptions of publication venues that follow will help you understand the issues you should be thinking about.

The Seminar

If you have completed your analysis in the context of a graduate seminar or working group, the most obvious first presentation of your results will be to that seminar. Such seminars usually bring together like-minded peers with similar backgrounds and expectations. Your presentation of results can often involve a full accounting of your analytic process and results.

The Conference

One of the most frequent venues for the presentation of results is the professional conference. On an annual basis, the members of your field will assemble to hear reports of one another's work. A variety of special interest conferences also exist that are sponsored on a one-time basis. In addition to conferences in one's own field, opportunities for presentation may exist at conferences in allied professions or in associations of practitioners for whom your results may have special meaning.

Calls for submissions to these conferences are not difficult to locate. Information about conferences associated with professional associations can almost always be found at the association's website. Calls for participation in one-time conferences are often posted on bulletin boards, linked to conference websites, mailed out to members of associations, or published in the back of the discipline's journals.

Most conferences allow presenters somewhere between 15 and 30 minutes to present results. In such a short time, it is impossible, of course, to give a full accounting of the basics as outlined in the previous section. Some conferences publish full papers in conjunction with the conference. In this case, the paper provides the full accounting and the presentation itself will simply review the highlights. In other conferences, the presentation time is all you've got.

Conferences usually allow for some level of peer review. If you are required to submit a full paper, reviewers will be able to provide a good review of the technical merit of your analysis. For this reason, conferences that require full papers for submission are often good places for a complete accounting of your work. If you are only asked for an abstract of your study, peer review is more often based on judgments about the significance of the problem and its relevance to conference attendees. In such cases, an abbreviated account may be more appropriate.

Research Journals

In many fields, the research journal is the standard place to present a full accounting of research results. They are always peer reviewed and reviewers will look at the adequacy of your analytic process as well as the nature and significance of your results.

Some of these journals follow standard scientific reporting practices. Others are more free-wheeling in their genre conventions. Nevertheless, every journal will expect you to place your results in the context of the archival literature of which that journal is a part. When planning to present your results in a research journal, it is, therefore, best to review back issues for the past few years to understand the conventions used by the journal as well as to identify specific research you will want to cite in your own presentation.

Other Journals

In many fields, journals exist that serve less to present research results and more to provide a forum in which to discuss theoretical issues or explore practical implications. If the results of your analysis have significant theoretical or practical implications, a theory or practice journal may be an appropriate publication venue for reporting your work.

In a theory or practice piece, details of the analytic process take second billing to the discussion of patterns in the results and their implications. Often readers are not willing or able to judge the technical merit of your analytic process. Details of segmentation, coding, reliability, and significance testing may be moved to appendices, endnotes, websites or through citations to more full accountings presented elsewhere.

In such venues, many authors leave out technical detail altogether. But such an approach can leave those who have a technical interest unable to judge your work and ultimately impoverish the literature. The best approach for presenting results in these other journals is to move technical detail out of the main body of the text to the periphery in endnotes and appendices. If your review of back issues suggests that technical detail is not found even in these peripheral places, you can at least provide readers with a pointer to how this detail can be obtained. In a footnote or author's note, for example, you can provide interested readers with an e-mail address or a website URL for a more complete accounting of the study's methodology.

12.3 Try It Out

Use the World Wide Web to locate two calls for proposals for conferences that might be interested in the analysis you have done. Compare their requirements.

For discussion: What are the pros and cons of choosing one or the other for the presentation of your results?

Options in Timing

In addition to options on where you present your results, you often have options on when to present them. When starting out, many researchers make the mistake of believing that a research project can only be presented once the full analysis is completed. While some fields do restrict presentation to final results, it is more common to find a number of intermediate opportunities for presentation along the way.

In the early stage of a project, you struggle with establishing the gaps in the literature, developing a design for collecting data, and establishing a methodology for analysis. Opportunities for presentation at this stage allow you to make a case that the phenomenon you have identified is of interest and that a particular methodology provides an appropriate approach. Such arguments can be especially powerful when combined with some preliminary data from a pilot study. Although early stage work is not often found in the research journals, it is often presented in seminars, at conferences, and even in theory journals. And, of course, it is the heart and soul of a dissertation prospectus.

By presenting early stage work, you accomplish a number of things. First, you provide a forum in which you need to articulate and examine your basic arguments. Such an experience can be very helpful in seeing holes in your own work. Second, you can develop connections with other researchers working on similar projects. These new colleagues can be good sources of advice and feedback. Finally, you begin to develop a track record of publications and presentations, establishing a trend and setting the tone for an active career of research and scholarship.

12.4 Try It Out

Make a list of journals in your field. Use discussion with your colleagues and a review of back issues to decide whether each one would be

a. A place for a full accounting of research such as you are completing
b. A place for an abbreviated accounting.

For discussion: Compare your list with the lists of your classmates. How did you decide how to classify a journal? What implications does this classification have for the presentation of your results?

Maxims of Presentation

The presentation of results is often a counterintuitive process. After burying our noses for months in data, we sometimes find ourselves blinded by the sunlight when we look up and try to describe to others what we have found and what it means. To help you avoid some of the more common pitfalls, this section presents some general maxims to guide your intuitions.

Follow the Phenomenon, Not Your Life History

Focused as we are on process and procedure, we are often tempted to present our results as our life history of the data—why we were interested in it, how we gathered it, how we struggle to analyze it, what we found, what it means to us.

Avoid this temptation. By and large, readers come to your presentation of results with the expectation of learning something about the phenomenon, not something about your life and times. Conventions of presentation in many fields now support and encourage the use of first person ("I coded the data . . ."), but even so, the focus of the story you tell ought to be on the phenomenon, not on you.

Acknowledge Your Agency

Even though you should avoid making the presentation of results a personal history, you should acknowledge your own agency in their development. These acknowledgments should be made judiciously, and in the contexts where they serve to increase your readers' understanding. Readers should understand how you got access to the data, what your relationship was to the site and its participants, how your assumptions structured the coding scheme, and so on. So, although you are not writing a personal history, it should have you as a person in it.

Provide Rationale as Well as Procedure

Many beginning researchers make the mistake of describing analytic procedures as they might have written up the steps in a sophomore biology report: just the facts, ma'am. A more sophisticated presentation will describe not only what was done but why. The rationale for analysis is as important as its description. Your goal is to have readers nodding their heads as they read through your process, saying "that makes sense."

Persuasion, Not Just Presentation

In the same vein, keep in mind that all research is persuasive. In presenting your results, you make a bid to make a contribution to your field. You must persuade your readers that that contribution is real. You must make points and lead your readers to your conclusions, not simply describe what you "found."

Balance Technical and Nontechnical

As you work through the conventions of your presentation venue, you need to make decisions about how much technical detail to provide and in what manner. Your guiding principle should be to seek a balance. On the one hand, provide the technical detail necessary to assess quality, but avoid swamping the reader with it. Appendices, notes, diagrams, bulleted lists, and other formatting and layout conventions can assist readers in skimming through details they may not be concerned with.

On the other hand, make sure to put in the main body of your discourse all material that is essential for readers' understanding. If, for example, readers are left to find your coding categories in an appendix or figure, they may overlook this critical information. Be strategic in where and how you present technical details.

Be Local, Not Universal

Suppose we were to claim that, "Cheryl dominates the talk in management meetings." What might be wrong with such a claim? The statement might, of course, not match the patterns in the data—maybe it was John who talked too much. But let's suppose that we're okay on the match. Is the form of the claim okay? Are we safe in saying that "Cheryl dominates . . ."?

I would suggest not.

Any analysis of verbal data is an analysis of a specific phenomenon, occurring in a specific context in a specific time. Statements like this one about Cheryl remove the claim from that local context by universalizing it. Written in the universal present tense ("dominates"), the claim makes a statement about Cheryl's talk that is true for all time. It is similar in scope to the suggestion that "all men are mortal"—it does not allow for the possibility that this condition will ever change. Like the butterfly pinned down in the collection, Cheryl is caught forever "dominating."

Yet, almost no verbal phenomenon has this eternal quality. And even if it did, no single analysis would be sufficient to establish it. As a general rule, then, you should make your claims as claims about the data you collected: "In the meetings examined,

Cheryl dominated the talk in those that were about management issues." Such claims are local claims. They are tied to the specific local context examined. They characterize the data as part of the historical record without making claims about the future or the eternals. They are usually more accurate and always more defensible.

12.5   Test Your Understanding

Rewrite the following universal claims (downloadable at the course website) to make them local.

1. Students using the asynchronous tool develop higher levels of interactivity than students using the synchronous tool (Deb Sarlin, unpublished manuscript).
2. The Hayes/Robinson song is the only one of the four studied that shows immediacy in terms of place (Virginia Martin, unpublished manuscript).
3. Here we see not a linear progression from information giving to information acceptance, but rather a nonlinear exploration of topics and strategic options. For example, the student expresses dislike for the essay prompt question. The tutor offers a few conceptual topics that the student might use in answering the question. The student doesn't pick up the topical directions from the tutor, who then looks for other options, saying, "Does it [the prompt] say the question is required?" The tutor finally suggests the student gather more information (Kelli P. Grady, unpublished manuscript).
4. While official expression defends the project more than half the time, it infrequently addresses the issue of the displacement of residents (Patricia Nugent, unpublished manuscript).

For discussion: What are the implications of making a claim local? Of making it universal?

Techniques of Presentation

Putting together a presentation of results uses your already-familiar skills. In fact, turning to presentation may be returning you to an environment—writing—which feels far more comfortable than your long sojourn in the land of spreadsheets. A couple of issues arise, however, about how you bring the evidence from those spreadsheets into the text. In this final section, we address these issues, first looking at techniques for inserting graphs and then for including details.

Inserting Graphs

In order to discuss the patterns you see in the graphs you create, you must move them from their individual Excel worksheets into a Word document as part of a coherent discussion. Placing graphs into Word is also the best way to look at multiple graphs at the same time for comparison purposes. The best way to do this is to freeze the graph as a graphic at the time of insertion. Once frozen, a graph will not change even if you change the source data.

To insert a frozen graph from a worksheet into Word, open both Excel and Word on your desktop at the same time. In the Excel file, click on the graph itself to select it. Make sure you have selected the entire graph including headings, etc. Use the copy command to put a copy into your clipboard.

Now move into your Word document and issue the Paste Special command. Excel will offer you the options shown in Figure 12.1. Rather than paste the graph as a Microsoft Excel Chart Object, the default option, select Picture. Also deselect the checkbox for Float over text to the right. This will keep your graph from floating around in your Word document. Click OK and your graph will be copied into the Word document at the insertion point.

If you later update your analysis or change your graph in Excel, these changes will not be reflected in the now-frozen graph in your Word document. Instead, you will need to manually recopy the new graph to replace the old one. I have found through long experience that this method is preferable to having your graphs changing in unpredictable ways as the result of activity in your workbook.

You may notice that once you have moved a graph into Word, that the scale for the text becomes unreadable. This usually happens when you move a graph in a relatively large Excel window into the comparatively smaller space in a Word document. A graph with unreadable text cannot communicate much to your readers, so it is important to keep your text in scale with the Word document itself.

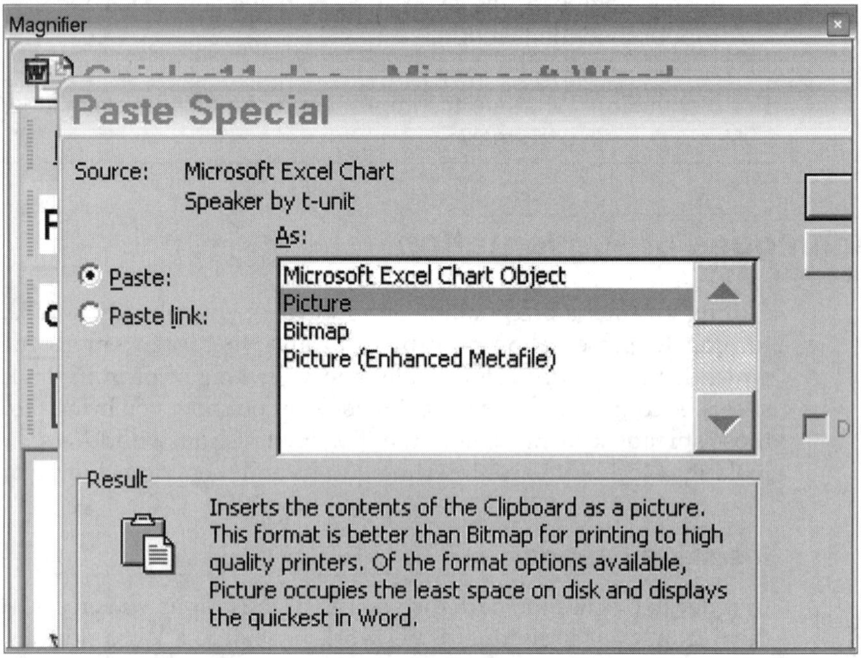

Figure 12.1   Paste Special to move a frozen graph into Word.

The easiest way to insure that your graphs scale appropriately when moved into Word is to fix the font to the size and style that you want to appear in your Word document. This requires turning off the autoscaling feature that Excel otherwise uses. To turn off autoscaling, double click the object with text (usually the x- and y-axis, the legend, the headings) and go to the Font tab as shown in Figure 12.2. Deselect the Auto scale check box in the bottom left-hand corner. Once this is done, the text will always appear in the size you have selected, no matter how big or small your Excel window.

Including Details

As you saw from Chapter 11, details strategically placed in a presentation of results can do worlds to illuminate patterns in data. Two rules of thumb should be followed when including them in your text: First, always identify the specific source of the data. Second, always characterize the data to clarify its relationship to the point you want to make. The following detail (Geisler and Lewis in press) follows both these rules:

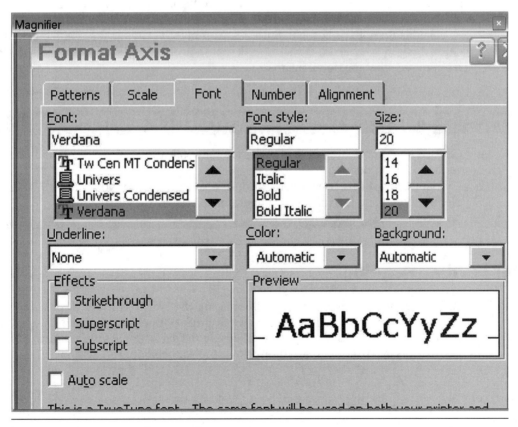

Figure 12.2   Turning off autoscaling.

Social narratives of the existing situation emerged in the earliest talk among Sam, Paul, Tim, and Jack as they recalled personal experiences with the disabled. Sam initiated this process with a narrative of a sixth-grade classmate in a powered wheelchair:

I knew a guy in my class in sixth grade, up through high school. He was in a powered wheelchair, and I don't know what he had, but he could move his right hand and his head and that was it. I mean, he could move his left arm a little bit, but it was an extreme effort just for him to kind of go like that [gesture] . . . And he had a little joy stick to move the wheelchair around, but that's all he could do. And his legs, I guess he couldn't move them. That's why he never got any exercise. They were really small. . . . (Team Meeting on 9/11)

With this narrative of an existing situation, Sam began to personify for himself and his teammates the social situation which they would try to improve. This story provided them with a concrete image of one kind of powered mobility device—the powered wheelchair—and it yoked together the assigned goal of providing mobility for the disabled with the more complex goal of providing them with exercise appropriate to their abilities. As we shall see, ability-appropriate exercise became a central feature of their eventual design.

Here, a parenthetical following the detail ("team meeting on 9/11") tells us exactly where the data comes from. The text following the detail reinterprets it ("Sam began to personify. . .") and relates it to the point we wanted to make ("this story provided them with a concrete image . . .").

Details do not speak for themselves. You must always make them speak. Include them in your text but also wrestle out their meaning for your readers. Help them to see what the detail means.

PROJECT: PRESENTING YOUR RESULTS

Choose an appropriate publication venue for your purposes and analyze its conventions for accounting.

Then follow these conventions to draft a presentation of your results. A sample full accounting is available at the course website.

For Further Reading

Geisler, C., and B. Lewis (in press). Remaking the World Through Talk and Text: What We Should Learn from How Engineers Use Language to Design. In R. Horowitz (Ed.), *Talking Texts: Knowing the world through the evolution of instructional discourse*. International Reading Association.

Table of χ^2 Distribution

df	.10	.05	.025	.01	.001
1	2.706	3.841	5.024	6.635	10.828
2	4.605	5.991	7.378	9.210	13.816
3	6.251	7.815	9.348	11.345	16.266
4	7.779	9.488	11.143	13.277	18.467
5	9.236	11.070	12.833	15.086	20.515
6	10.645	12.592	14.449	16.812	22.458
7	12.017	14.067	16.013	18.475	24.322
8	13.362	15.507	17.535	20.090	26.125
9	14.684	16.919	19.023	21.666	27.877
10	15.987	18.307	20.483	23.209	29.588
11	17.275	19.675	21.920	24.725	31.264
12	18.549	21.026	23.337	26.217	32.910
13	19.812	22.362	24.736	27.688	34.528
14	21.064	23.685	26.119	29.141	36.123
15	22.307	24.996	27.488	30.578	37.697
16	23.542	26.296	28.845	32.000	39.252
17	24.769	27.587	30.191	33.409	40.790
18	25.989	28.869	31.526	34.805	42.312
19	27.204	30.144	32.852	36.191	43.820
20	28.412	31.410	34.170	37.566	45.315
21	29.615	32.671	35.479	38.932	46.797
22	30.813	33.924	36.781	40.289	48.268
23	32.007	35.172	38.076	41.638	49.728
24	33.196	36.415	39.364	42.980	51.179
25	34.382	37.652	40.646	44.314	52.620

(continued)

df	.10	.05	.025	.01	.001
26	35.563	38.885	41.923	45.642	54.052
27	36.741	40.113	43.195	46.963	55.476
28	37.916	41.337	44.461	48.278	56.892
29	39.087	42.557	45.722	49.588	58.301
30	40.256	43.773	46.979	50.892	59.703
31	41.422	44.985	48.232	52.191	61.098
32	42.585	46.194	49.480	53.486	62.487
33	43.745	47.400	50.725	54.776	63.870
34	44.903	48.602	51.966	56.061	65.247
35	46.059	49.802	53.203	57.342	66.619
36	47.212	50.998	54.437	58.619	67.985
37	48.363	52.192	55.668	59.893	69.347
38	49.513	53.384	56.896	61.162	70.703
39	50.660	54.572	58.120	62.428	72.055
40	51.805	55.758	59.342	63.691	73.402
41	52.949	56.942	60.561	64.950	74.745
42	54.090	58.124	61.777	66.206	76.084
43	55.230	59.304	62.990	67.459	77.419
44	56.369	60.481	64.201	68.710	78.750
45	57.505	61.656	65.410	69.957	80.077
46	58.641	62.830	66.617	71.201	81.400
47	59.774	64.001	67.821	72.443	82.720
48	60.907	65.171	69.023	73.683	84.037
49	62.038	66.339	70.222	74.919	85.351
50	63.167	67.505	71.420	76.154	86.661
51	64.295	68.669	72.616	77.386	87.968
52	65.422	69.832	73.810	78.616	89.272
53	66.548	70.993	75.002	79.843	90.573
54	67.673	72.153	76.192	81.069	91.872
55	68.796	73.311	77.380	82.292	93.168
56	69.919	74.468	78.567	83.513	94.461
57	71.040	75.624	79.752	84.733	95.751
58	72.160	76.778	80.936	85.950	97.039
59	73.279	77.931	82.117	87.166	98.324
60	74.397	79.082	83.298	88.379	99.607
61	75.514	80.232	84.476	89.591	100.888
62	76.630	81.381	85.654	90.802	102.166
63	77.745	82.529	86.830	92.010	103.442
64	78.860	83.675	88.004	93.217	104.716
65	79.973	84.821	89.177	94.422	105.988
66	81.085	85.965	90.349	95.626	107.258
67	82.197	87.108	91.519	96.828	108.526
68	83.308	88.250	92.689	98.028	109.791
69	84.418	89.391	93.856	99.228	111.055
70	85.527	90.531	95.023	100.425	112.317
71	86.635	91.670	96.189	101.621	113.577

(continued)

df	.10	.05	.025	.01	.001
72	87.743	92.808	97.353	102.816	114.835
73	88.850	93.945	98.516	104.010	116.092
74	89.956	95.081	99.678	105.202	117.346
75	91.061	96.217	00.839	106.393	118.599
76	92.166	97.351	01.999	107.583	119.850
77	93.270	98.484	03.158	108.771	121.100
78	94.374	99.617	04.316	109.958	122.348
79	95.476	100.74	105.473	111.144	123.594
80	96.578	101.87	106.629	112.329	124.839
81	97.680	103.01	107.783	113.512	126.083
82	98.780	104.13	108.937	114.695	127.324
83	99.880	105.26	110.090	115.876	128.565
84	100.980	106.39	111.242	117.057	129.804
85	102.079	107.52	112.393	118.236	131.041
86	103.177	108.64	113.544	119.414	132.277
87	104.275	109.77	114.693	120.591	133.512
88	105.372	110.89	115.841	121.767	134.746
89	106.469	112.02	116.989	122.942	135.978
90	107.565	113.14	118.136	124.116	137.208
91	108.661	114.26	119.282	125.289	138.438
92	109.756	115.39	120.427	126.462	139.666
93	110.850	116.51	121.571	127.633	140.893
94	111.944	117.63	122.715	128.803	142.119
95	113.038	118.75	123.858	129.973	143.344
96	114.131	119.87	125.000	131.141	144.567
97	115.223	120.99	126.141	132.309	145.789
98	116.315	122.10	127.282	133.476	147.010
99	117.407	123.22	128.422	134.642	148.230
100	118.498	124.34	129.561	135.807	149.449

Key Formulas in Excel

Purpose	Formula	Chapter Introduced
Random number list	=ROUNDUP((RAND()*SIZE),0)	Chapter 2
Automatic coding	=IF(ISERR(SEARCH(PATTERN,SEGMENT)),0,1)	Chapter 4
Agreement checking	=IF(Value1 = Value2,1,0)	Chapter 5
Simple agreement	=sum/count	Chapter 5
Count	=COUNT(range)	Chapter 5
Frequency	=DCOUNTA(database,"dataColumn",criteria)	Chapter 6
Marginal sum	=SUM(range)	Chapter 6
Average	=AVERAGE(range)	Chapter 7
Assigning numeric value to codes	=IF(FirstCategory, 1, (IF(SecondCategory, 2, (IF(ThirdCategory,3, (IF(FourthCategory,4)))))))	Chapter 9
Separating data by code	=IF((Value = "Cheryl"),1,0)	Chapter 9
Cumulative count	=IF(ISNUMBER(DemarcationColumn),NewCount, CurrentCount + NewCount)	Chapter 9
Expected frequency	=(RowMarginal * ColumnMarginal)/GrandTotal	Chapter 10
χ^2	=((Observed − Expected)*(Observed − Expected)) /Expected	Chapter 10

Course Website Resources

Website URL

http://www.ablongman.com/geisler

Video Clips

Video clips, in the form of QuickTime movies, are available at the course website to help you with the techniques introduced in this book. In the chapters, they are marked with the symbol shown above and are listed here in the order they appear along with the page numbers on which the techniques are introduced.

Topic	Video Clip	Discussion
Finding an anchor	Doing a Cited Reference Search	Page 3
	Searching a Bibliographic Database	Page 5
Selecting a random sample	Generating a Random Number List	Page 20
Setting up a data workbook	Adding a Worksheet	Page 25
	Naming a Worksheet	Page 26
Segmenting data	Inserting Segmentation	Page 45
	Removing Unwanted Carriage Returns	Page 45
	Making a Macro	Page 46

(continued)

Topic	Video Clip	Discussion
Moving data from Word to Excel	Creating a Style in Word	Page 48
	Modifying a Style	Page 48
	Shaping Conversational Data	Page 49
	Moving Text from Word to Excel	Page 51
Labeling data	Numbering Segments	Page 52
	Labeling Segments	Page 52
Coding data	Viewing Data and Coding Scheme Together	Page 59
	Using an Autofilter	Page 65
	Sorting Data	Page 65
	Automatic Coding	Page 68
Preparing for a second coding	Hiding a Column	Page 76
	Using the Format Painter	Page 76
	Freezing Panes	Page 76
Calculating reliability	Comparing First and Second Coding	Page 79
	Using the Cohen's Kappa Website	Page 84
Revising a coding scheme	Using Autofilter to Inspect Disagreements	Page 86
Calculating frequency	Naming Data	Page 94
	Copying Fixed Values	Page 97
	Copying Formulas	Page 98
	Calculating Frequency	Page 100
	Filling a Frequency Table	Page 101
	Calculating a Marginal Sum	Page 102
	Calculating a Relative Frequency	Page 102
Making a frequency graph	Making a Frequency Graph	Page 108
	Modifying the Scale	Page 109
	Changing Plot Color	Page 109
	Making a Chart Style	Page 110
	Applying a Custom Chart Style	Page 110
Refining patterns	Collapsing Cases	Page 120
	Calculating Averages	Page 122
Adding a second dimension	Adding a Second Dimension	Page 127
Using a block chart	Creating a Block Chart	Page 132
	Rotating a Chart	Page 133
	Setting Rotational Angle	Page 133
Creating a clustered display	Creating a Clustered Display	Page 135
	Changing the Color of a Column	Page 136

Topic	Video Clip	Discussion
Checking patterns	Calculating Overall Frequency	Page 140
	Changing Axis	Page 141
	Selecting Nonadjacent Data	Page 142
Making a temporal index	Assigning Numeric Values to Codes	Page 158
	Making a Temporal Index	Page 159
	Relabeling the Categorical Dimension	Page 161
Aggregating temporal data	Demarcating an Aggregate	Page 162
	Numbering Aggregates	Page 163
	Separating Data by Code	Page 165
	Doing a Cumulative Count	Page 166
Doing a χ^2 test	Computing a χ^2 test	Page 177
	Looking up a χ^2 Value	Page 179
	Pinpointing Greatest Differences	Page 179
	Calculating Expected Marginals	Page 184
Choosing details	Marking Filtered Data	Page 199
Presenting graphs	Inserting a Frozen Graph	Page 213
	Turning off Autoscaling	Page 215

Sample Workbooks

Sample workbooks are available at the course website to provide you with a template for completing major analytic procedures. You can download them and edit them to suit your purposes.

Topic	Chapter	Workbook
Reverse engineering	Chapter 1	Reverse.xls
Data workbook	Chapter 2	Data.xls
Segmented data	Chapter 3	Segment.xls
Coded data	Chapter 4	Coding.xls
Reliability workbook	Chapter 5	Reliability.xls
Frequency table	Chapter 6	Frequency.xls
Distribution graphs	Chapter 7	Distribution.xls
Dimensional exploration	Chapter 8	Dimension.xls
Temporal analysis	Chapter 9	Temporal.xls
Significance testing	Chapter 10	Significance.xls
Full accounting	Chapter 12	Accoounting.xls

Answer Key

Answers for Test Your Understanding exercises can be found at the course website as follows:

INDEX